GUY STANDING

# Plunder of the Commons
## A Manifesto for Sharing Public Wealth

A PELICAN BOOK

PELICAN
*an imprint of*
PENGUIN BOOKS

## PELICAN BOOKS

UK | USA | Canada | Ireland | Australia
India | New Zealand | South Africa

Penguin Books is part of the Penguin Random
House group of companies whose addresses can
be found at global.penguinrandomhouse.com.

Penguin
Random House
UK

First published 2019
001

Text copyright © Guy Standing, 2019
The moral right of the author has been asserted

Book design by Matthew Young
Set in 10/14.664 pt FreightText Pro
Typeset by Jouve (UK), Milton Keynes
Printed and bound in Great Britain by
Clays Ltd, Elcograf S.p.A.

A CIP catalogue record for this book is available
from the British Library

ISBN: 978–0–141–99062–0

MIX
Paper from
responsible sources
FSC® C018179
www.fsc.org

Penguin Random House is committed to a
sustainable future for our business, our readers
and our planet. This book is made from Forest
Stewardship Council® certified paper.

www.greenpenguin.co.uk

# Contents

# Preface

As she basked in a landslide victory in the 1987 General Election that had followed a split in the opposition, albeit with only 42 per cent of the vote, Margaret Thatcher gave a rambling interview to *Woman's Own*. During it, she made and repeated the revealing remark that summed up her ideology. 'There is no such thing as society', she said, adding 'there are only individuals and families'. One senses that she would have made no objection had the tense been changed so as to read 'There should be no such thing as society.'

What lay behind the remark? When elected leader of the Conservative Party in 1975, at the first meeting of her Shadow Cabinet, she took out from her bag a copy of Friedrich August von Hayek's *The Constitution of Liberty* and slammed it on the table, saying, 'This is what we believe!' It must have crowded out other things, since it was a hefty tome of 576 pages. Hayek was Thatcher's guru and was Ronald Reagan's too.

The Austrian economist had set up a mostly right-wing group of economists and other scholars as the Mont Pelerin Society in 1947. He was not a conservative in the traditional sense, but believed fervently in a 'free market' economy. His mentor was Ludwig von Mises, another Austrian. What von Mises taught Hayek, and what Thatcher digested, was that economic value was measured only by price; what had no price had no value.

In the political hands of Thatcher and Reagan, this view was to evolve into a wholesale agenda of privatization – nothing less than the dismantling of public institutions and bodies that stood against market forces. And if something has no value, it can be given away for free or abolished or converted into something that does have value, a price.

'Thatcherism' cannot be understood without understanding Hayek and von Mises. In 1976, Hayek was awarded the Nobel Prize in Economics, reflecting the capture of the mainstream economics profession by 'neo-liberalism'. In 1984, Thatcher arranged for Hayek to be given the rarely awarded Order of the Companion of Honour by the Queen, which Hayek described as the 'happiest day' in his life. He presumably did not see the irony that the monarchy was hardly a testament to a free-market economy. Reagan said Hayek was one of the three people who most influenced him, and in 1991 George H. W. Bush awarded him the US Presidential Medal of Freedom. Truly a prophet honoured in his lifetime.

Hayek's Mont Pelerin Society still meets regularly around the world and continues to influence mainstream economics. This book is about what is probably the most destructive aspect of the neo-liberals' economic ideology. In their view society has no price and so has no value; therefore the institutions that make up society can be dismantled. For good measure, because only the market determines prices and value, anything that stands apart from or against the market is not just value-less but market-distorting.

Thus began a war – and no other word captures what has

been involved so well – against all organizations and mechanisms of society embodying values of social solidarity, which have no price. The war has been conducted most vehemently and incessantly against what historically has been known as the commons. The commons has a lovely ancestry, as this book tries to remind us. But it is also vital today.

The commons refers to all our shared natural resources – including the land, the forests, the moors and parks, the water, the minerals, the air – and all the social, civic and cultural institutions that our ancestors have bequeathed to us, and that we may have helped to maintain or improve. It also includes the knowledge that we possess as society, built on an edifice of ideas and information constructed over the centuries. This book is about how the commons have been depleted by neglect, encroachment, enclosure, privatization and colonization. It is also about how appreciation of the commons leads to a rationale for a new progressive policy.

The devaluation of society and the disdain for the commons were at the heart of Thatcherism. She went on to become Baroness Thatcher and when she died in April 2013, she was given what amounted to a state funeral, costing the public (society) £3.6 million. It was attended by the Queen and all four of Thatcher's successors as prime minister, most notably Tony Blair, often dubbed 'son of Thatcher'. No such honour was given to her predecessors, such as Harold Wilson who had won four general elections, one more than she did. It signified that not only her own party but New Labour too had been converted to her doctrine. Those she had defeated were lining up to pay homage.

Her biggest economic decision had been to privatize

North Sea oil operations and splurge the oil taxation revenue on income tax cuts and current spending. This was in contrast to Norway, which retained government stakes in its share of North Sea oil and invested the revenues from taxes and dividends in a national capital fund. By the time of Thatcher's death, it was the biggest capital fund in the world, guaranteeing the welfare of every Norwegian today and of future generations. Meanwhile, much of Britain's oil was in the hands of Chinese state (communist) enterprises, which is hardly what Thatcher had intended.

Thatcher's successor as Prime Minister, John Major, privatized British Rail. One extraordinary aspect of the legislation was a clause ruling out just one possible operator, the British government. Profitable bits of the railways came to be owned by French and German state operators, acting on behalf of their societies. It should have been clear by then that privatization was little more than an invitation to foreign capital to colonize Britain's commons. But worse was to follow. Thatcher began the privatization of the most precious part of Britain's social commons, the National Health Service, through what her economic advisers called the 'micropolitics of privatization'. The idea was that the government should gradually cut resources for a popular service so as to undermine faith in its capacity to deliver, leading to acceptance of privatization. But the Blair government did most to accelerate NHS privatization and colonization.[1] By 2018, much of the NHS was in the hands of private providers, even though the pretence was preserved that it was still a public service and an embodiment of the traditions of universalism.

Finally, as this book will show, the Coalition government

of the Conservatives and Liberal Democrats, and the sub-sequent Conservative governments, accelerated the privatiz-ation and plunder of the commons under the umbrella of 'austerity'. That has further devalued society and accentu-ated inequality. In discussing what has happened, why it has happened, and what impact it has had, there is one under-lying message: We want our commons back!

*

The writer of this book lives, as much as he can, in what was once a watermill on a stream. It has long since ceased being a mill. It was operational from the fourteenth century to about 1960. Then it fell into ruin, the wheel was removed, and the roof and walls crumbled. When I first went to see it, there was no kitchen, no dining room and three bedrooms that estate agents like to call 'cosy'.

The mill is set deep in a gorge in woods. On that initial visit, there was no road of any sort, and it being a rainy Oct-ober day, by the time I reached it I was soaked, muddy and rather sceptical. Then I saw the waterfall, ten metres across at the top and with a drop of nine metres, the spray of the water crashing onto the rocks drifting twenty metres downstream. I took one look at it and muttered, 'If I do not buy this, I will never forgive myself.'

It took two years to complete the purchase, and it has taken about twenty years to renovate it as a living place. It is nothing grand. But it has some distinguishing features. Although the mill is my private property, I am not allowed to make any structural change to the building without prior permission from the local authority, and any change must not compromise the original character of the building. That has made the renovation more expensive, and slower, but is a rule worthy of respect. It is a rule that helps protect the commons.

The restrictions do not stop there. We have sole usufruct rights to about 350 square metres around the building (I do not own the land but can use it), and rights in common to woodland beyond it. More significantly, the stream that runs alongside the mill is part of the commons. Anybody has the right to walk along it, go into it and use it.

When I first moved to the mill, the stream flowed continuously, all year round. Since the fourteenth century it had been a force of nature, strong enough to drive a large mill wheel and the heavy grindstone above that ground the flour for the village's needs. The water level rose in the winter, and fell in the summer, but not by much either way, except in rare years of heavy persistent rains in the winter months.

When I first went there, I had a young son with whom I went fishing in the stream in the summer. At the time, there were nine species of fish, including rainbow trout and several rare types of little fish, as well as the occasional fresh-water crab and shrimps. We never ate what we caught.

Then global warming started to do its work. The tragedy did not happen rapidly, initially. It happened year after year, slowly but visibly, until a dangerous threshold was reached. The first alarm signal was the growing seasonal variability in water levels, with the stream's banks flooded and more trees brought down in winter and with the flow of the stream reduced to a trickle in the summer.

One after the other, the fish species were depleted, before disappearing. I remember a fleeting moment of joy when I saw a gudgeon, which was so common in the earlier years. But I did not see it again. Within a decade, seven of the nine species had ceased to exist in the stream, gone for ever. Each year, I tried to rescue some of the remaining species from being trapped in shrinking pools without a flow, with limited success. The crabs and shrimp were long gone. Last year, I thought I saw a barbel. But I may have been mistaken. One day, when transporting a few small specimens from a drying pool to the one remaining deep hole under the waterfall, I found four bloated trout dead on the surface, surely the last, all having expired in the water, deprived of oxygen.

Today, the floods of winter are a source of intensifying fear, the torrent shifting huge boulders and in one year destroying a terrace we had built and bringing down the full-grown walnut tree that had provided cover for decades.

The barren stillness of midsummer is a source of melancholy. It seems to have altered the mood and behaviour of the village. Not so long ago, teenagers used to go down or up the stream and find rocks and bushes behind which to kiss or make love, or smoke and drink and lie out in the dappled sunshine. They mostly took their stuff home or at least to a nearby rubbish dump. But over the years a carelessness has come to characterize those visits; a tendency to throw rocks and stones has accompanied a raucous disdain for the nature of the place. The decay in nature is being reflected in the decay of respect.

What has happened to this stream, and to the species that lived in or on it, is a microcosm of what is happening to the natural commons in many parts of the world. It need not be happening. Solving and preventing such brigades of decay would be relatively easy, if only we and the politicians who represent us placed the crisis higher in our collective priorities. This crisis is undeniably due to the crassness and dogma behind the neo-liberal economics that has dominated politics for the past four decades.

The unfolding tragedy of that stream arises directly from the fact that it belongs to the *unmanaged* commons. Limited financial and administrative regulatory resources are concentrated on what voters and local lobbyists specify as their priorities. If the choice is between improving storm drains in the town and the upkeep of a stream curving its way through the woods outside the town, one can predict the winner in competing for limited resources.

The logic of austerity has made that calculation much worse. For many decades, resources would have been found for both drains and stream. But as governments have pursued the goal of balanced budgets while cutting taxes for the affluent, they have steadily tightened the squeeze on public spending. The commons has been the first to be chopped, belying the rhetoric of local or national politicians in praise of the wonders of the countryside.

The stream has then suffered from a double blow. Because the probability of flooding in winter has risen dramatically, threatening houses and roads around the outskirts of the town, the authorities have diverted the shrinking financial, administrative and human resources for the upkeep of the stream and its surrounds to building flood-control basins further down the stream. That has tended to increase the flow of water further up, which in turn has gradually lowered the level of the water basin high up in the hills. More and more, the water that passes by where I live is rainwater. One consequence is that after rains the water colour turns coppery brown, since most of the water is being swept off the fields. Usually, the immediate effect is a rush of soapiness, due to the prevalence of fertilizers and herbicides in the fields upstream.

The measures taken to control flooding have had other negative effects. They have left even less money for spending on other protective measures, and that has meant that the drought upstream in the summer months comes earlier, lasts longer and is much worse in between periods of flooding.

There is still one potential solution: individual action by those living near the stream. But here is the classic conundrum of collective action. If one person tried to introduce safeguards in the patch of stream adjoining their patch of land, that action might temporarily revive fish stocks and vegetation. But it would also speedily encourage fishermen to go to that patch and teenagers to seek it out as their preferred location for swimming and recreation, not only defeating the ecological objective but probably making the damage worse.

The only way to make progress would be to obtain special dispensation from the local authority to introduce such measures and have a 'usufruct monopoly' (i.e. have sole control to manage the conservation) over a specified area that could be enforced. Fat chance. Because of cuts to staff and resources for the maintenance and revival of the commons, there are few if any staff in local authorities who are in a position to consider, let alone decide on granting any such usufruct right.

As we know, letters and emails go unanswered, and probably unread; queues to see somebody lead to frustration and possible form-filling without any follow-up. The failure in one's ability to do anything leads to energy seeping away. Nobody is responsible, nobody is held accountable. The stream dies. The arteries of rural life stiffen and decay. *A luta continua.*

No book is the work of one person. It draws inspiration from many sources and people. While it is often invidious to single out a few for mention, it is a pleasure to acknowledge and thank the following, with apologies for any inadvertent omissions – Kate Ashbrook, Rahul Basu, Gordon Bathe, Maria Bedford, Tom and Jacqui Connor, Brian Davey, Dave Dewhurst, Andrea Fumagalli, Liz Hames, Christian Liddy, Peter Linebaugh, Mothiur Rahman, Guy Shrubsole, André Standing, Julie Timbrell, Dave Wetzel, Alan Wheatley, Carol Wilcox and most of all Frances, who has painstakingly edited the whole manuscript and helped with ideas at every stage. This book is dedicated to her, and to the stream that evokes Bertrand Russell's metaphor of life. We begin life as a bubbly spring, which gathers strength as it descends, being joined by others; as it gathers water from elsewhere it grows deeper and stronger, being strengthened by joining with others in sharing knowledge, learning and experience. It becomes a river, deep and powerful, and as it flows down towards the sea it widens and slows, losing direction and force, until it flows into the sea. It is also a metaphor for the commons.

A special thanks is due to the denizens of the Runnymede Eco-Village, who occupied and lived in the commons in the woods above the Runnymede meadow for three years before their eviction to make way for a luxury property development. I will always recall the invited lecture I gave in those woods as the official celebration of the 800th anniversary of what later became the Magna Carta was taking place in the valley below, attended by the Queen, Prime Minister and elite of the land. The gentle conviviality and the great collective hug at the end belied the need for the heavy police presence outside the woods.

Finally, a few words on the Charter of the Commons are in order. Some of the ideas were discussed during a series of events in late 2017 designed to celebrate the 800th anniversary of the Charter of the Forest. They included a day-long barge trip from Windsor to Runnymede, during which workshops were held on various ideas relating to the commons. The trip ended with an 'assembly' in Runnymede Meadow around the twelve bronze chairs of *The Jurors*, an artwork that makes reference to Clause 39 of the Magna Carta, and then under the great Ankerwycke Yew, which is over 2,000 years old.

This was followed by a special evening event in the Speaker's Chamber in the House of Commons on 5 November 2017, and what was a personally humbling event in Durham Cathedral on the actual anniversary day of 6 November, where I was invited to make a presentation of the material that has now become Chapter 1 of this book. The cathedral and Lincoln Castle share the honour of being the only two remaining originals of the Charter of the Forest. So it was fitting that the final event was a well-attended public celebration in Lincoln on 11 November 2017. I am sure my co-organizers would agree that it is appropriate to thank David Bollier, Noam Chomsky, Peter Linebaugh, Caroline Lucas and John McDonnell for their support and encouragement of all those events. Now, we really must put our energies into rescuing and reviving the commons.

Inspired by the Charter of the Forest, this book tries to lay out core elements of a Charter of the Commons for Britain today. Readers will have their own ideas and alternative priorities; that is how it should be. For other countries, there would be different priorities and different institutional specifics. But a Charter of the Commons should be drawn up for every country.

The virtue of a Charter is that it should focus on necessary elements of a transformative strategy. Chapter 2 concludes with a preamble for the Commons Charter, while subsequent chapters put forward articles relating to the five types of commons. Chapter 8 proposes a way of mobilizing resources from the commons to increase environmental sustainability, economic security, freedom and equality in rebuilding what we mean by society, in the wake of the ravages of the austerity era. That era was so unnecessary and so destructive; it was a war on commoners. However, we need to realize that great transformations have historically come in the wake of wars. There is good reason for believing that such a moment lies ahead.

# CHAPTER 1

# The Charter of the Forest

> Know ye, That We . . . have given and granted . . . to all
> Freemen . . . these Liberties following, to be kept in our
> Kingdom of England forever.
> — Preamble, The Charter of the Forest, 1217[1]

Imagine the scene. On 6 November 1217, on a dank cold morning in the original St Paul's Cathedral in London, ten-year-old King Henry III watched his uncle, William Marshall, Earl of Pembroke, acting as Regent, and an Italian cardinal, representing the Pope in Rome, put their seals to two documents, each consisting of a large single piece of parchment crammed with elegant Latin script that the boy-king would scarcely have understood. What was being done in his name was nothing less than momentous.

One of those parchments has resounded down the ages to become the inspiration for national constitutions and the protection of human rights around the world. It had begun life on 15 June 1215 as the Charter of Liberties, sealed by King John under duress from the barons in the meadow at Runnymede by the River Thames, only to be hastily abrogated by him and by the Pope. On that November day in 1217, in a somewhat reduced form, it became the Magna Carta.

The second document is scarcely known today, but at the time of its sealing was regarded as equally fundamental. This was the Charter of the Forest, or *Carta de Foresta*. And it lasted longer on the British statute books than any other piece of legislation, only being fully repealed 754 years later.

For generations after the Charter of the Forest was promulgated, all churches in England were required to read it out in its entirety on four public occasions each year – at Christmas, Easter, the feast of St John in summer and the feast of St Michael in the autumn. It was regarded as that important. In 1297, King Edward I declared it and the Magna Carta to be the common law of the land, in the Confirmation of Charters.

Yet today its principles are ignored, and few will have heard of it. In 2015, when the British government ordered a copy of the Magna Carta be sent to all 21,000 state primary schools, along with simple guides on what the text meant, it certainly did not do the same for the Charter of the Forest. No wonder, since, although it continues to inspire those who bother to read it, the exemplary values and principles it enshrined have been abused over the centuries by monarchs, elites and governments.

This chapter outlines the Charter's rise and rocky road through history from the perspective of its values, or ethos, and objectives. These remain relevant today.[2] The Charter is not about preserving a primitive, idealized state of nature. It is about a way of living as an individual in society, about 'commoning' as a collaborative and collective activity in the commons, and about the rights of commoners to use and manage common resources.

## The Charter in history: from 1217 to 1971

The Charter – as it will be called throughout this chapter – was short, consisting of just seventeen articles, all compressed onto a single piece of parchment. It is impossible to understand today if read literally, simply because many of its key words and concepts have themselves drifted into history. That is a pity, since they had very precise meaning and purpose at the time and for hundreds of years afterwards. The values they capture are eternal.

The Charter stemmed from the original Charter of Liberties, which in its 1215 version stated that 'All evil customs relating to forests' were to be stopped, without saying what those evil customs were. In the 1217 version of what became the Magna Carta, this and some other clauses were removed, shortening it to forty-seven articles from sixty-three in 1215. It was left to the Charter of the Forest to define those evil customs and to say what should be done instead.

The etymological root for 'forest' is the same as for 'forbidden', and the Latin *foris* means 'outside'. This was reflected in the thirteenth-century meaning of forest to describe areas of land appropriated by the monarch for his own purposes (usually hunting), thereby denying commoners their customary rights to access common land and use its resources to support themselves and their families. The concept of forest was much broader than implied by the modern usage as a large expanse of trees. For example, Dartmoor and Exmoor, treeless areas of heather and gorse, were part of the 'forest' covered by the Charter. 'Forest' could also include fields and even farms and villages. The historical ecologist

Oliver Rackham estimated that only about half of the land regarded as medieval forest actually comprised wooded areas.[3]

To a certain extent, the Charter can be regarded as an outcome of the first class-based set of demands on the state made by, and on behalf of, the common man (and woman), asserting the common or customary rights of 'freemen'. Like the Magna Carta, the Charter neglected the rights of serfs, who at the time comprised about a third of the population. However, their numbers were to shrink over the next three centuries until the few remaining were freed ('manumitted') by Elizabeth I in 1575. And the Charter also heralded the principle of universalism, for in its final article it said liberties should be extended to all men (*concessimus omnibus*).

The Charter was such a class-based advance that it has often been called the Charter of the Common Man. It was a truly radical document, guaranteeing freemen the right to the means of subsistence, the right to raw materials and, to a limited but substantive extent, a right to the means of production. For the first and perhaps only time, it thereby gave real meaning to the notion of 'the right to work', later interpreted as little more than a duty to labour, as implied in the Universal Declaration of Human Rights, for example.[4] Thus it enabled the poor to hire themselves out by the day, rather than submit to long-term employment 'in service', a significant freedom that social democrats were to forget in the twentieth century.

The Charter was also among the first statutes of environmental law in the history of any nation.[5] It placed implicit limits on the exploitation of natural resources and paid attention to the need to reproduce and preserve those resources.

It established norms for their use, an essential attribute of environmental rights which, as Chapter 3 will show, have been blatantly abused in modern times. Giving any one type of use of land priority or monopoly over others goes against the principles contained in embryonic form in the Charter.

It could also be called the first feminist charter, as it coincided with the first advance in women's rights, in a modified Article 7 of the Magna Carta, which could equally well have been in the Forest Charter. The new Article 7 gave widows the right to refuse to be remarried, to retain some of their husband's land and to have reasonable *estovers* on the commons, that is, to take the means of subsistence.[6] In effect, widows were given the right to a basic income. This was a remarkable advance for the time, when women were treated as little more than chattels. King John had even sold his ageing wife to a reluctant baron, who was forced to pay for the privilege.

Supporting these rights was the obligation on the monarchy to return enclosed land to the commoners – to 'disafforest' – and desist from further land grabs. Fundamentally, the Charter was a manifesto for the 'property-less'. It further provided for reparations for those deprived of their common rights. And it recognized the commons, or forest, as a place of refuge, for those who had fallen on hard times or who were excommunicated from their community for whatever reason.

Above all, in the wake of protracted civil strife and the misdeeds of one of the most detested monarchs of British history, King John, the Charter stood against the usurpation of the commons by elites and the state, which had been all too widespread and capricious in the twelfth century and early part of the thirteenth century. In 1086, the Domesday Book recorded twenty-five royal forests. By 1215, there were 143, as successive kings encroached on common land to increase their revenue, for example from the sale of timber, as well as their hunting space.

One of King John's most resented acts was his order in 1209 to destroy all unauthorized ditches and hedges on forest land to give free range to deer and wild boar for hunting. This single action reduced the ability of commoners to obtain subsistence from the commons, because wild animals – including the deer so prized by the monarchy and the barons – destroyed vital crops and vegetation. The Charter in effect reversed this and other orders, not only requiring 'disafforestation' of formerly common land, but also the restoration of common rights on forest land considered rightfully the monarch's own. This is the essence of the Charter – its insistence on respect for, and demand for, the restoration of ancient or customary common rights.

The removal of designated forest areas from the royal domain also removed them from royal forest law, which was beyond the reach of common law. So in restoring land to commoners, the Charter expanded the realm of common law and established appeal to tradition and old customs and practices as the basis of justice. To this day, common law is based on precedent, in Britain and around the world.

The Charter also marked an important advance in civil rights, going beyond the great advances in the Magna Carta. It abolished the monarch's power to impose the death penalty for poaching deer, though offenders could still be fined or imprisoned. It also abolished mutilation, which included castration and blinding, as a lesser punishment. And it stopped summary justice by the hated royal foresters, instead handing judicial powers to local courts administered by 'verderers'. Verderers were low-level locally elected officials charged with protecting beasts of the forest, notably deer and boar, and their habitat. They dealt with forest offences such as taking venison, excessive cutting or destruction of woodland, and encroachment through unauthorized enclosure and buildings.[7] They were thus 'gatekeepers' for the commons, a role recognized formally for the first time in history. Every age and every commons needs its gatekeepers, to help to manage the commons and ensure commoners' rights are respected.

Again, for the first time in history, the Charter recognized the role of stewardship: formal ownership also entailed a societal responsibility towards the commons and commoners. In an implicit reciprocity between the state and commoners, the monarchy was granted lands taken by William the Conqueror (though not by his more recent successors), but in return the king was obliged to respect all traditional uses of that land by commoners. And although commoners' rights were to be flouted egregiously by the monarchy over the succeeding centuries, the Charter inspired dissidents and social movements too.

The Charter also recognized the need for governance and regulation of the commons. It made the king's foresters and the verderers the primary gatekeepers of the commons, but effectively transferred much of the authority over the commons from the state to the commoners themselves. In so doing, it introduced the principle of local governance of the commons, and provided the foundation for the modern concept of community stewardship of shared resources and the means of subsistence. Whatever a commoner did with his assets could only be done 'on condition that it does no harm to any neighbour'.

The Charter was born of struggle by an informal coalition of classes, embracing discontented barons, an array of ecclesiastical bodies and the mass 'working class' of the time – the commoners. They were sick of the arbitrary, venal and extortionary behaviour of the king's sheriffs and the continuing extension of the royal forests, policed ruthlessly by the royal foresters. Together they had one clear distributional objective: to limit the power of the monarch and his entourage or court.

The story of Robin Hood and his merry men and women battling against the oppressive Sheriff of Nottingham in local folklore was an expression of a widespread mood among the yeomanry and peasantry that traditions and former customs, perceived correctly to have been usurped by successive kings, should be restored.[8] The Charter forced the monarchy to return land that had been afforested to the commons. It was perhaps the single greatest victory for the common man in British history.

The Charter's historical significance lies in part in appreciating the vital importance of the forest in securing subsistence for commoners and rural dwellers, aptly described as 'the poor's overcoat'.[9] It provided farmers – yeomen and peasants, and even some serfs– with land to release livestock to forage or to graze; it allowed the poorest to pick up deadwood; it allowed people to collect or cut gorse to fire brick or pottery kilns or bread ovens; and it permitted commoners access to hazel poles for weaving into gates and fences and fishing weirs. Wood could be lopped off trees to make doors, furniture, house frames, wagons and other useful items. Peat could be cut for fuel, mushrooms could be picked and rabbits snared. Fish could be caught, honey and medicinal herbs could be gathered, and soft fruit could be taken. And the under-appreciated practice of coppicing – cutting certain tree species down to the ground and then allowing regrowth – provided a continuous supply of wood while preserving the trees.[10] The 'forest' gave common access to 'waste': unenclosed land where animals could be grazed and wood, nuts and berries could be gathered. Waste had positive value then, but over the centuries, thanks to capitalism, the word has come to signify something negative that is generated on a vast and frightening scale.

These practices generated the occupations and common surnames that even today testify to their centrality in society – names like Carpenter, Cooper (barrel-maker), Cutler, Fowler, Marler (clay-pit worker), Potter, Sawyer, Smith (and variants), Taylor, Turner (maker of turned instruments, including cups), Wheeler and Wright.[11] Then and now, we define ourselves by what we do and how we relate to each other.

The Charter protected commoners not only against deprivation and homelessness but from outside surveillance and control. In the early nineteenth century – over five centuries later – William Cobbett, on his tours of the English countryside, noted that the 'labouring people . . . invariably do best in the woodland and forest and wild countries. Where the mighty grasper has all under his eye, they can get but little.'[12]

It put limits on both 'agency power', by stating what

property owners and their agents could not do, and 'system power', by curbing the power of property owners over the property-less. By stating explicitly that people could exercise their common rights in the forest 'without danger', it thus limited not only actual but potential power, a principle of so-called 'republican freedom'. ('Republican' here refers to civic liberties and does not necessarily mean non-monarchical government.) Republican freedom does not exist if somebody must be asked for permission to do something that in itself is legal. Republican freedom means deciding for oneself, without fear of retribution if that does not please somebody else. It is a form of freedom that too few policymakers respect.

In 1225 the eighteen-year-old Henry III was obliged to put his own seal on the Charter, which was reissued with minor changes alongside the Magna Carta, in what became the definitive version. Admonishing William Brewer, a baron who had urged King Henry to reject the Charter, Archbishop Langton, the main architect of the Charter of Liberties in June 1215, said: 'William, if you love the king, you should not impede peace of the kingdom.' He knew that the commoners would not tolerate another era of land-grabbing by the monarchy and favoured barons. Nevertheless, over his fifty-six years on the throne, Henry made numerous attempts to revoke the Charter. He failed every time, although as early as 1235 the Statute of Merton gave lords the right to take over forest commons on their estates, with the vague caveat that enough should be left for tenants.

Subsequent monarchs and ruling elites tried with rather more success to enfeeble the Charter's protections and principles. A second wave of enclosures came with the Tudors, notably Henry VIII, who confiscated land partly to expand his area for hunting and partly to raise income to cover his mounting debts. History books focus on his destruction of the monasteries and the confiscation of 10 million acres hitherto owned by the Church, land which had also provided some means of subsistence and shelter for commoners. Today's British landscape is pock-marked with ruins of monastic dwellings that testify to the vehemence of his ruthless campaign. But his cavalier disbursement of huge tracts of that land to his favourites was no less consequential. The arbitrary mass transfer of what had been a form of commons was to scar permanently Britain's class structure. It led to an extraordinary degree of concentration of land ownership that persists to this day.

The transfer of land ownership during the Tudor era coincided with the realization by landowners that fortunes could be made from enclosing commons for large-scale sheep-farming. The resultant enclosures, which led to widespread impoverishment in the countryside, were famously denounced by Thomas More in his epochal *Utopia*:

> Your shepe that were wont to be so meke and tame, and so small eaters, now, as I heare saye, be become so great devowerers and so wylde, that they eate up and swallow downe the very men them selfes. They consume, destroye, and devoure whole fields, howses and cities . . . Noble man and gentleman, yea and certeyn Abbottes . . . leave no ground for tillage, thei inclose all into pastures; they throw down houses; they pluck down townes, and leave nothing standynge but only the churche to be made a shepehowse.

Commercial needs also began to encroach on forests. The use of paper was growing and the expanding Royal Navy demanded timber. Other enclosures were rationalized on grounds of 'improvement', initially for sheep-farming and later commercial agriculture, which displaced the open (strip) field system that had prevailed for centuries.

The steady plunder of the commons, sometimes by force but usually by class domination of politics, marked the ensuing centuries. In a third phase of enclosure in the seventeenth century, Oliver Cromwell handed over much of the public land taken from the monarchy to his followers. A fourth phase of legalized theft of land via the enclosure Acts followed between 1760 and 1870.

The courts, too, played their role. Over time, the rights of landowners came to supersede the rights of commoners, while fewer and fewer people were deemed to have any such rights. The idea that ownership conferred *exclusive* rights to use and dispose of property took shape in the seventeenth century, aided by the influential, though much disputed, philosophical justification of private property rights by John Locke. Enclosures not only denied commoners the use of land but, from the 1604 Inclosure Act onwards, also limited the right to possess land. This essentially dispossessed cottagers, a category of farm labourers who previously were allotted some land for their exclusive use.

The most class-based action of all came in August 1845, when the British parliament, overwhelmingly dominated by aristocratic landowners, passed a General Inclosure Act and appointed Enclosure Commissioners who were authorized to enclose land without, as previously, submitting a request to parliament. But decisive though this was, the Act was only one of many designed to snatch the commons. Between the seventeenth and twentieth centuries, parliament passed over 5,000 enclosure Acts, enclosing more than 6.8 million acres of what had been common, public land.[13]

While enclosure Acts were legalizing the wholesale encroachment of the commons by landowners, the government in 1838 criminalized petty enclosure by commoners, including activities that the Charter of the Forest upheld as rights. There were numerous convictions and heavy fines for such acts as opening quarries, erecting small cottages and encroaching on land for planting crops or pasturing animals. And it was left to the verderers' courts to undertake the prosecutions, the very bodies that had been set up to protect commoners' rights in the Charter.

To the list of egregious enclosures of the natural commons should be added the despicable process in Scotland now known as the Highland Clearances, when the likes of the Duke of Sutherland evicted thousands of crofters, small-scale tenant farmers, burning down their homes to force them out. Many were summarily deported to North America and Australia. Descendants of that duke were to become the biggest landowners in Britain, with well over a million acres. His forebears traded in much of that land and now the current duke has amassed one of the greatest art collections in the country, some of which he magnanimously allows the public to see.

By the late nineteenth century land concentration in Britain had reached the extreme levels we still see today. A survey in 1873 found that less than 5 per cent of the population owned all the land while the rest owned nothing at all. Though large tracts of land are now in public or corporate ownership, and home ownership is widespread, a third or more remains in the hands of a few thousand aristocrats and gentry, mostly descendants of the land-owning families in 1873.

Commons now make up a tiny 5 per cent of land in Britain, against roughly half in the Middle Ages, while only 2 per cent of what was wooded forest in medieval times is forest now. And a fifth wave in the plunder of the commons is underway, accelerated by globalization and the austerity regime imposed after the financial crisis of 2007–8. It is not just land. Everything we hold or use in common or intended for public benefit – from parks to police, from schools to sewers, even the air we breathe – is under attack.

## Enclosure, camping and other riots

> Thus came inclosure – ruin was its guide,
> But freedom's clapping hands enjoyed the sight
> Though comfort's cottage soon was thrust aside
> And workhouse prisons raised upon the site.
> — John Clare, 'The Fallen Elm'

In the first half of the nineteenth century, John Clare, 'the peasant poet', epitomized the lament for the disappearing commons. But this was not for want of opposition to the erosion of the commons and the ideology of private property rights used to rationalize it. The 800 years since the Charter have seen numerous protests, riots, petitions and movements in defence of the commons, led by oppressed and isolated commoners who often paid a heavy price for doing so.[14]

From the sixteenth century onwards the emerging middle classes of private property-owners joined the aristocracy in treating the rural commons as subversive, a zone of idleness, sinfulness and debauchery. One seventeenth-century observer, no doubt keenly supporting privatization of the commons, sneered that forests were:

> so ugly a monster as of necessity will breed . . . more and more idleness, beggary and atheism, and consequently disobedience to God and the King . . . wherein infinite poor yet most idle inhabitants have thrust themselves, living covertly without law or religion, *rudes et refractori* by nature, among whom are nourished and bred infinite idle fry, that coming ripe grow vagabonds, and infect the Commonwealth with most dangerous leprosies.[15]

In reality the commoners were struggling, deprived of the capacity to work and obtain adequate subsistence in the commons. Riots and rebellions in defence of the commons spread around the country. In the late fifteenth and early sixteenth centuries unrest broke out in towns and cities all over England over enclosures of common land their urban inhabitants still relied upon.[16] In the summer of 1549 two rebellions, in the West Country and in East Anglia, saw tens of thousands of protesters set up campsites in the countryside in a sixteenth-century precursor of the Occupy Movement remembered as the 'camping' time.[17]

It was around this time that the terms 'commons' and 'commoners' lost their dignifying and universalistic character and instead began to signify lower-class and inferior. This helped the elite to justify ignoring commoners' expressed views and interests.[18] By the Tudor era commoners were expected to know their place and do jobs for employers as the way to uphold the 'commonwealth', instead of sustaining themselves in the commons. But commoners did not give up silently.

Social discontent came to a head in the years leading up to the Civil War in the early seventeenth century and contributed to support for the English Revolution and the victory of the Parliamentarians. The sale of royal forest land by Charles I, for enclosure by its new owners, led to a series of riots known as the Western Rising, including Gillingham Forest, Braydon Forest and the Forest of Dean, as well as unrest elsewhere. Rioters, mostly artisans (and miners in the Forest of Dean) who relied on the forests for their livelihoods, staged mock parades and tore down newly erected barriers. In Gillingham they killed deer and destroyed plants for use in the enclosures. More violent protests erupted in the Forest of Dean where rioters armed with guns and pikes filled in iron ore pits and attacked houses for enclosure workers. Officials sent by the Star Chamber to put down the Braydon riot were shot at and sent packing. In the end, however, the sales and enclosures mostly went ahead, with no compensation for the commoners who had lost their means of support.

In the Grand Remonstrance of December 1641, which summarized parliament's opposition to Charles I's policies in 204 'points of remonstrance', number 21 refers to 'the enlargement of forests, contrary to *Carta de Foresta*'. However, parliament was primarily concerned with the interests of the well-to-do rather than the poor. Not long after the execution of the king, it passed legislation authorizing the sale and enclosure of all remaining royal forests.

During the English Revolution the Levellers and Diggers had been the most organized protestors on behalf of the common man and woman. Both were suppressed; the Diggers were massacred. In 1649 the Diggers planted parsnips, carrots and beans on the commons on St George's Hill in Surrey, and occupied wasteland elsewhere, in their campaign to reclaim lost commons land, which they believed had been taken by the 'Norman Yoake'. They claimed that until the Norman Conquest in 1066, most of England had been common land which was then appropriated by William the Conqueror, his barons and their successors. Their manifesto stated:

> The Earth (which was made to be a Common Treasury
> of relief for all, both Beasts and Men) was hedged in to
> In-closures by the teachers and rulers, and the others were
> made Servants and Slaves . . . Take notice, That England is
> not a Free People, till the Poor that have no Land, have a free
> allowance to dig and labour the Commons, and so live as
> Comfortably as the Landlords that live in their Inclosures.

The commons were also defended by the Levellers, a name formerly applied to those who levelled hedges in enclosure riots, whose goal was 'the right, freedom, safety and well-being of every particular man, woman and child in England'. In 1648 they submitted a petition to parliament, signed by 40,000 people, that included a request for 'the opening of all late enclosures of Fens and other Commons'.

In what became known as the Putney Debates of 1647 on

a new British constitution, Levellers in the Parliamentarians' New Model Army argued unsuccessfully for near-universal male suffrage. Instead, Cromwell and his allies insisted on limiting the vote to men of property and once in power greatly expanded the property-owning middle class or 'gentry' by privatizing large swathes of land. Still, the Levellers and the Diggers have gone down in English history as doughty defenders of customary rights and economic freedom.

Protests did not stop there. In 1680, faced with the impending enclosure of Ashdown Forest, the commoners petitioned against the implied loss of their rights to graze animals, collect firewood, and take stone and clay for building and other purposes.[19] Fifty years of protest and negotiation followed, such that even today much of the Ashdown Forest remains a commons. But it was a rare victory.

After the Restoration in 1660, longstanding customary rights were criminalized and the commercialization and commodification of land became integral features of a capitalist society. It was not just access to land that was restricted. Parliamentary Acts in 1663 and 1671 made it an offence to gather wood from royal forests. And in 1766, reflecting the growing market for wood, it became a crime to cut or break branches off ash, beech, oak or other trees used for timber.

In the eighteenth century, 'blacking' protests against enclosure and encroachment of the commons – so called because protesters blackened their faces – so alarmed the aristocratic elite that parliament hastily passed the Black Act in 1723, imposing the death penalty for over fifty criminal offences related to the forest, including being found in a forest while disguised.[20] As if this was not enough, Robert

Walpole, Britain's first prime minister, installed man-traps in Richmond Park to deter commoners from entering forbidden territory. Originally enclosed for a hunting park by Charles I, who seized common land from several parishes, it later became a lucrative sinecure for whoever held the post of Park Ranger, in Walpole's case his son. Walpole turned the park into a resort reserved for royalty and nobility, instituting a ticket and key system that locked out commoners and other hoi polloi.

The two years following 1723 saw skirmishes between poachers and gamekeepers that led to the execution of at least two poachers. However, commoners continued to protest against the loss of their rights of way. They staged a mass invasion of the park in 1751 and a few years later they won a famous legal victory against Walpole's successor as Park Ranger when the court ordered Richmond Park to be opened to all.

By the turn of the nineteenth century common land had already been reduced to a modest part of the countryside. However, enclosures continued, again sparking sporadic riots, which were put down by force. In 1831, at the height of the Industrial Revolution, more than 2,000 miners in the Forest of Dean tore down fences enclosing thousands of acres of land for coal and timber production where they formerly had commons rights to dig coal, as well as grazing and foraging rights. The military was called in and Warren James, the miners' leader, was arrested. Initially condemned to death, his sentence was commuted to transportation to Australia, where he died. By the time the Great Reform Bill was enacted in 1832, most of the land in England and Wales had been enclosed and privatized. In Scotland, the process was even more draconian. The Highland Clearances forcibly pushed more than 50,000 crofters off the land and replaced them with sheep. It was class politics at its most vicious.

Still, the ethos of the commons and commoning did not die, and nor did the resistance to further encroachments. And by the mid-nineteenth century the urbanizing bourgeoisie had developed a more romantic image of the forest, which began to inspire middle-class efforts to halt the assault on Britain's dwindling commons. Reflecting the growing popularity of medieval themes in literature (Sir Walter Scott's *Ivanhoe*), art (the Pre-Raphaelites) and architecture (the Gothic revival), the forest and the Charter were seen as capturing the spirit of 'greenwood'– a zone of freedom and a backdrop for the chivalry and courtly love depicted in *Ivanhoe* and the increasingly sentimentalized tales of Robin Hood.[21]

In the long Victorian era the forest increasingly became a place for recreation where people could escape from the noise, bustle and pollution of newly industrialized cities. This led to a popular interest in natural history, including the conservation of nature and biological diversity. The Royal Society for the Protection of Birds was founded in 1889, initially to counter the trade in plumes for women's hats for which thousands of birds were slaughtered. The National Trust, Britain's largest conservation organization, was created in 1895. But while the emphasis on nature was welcome as a nascent demand for ecological protection, it proved a distraction from the core of the Charter: its role in assuring a right to subsistence from activities and resources in the commons.

During the nineteenth century and early part of the

twentieth, many principles of the Charter were either lost or embedded in other legislation, including the Commons Act of 1876, which ruled that enclosure should be allowed only if there were public benefit, a sadly elastic concept. A fundamental assertion of common rights was turned into a generalized plan to transform nature into resources for use and profit. From the Charter's origins as a great act of 'de-commodification' of commoners, allowing them the means of subsistence outside the marketplace, it gradually evolved into a body of legislation and institutions for the managed com-modification of natural resources.

The protests and campaigns of the late nineteenth cen-tury were largely attempts to transform what remained of the natural commons into something rather different: public amenities for recreation. In the 1860s and 1870s, local com-moners, supported by the recently formed Commons Preser-vation Society, successfully opposed the enclosure of parts of Epping Forest, resulting in the Epping Forest Act of 1878.[22] This transferred ownership of the forest and the rights over it to the City of London, which has maintained it to this day as a recreational area. Still, Epping Forest was transformed from a commons, over which rights of access and resources were confined to a specific group of local residents as com-moners, to a public amenity, accessible to all but with more limited rights.

The change was more than symbolic. George Shaw-Lefevre, the leading light behind the Commons Preservation Society, described the commons as 'natural parks over which everyone may roam freely'. This was a far cry from their role as described in the Charter of the Forest, where they had a clear economic purpose as well as a social and political one. The whittling away of the natural commons as zones of subsistence accompanied aggrandizement of aristocratic and other landed estates. By the late nineteenth century much of the best land in the country was owned by a handful of people. In 1872, Lord Derby, himself a major landowner, asked the government to conduct a survey of landholding across the country, hoping to refute claims by the Liberal MP John Bright that land ownership was highly concentrated. But the survey report, *The Return of Owners of Land, 1873*, known as the second Domesday book, deeply embarrassed the noble lord and the governing aristocracy in general. The report showed that just 710 aristocrats – that is, Lord Derby and his friends – owned a quarter of the whole country and 4,000 families owned half of it, much of that land obtained from the commons and from gifts from successive monarchs. Its findings were hastily suppressed and copies of the report were hidden or destroyed. That was the last time an official record of land ownership in Britain was attempted.

In the twentieth century, the Charter's influence lingered, albeit weakly. There was one symbolic act of defiance. By chance, in July 1921 Britain's first woman barrister, Helena Normanton, noticed that the coalition government under David Lloyd George had put up for auction the Runnymede meadow itself, designated as commons since the thirteenth century. Intended for property development, the meadow was simply listed as 'Lot 8'. However, it had failed to reach its reserve price. Normanton wrote letters of protest to *The Times* and others and mobilized a public campaign against any further attempts at a sale. Public outrage inspired by her campaign reached such a pitch that only a month later the government announced it would not sell Runnymede after all. Eventually the Runnymede meadow and its surroundings were bequeathed to the National Trust, and its ninety-nine acres remain part of the natural commons to this day. The many people who roam casually over it now owe thanks to Helena Normanton for what she did.

The Forestry Commission, established in 1919 and today Britain's biggest landowner, has a mandate to preserve and expand Britain's forests and woodlands, including as a public amenity, but it was never tasked with preservation of the rights of commoners or the right to subsistence in the commons. Subsequent legislation, too, has emphasized nature, recreation and ownership rather than the economic, social and political values of commoning and the commons that are integral to the Charter.

The formal end of the Charter itself came with a whimper. It was simply replaced with the Wild Creatures and Forest Laws Act of 1971.[23] Commercial bourgeois values had triumphed. The Charter from its outset had been a vehicle for asserting the values of the commons and the rights of commoners against the state and against the forces of commodification. The Act that replaced it in 1971 was about the protection of nature and managing the commodification of our natural resources. It omitted the radical ethos that made the Charter so important – the preservation of the commons assuring citizens of sustainable subsistence, as rough equals.

## The Charter uncelebrated

The law locks up the man or woman
Who steals the goose from off the common,
But lets the greater villain loose,
Who steals the common from off the goose.
— Anon, seventeenth century[24]

In June 2015, in the House of Lords, Liberal Democrat Baroness Miller of Chilthorne Domer asked if the Conservative government would be marking the 800th anniversary of the Charter of the Forest in 2017. The 800th anniversary of the Magna Carta was being celebrated with great fanfare that same year, with exhibitions, events and media programmes across the country. The Justice Minister responded: 'Although the provisions of the Charter of the Forest remained in force for a number of centuries, it has not enjoyed the same lasting and worldwide recognition [as the Magna Carta]. Consequently the Government has no plans to mark and celebrate the 800th anniversary of the Charter of the Forest.'

Yet the Charter of the Forest had been on the statute books for longer than any other piece of legislation, and even in 2015 there were parts of the country that still adhered to rules and procedures emanating from the Charter. Verderers' courts, set up to enforce the Charter and ensure sustainable management of forest resources, still exist in the New Forest and the Forest of Dean where commoners continue to have 'rights of common', including grazing animals and collecting firewood.[25] The Charter's lasting legacy lies in asserting the rights of commoners, in a far more specific and meaningful way than in the Magna Carta. It laid down the idea of citizenship as the 'right to have rights', a term that Hannah Arendt made famous. It made clear that all commoners had rights in the commons, not just permission to access and use it that could be withdrawn at any time. This emphasis on non-withdrawable rights is part of what defines a commons. The Charter was also subversive. It was not about the rights of the poor, but about the rights of the free. For its time and place, it was a radical assertion of the universality of freedom, its commonality.

The Charter in itself was not a complete defence of the commons or the commoners. But it was a coherent defence as well as a harbinger, a step on the journey and a benchmark from which the commons could be constructed and defended.

# CHAPTER 2

# The Commons, Commoners and Commoning

Nature knows no sovereignty.

— Hugo Grotius, *Mare Liberum*, 1609

The Charter of the Forest was a reverential celebration of the commons and commoners in a society under reconstruction. However, it should not be seen as just an interesting historical document relating to long-past tussles over common land but, like the Magna Carta, as expressing eternal universal values. A thriving commons – encompassing not just the natural environment and its uses and resources, but our public services and amenities, our social and justice systems, and our cultural and intellectual life – is just as vital for a good society today as access to the commons was in medieval times. That is why we must resist contemporary attacks on the commons, which are lowering living standards, reducing the quality of life and corroding values of solidarity, sharing and community.

## Commons, commoning and commoners

'Common' stems from early English 'commune', signifying something that is general, universal or shared. Scarcely used today, the archaic verb 'to common' and the associated 'commoning' relate to the collective activity of working in the commons. Edward Coke, the jurist who rescued the Magna Carta from obscurity and neglect in the early seventeenth century, stressed the commoning aspect of the commons as a place where commoners undertook collective customary activities.[1] In this sense, the commons can be any setting where commoning – participative, communal activity – takes place. This is what defines a community. Without a commons and commoning, there is no community; without a community, there cannot be a commons.[2]

The other way of looking at the commons is as a communal resource, for use by a designated group, commoners. They can determine – or allow a nominated agent to determine – who has access to it, who has use of it, how it can be shared, and how it should be maintained, preserved and reproduced.

Many years ago, Ivan Illich, a distinguished social observer, made the tantalizing remark that the environment as commons should be distinguished from the environment as resource, the former being for people's subsistence, the latter for the production of commodities.[3] He lamented the loss of the distinction in the English language. However, subsistence should include preservation of the environment and the increasingly delicate balance of human and other natural species. The commons is about reproduction of resources, not depletion of them in the pursuit of economic growth and profits.

The commons have always stood for a collaborative way of living, suggesting shared access by rough equals. They are not just public in terms of use; they are zones of freedom from private restriction and domesticity. Handed down through the generations, they represent what has been gained for society. Many have been created for posterity, bequeathed as acquired rights, such as the Royal Parks given to the nation by Queen Victoria, or Stonehenge, gifted by the owner in 1918. They cannot legitimately be taken away by private interests or exploited for private profit, or sold or commercialized, without prior democratic approval of the commoners.

The word 'commoner' has also conveyed different meanings over the years. Now it brings to mind an image of someone living off the land, particularly those living on manorial property, affectionately depicted in the bucolic novels of Thomas Hardy and lauded in early photographic accounts of village life.[4] But 'commoner' had locally derived meanings in early towns of England as well.[5] Sometimes it encompassed the 'common people' in general and their rights to access urban streets, squares and greens, but often commons rights – for example to graze animals on common land outside city walls – were restricted to those citizens who had been granted the 'liberty of the city'. This image of the commoner is still portrayed by City of London livery companies, where the term signifies someone with special civic rights.

Commoners can be defined more broadly as all those who have access to the commons, who rely on them for their livelihood or way of living, and who participate in the governance, preservation and reproduction of a commons. All of us are commoners in that we all have access to some, perhaps many, kinds of commons. Most of us aspire to be commoners in a deeper sense. We want to belong, to share and to think of passing on what we and others have preserved. We have a responsibility to hand on resources, the environment, a landscape, a community as least as good as the one we were handed by those who forged it before us. At our best we are custodians.

This idea of the commons is ingrained in our culture, a reflection and reminder of our history. It is both anti-market and anti-government – or at least it stands against too much market, which elevates competition and individualism, and too much government, with its inherent bureaucracy and paternalism. The commons does not refer only to common or collective property. It also encompasses private property to which commoners (non-owners) have certain rights of access and use (usufruct rights). Some see the commons as 'areas where certain people, who do not own the land, have rights to share grazing or to gather fuel and animal bedding'.[6] But the Charter of the Forest went beyond this narrow definition. The important point is that certain people, who do not own the commons, have a right to share it.

The commons are neither a pristine untouched state of nature, where no one has rights, customary or otherwise, nor are they property acquired by the state for its own purposes, such as offices or military barracks, which governments can use as they see fit, since commoners' rights are not infringed. Shrinking or commercializing a commons, by contrast, erodes our common rights.

There is some arbitrariness in defining commons boundaries. David Bollier, an American writer and commons activist, includes 'tangible assets such as public forests and minerals, intangible wealth such as copyrights and patents, critical infrastructure such as the Internet and government research, and cultural resources such as the broadcast air-waves and public spaces' – resources, social institutions and cultural traditions paid for by taxes or inherited from previous generations.[7] However, many of these assets have been privatized and no longer fall into the category of commons. For instance, patents and copyrights are powerful means of *denying* an intellectual commons, turning a public good – ideas – into private property.

Other ways of defining the commons focus on collective governance and management of a shared resource, with special regard for equitable access, use and stewardship.[8] Here, too, there are boundary issues. Public utilities such as electricity and water are treated as commons in this book, but some writers exclude them because they are not directly managed by commoners.

In an attempt to define the commons, *The Economist* has argued that they share elements of both private property and public goods.[9] Like public goods such as street lighting, people cannot easily be excluded from using them. But like private property, use by one person diminishes – 'subtracts' from – access by others. Again, this is moot. Traditionally, non-commoners were denied access to common land, in which only designated commoners had rights, and this is still the case for some common land today. Local public services, such as elder care, are also normally restricted to local residents. So commons can be 'excludable'. However, restriction of access is often impractical. While many recreational commons were originally intended for locals only, no one is going to check users' postcodes.

A commons may not be 'subtractable' either. This

particularly applies to the intellectual commons – the realm of ideas and knowledge. You knowing something does not, or should not, subtract from the possibility of me knowing it as well. And where a commons is 'subtractable', usually termed a 'common pool' resource, access and use is normally shared in a pre-defined way, and is free or, if paid for, does not profit private interests.

Elinor Ostrom, who received the Nobel Prize in Economics for her work on management of the commons, was first inspired by an irrigation commons that still exists in the Swiss mountain village of Törbel. Water from the *bisses* (watercourses) has been reserved for the villagers as a common pool resource since the fifteenth century. In return for the right to take water from the *bisses*, the commoners must contribute their time to maintain them and not exceed their personal water allocation.[10]

Defining the commons in purely economic terms of 'excludability' and 'subtractability' fails to recognize the variety of the commons, and how they are used and come into being. A commons can also be defined by heritage or customary use established over time. There is something comforting about a commons. It has a quality of just being there – part of our society – that adds to our sense of belonging.

The commons 'belongs' to the commoners, traditionally a group defined by custom, but often in modern times the general public. They may use it, but are subject to known rules and procedures. They cannot do with it whatever they want. One enduring legacy of the Charter of the Forest is that it set conditions for collective action and governance of the commons alongside a commitment to preserve them.

This is why Garrett Hardin's 'tragedy of the commons' profoundly misunderstood the essence of a commons – that is, agreed rules and practices for managing a shared resource. In a famous article of 1968, Hardin claimed that the commons was doomed to depletion because every user had an incentive to maximize what they could take out of it. Although the argument had been made before, it was seized upon by neo-liberal economists to justify privatization. Yet the claim was always contested. Indeed, shortly before he died, Hardin confessed he should have called his article 'The tragedy of the *unmanaged* commons'.

Fundamental features of any commons are control of access, control of use, management rights, and rules for transferring or removing rights.[11] First, there must be rules for who has the right to access or use some common asset. To ensure sustainability and prevent over-exploitation, this may not be 'open access' for all at any time. As Elinor Ostrom emphasized, there are usually conventions that specify who can use commons resources and when.[12] Commons fisheries and grazing land are often cited as examples, but the principle applies more widely. Imagine if there were free and unlimited access to the two original copies of the Charter of the Forest. Excessive exposure would damage them and in the long term fewer people would be able to enjoy them.[13]

There also need to be rules on the 'right of withdrawal' that determine what commoners can take from the commons. In many commons there are limits on how much can be 'harvested' from a common asset. Fisheries and pasturing livestock again come to mind, but the same principle applies to consumption of water or use of a public library. Rules of sustainability are crucial. Ideally, harvesting should be allowed only up to a point where further use would threaten the sustainability or reproduction of the asset. This compares with private property, where the owner can choose to exploit a resource to extinction, as in mining.

The 'right of management' means the right to regulate the uses allowed in the commons, including the right to make improvements or modifications. Commoners do not need to manage the commons directly, as some insist.[14] Instead, they can delegate to a chosen agent or sub-set of commoners, accountable to the wider group. But management should be democratic; the commoners should be consulted and should have a voice in the outcome.

Finally, there should be rules on the 'right of alienation' – the transfer of common rights by sale, gift or lease. A rule may simply state that transfer of ownership or stewardship is not allowed. Historically, a real tragedy of the commons is that rules have often been too vague, allowing the powerful to take advantage of vulnerable groups to enclose, privatize, commercialize or run down a commons. In the seventeenth century, lords of the manor employed surveyors who were adept at citing written material to justify taking commons for their own use, whereas illiterate commoners could only rely on their recall of customary rights. But both state and market mechanisms have been used to undermine collective commons, by allowing their alienation or by relaxing protective regulations.[15]

The principles for sustaining the commons may be summarized as follows:

1. There should be well-defined boundaries. In medieval times these were confirmed and enforced by the practice of regular perambulations, or 'beating the bounds', when commoners would walk around customary boundaries of common land to identify and rectify surreptitious encroachments.

2. There should be 'collective choice arrangements' – that is, democratic governance. Commoners should have a say in the rules governing access and use. But the rules have often been so vague that they have allowed special interests to capture and exploit them for commercial gain. Egregious examples include extraction of minerals and bio-piracy – the plunder by pharmaceutical companies of indigenous know-how on medicinal uses of plants to make and market profitable drugs.

3. The commons should be monitored. This is not the same as governing or managing and should not involve the same people. Those nominated to monitor access and use – 'gatekeepers' – should be accountable to the commoners, not to any other authority, such as the government or landlords.

4. There should be rules on infractions by commoners, with known and proportionate penalties for proven infractions and clear due process procedures. Sanctions may include suspension of access or use of the commons in question. For example, someone failing to return library books can be fined and barred from further borrowing until the books are returned.

5. There should be mechanisms for resolving conflicts. To maintain trust and equity in the governance of the

commons, these mechanisms should be localized and low-cost.

6. Higher-level administrators and managers must recognize and respect commoners' rights, including their right to help make the rules.

7. While local commons may be part of a national system, they should be allowed to adapt rules to local conditions and traditions, a version of the principle of subsidiarity.

Failure to abide by and enforce these basic principles is at the root of the plunder of the commons – historically and in the present day.

## The right to subsistence

The Charter of the Forest emerged at a time when livelihoods and customary ways of living were under threat from civil war and 'afforestation'. It asserted not just rights of access to the commons but the rights of commoners to obtain subsistence in them. This is the implication of Article 9, which began as follows:

> Every Free-Man may Agist his own Wood within Our
> Forest, at his Pleasure, and shall take his Pawnage. Also,
> We do grant, That every Free Man may drive his Swine
> freely; without Impediment, through our Demesne Woods,
> to Agist them in their own Woods, or where else they will.

These were the ways commoners obtained subsistence, and the Charter depicted them as economic rights. The key words, incorporated into the Magna Carta as well, have long been erased from the English language, but their practice was central to a commons, referring to what the monarchy (as the state) conceded to commoners (the property-less) as common rights. While those rights reflected their time and place, the principles underpinning them are timeless.

Article 1 referred to 'common of herbage'. Commoners had a right to pasture their animals in the forest, which was linked to the 'right of agistment' – the right to graze livestock. The 'right to piscary' was the right to take fish from rivers and lakes. Like other subsistence rights, this was usually ruled by quota limitations. Fish has always been an important part of our diet, and it was recognized from early times that stocks had to be managed cooperatively in order to sustain them. 'Pawnage' (or 'pannage') referred to acorn, chestnut and beech-nut pastures set aside for pigs – also known as 'common of mast'. The right to let pigs loose in the woods in autumn usually entailed paying a fee to the lord of the manor. Commoners struggled for free access and tended to gain or lose it depending on changes in economic conditions and the needs of landlords. In medieval England, the value of pannage was a factor in determining the value of woodlands, and some woods recorded in the Domesday Book of 1086 were valued by the number of pigs in them.

The 'right to estover' was a right to collect firewood and wood, bracken and heather for everyday needs. Wood could be taken for 'housebote', 'cartbote' and 'firebote', usually with a quota intended to ensure equity and reproduction. The right to estover was probably the most important in the Charter, deriving from ancient Norman French to imply access to the necessaries for living. In the centuries following the sealing of the Charter, the right to estover merged with a community entitlement to 'glean': to pick grain and other useful outputs from fields after the harvest. This 'commoning' practice, the antecedents of which go back to biblical times,[16] was almost invariably done by women, often with children to assist. The 'right to turbary' was the right to cut peat for fuel. This has persisted in various places to this day, notably in Scotland, which came under the protection of the Charter when the Union was established in 1707. And the 'right to marl' – the right to dig and use clay – was more important than is often appreciated.[17] Freemen were allowed to construct a marl-pit and use the clay to line ponds, make domestic pots, and build walls (as in cob) for homes.

Although these historical rights of subsistence are little exercised today, as common land has shrunk, the principle endures that commoners have rights of subsistence from the commons.[18] But in the twentieth century, the state steadily converted common rights into labour-based entitlements. Rather than rights extended to all commoners, these entitlements were only provided to those doing labour and their immediate families. This was a momentous change, for it left the commons exposed and undefended.

## Social income

Discussing the right to subsistence should lead us to consider the meaning of income. When we think of income, most of us think of money. Indeed, mainstream economics has narrowed income to a monetary metric and national statistics have reflected that. Work that is not paid, such as caring for children and the elderly, or voluntary work in the community, has been made invisible and given a value of zero.

A political consequence is that governments have tried to maximize the number of people doing paid jobs, not caring that this might reduce their valuable unpaid work. We must broaden the idea of income to encompass all the resources available to us that contribute to our living standards and quality of life. Income is not just money.

That broader concept of 'social income' can be broken down into seven components, with some people having just one of these sources of income and very few having all seven: own production, such as growing one's own food; money wages; non-wage benefits paid by employers such as pension contributions, paid holidays and sick leave; occupational benefits, paid or available for those belonging to an occupational community (a form of commons); state benefits such as pensions, unemployment benefits and disability benefits; private benefits such as interest from savings and investments; and community benefits.

The last source of income can be split between social support from family, friends, neighbours or community, and commons benefits such as sources of subsistence gained from the commons. These may be opportunities to produce from commons resources (allotments, say), or aspects of the commons that reduce living costs or improve the quality of life, such as public services and amenities.

Social income provided by the commons can mitigate inequality and insecurity, giving people equal access to free or low-cost services, amenities and support. They can ensure that everyone is treated as an equally valued member of society, lowering the risk of falling into destitution or becoming a social outcast. As the Charter of the Forest recognized, the commons provide a lifeline that increases personal and community resilience to weather setbacks, shocks and hazards. Taking away the commons makes society more fragile and lowers social income, both directly and by removing a form of social insurance. The beauty of the commons is that while it may not be used, it is there for use if needed.

In recent decades, most components of social income have become more unequal, with rising salaries, perks and capital income for the affluent, and stagnant or falling wages and state benefits for the majority. A central proposition of this book is that the erosion of the commons in this period has increased social income inequality. Conventional income statistics have concealed that trend.

## How commons are created and preserved

of olde custome tyme owte of mynde

. . .

the syd costom hath been used inviolably . . . tyme out
of mynd of man
— Sixteenth-century sayings[19]

All commons have a history. Natural resources – land, water, the air, sources of energy and minerals – belong to all of us, bequeathed to commoners by virtue of being part of the natural commons. However, a commons can also be created through inheritance, bequeathed by virtue of its development and preservation over generations, or through a gift to posterity or to a particular community. A commons can also be created through a bargain between a property-owner and the surrounding community. In the Middle Ages, villagers often agreed to do labour services in return for common rights.

However created, a commons comes into existence because – in the words used by commoners for hundreds of years in villages, manors and towns across England – it has been that way since 'time immemorial' or 'time out of mind of man'. But for a commons to be secure, that memory must have been uncontested for a prolonged period, or if contested it must be resolved in some legal way in favour of the common rights.

In the early Middle Ages reference to accepted custom was based mainly on word of mouth and relied on recollections by older people that a commons had existed since 'time immemorial' – further back than anyone could remember or hear tell. At first, 'time immemorial' in a legal sense meant before the Norman Conquest in 1066, after which William the Conqueror declared that all land belonged to the Crown. As this date receded into the distant past, it became more and more difficult to claim. In 1275 Edward I brought in the first Statute of Limitations, which fixed time immemorial as being what was done and accepted before 1189, the coronation year of Richard I. If a custom or commons was held to exist before that date, it qualified as being since 'time immemorial'. In contested cases, elderly community members could be summoned as witnesses and their testimony taken as adequate proof. Much later, in the Limitation Act of 1623, 'customary' was given a less exacting definition, to mean a practice that had been uncontested for at least twenty years.

Once a commons is accepted as such, the owner, whether private or a government or public body, is at most the trustee or 'steward' of the commons, not a full owner with all the rights associated with private property. No part of the commons should be 'alienated' – sold or commercialized – without the prior approval of, and proper compensation to, the commoners. These constitutional principles were enshrined in the Charter of the Forest, which is why ruling interests and those who serve them have been so keen to whitewash it out of British history. The commons give substance to the universal and equal right of subsistence, contributing to living standards and the quality of life. They are not property that can be legitimately disposed of or otherwise blocked from being used for that purpose.

The creation of a commons should be distinguished from its preservation. Historically, preservation has involved partly symbolic collective actions that were also acts of socialization and intergenerational bonding. Annual perambulations and 'beating the bounds' were ways of indicating legitimacy and social solidarity, teaching successive generations what the commons entailed, and telling would-be encroachers, enclosers or privatizers that a commons was inviolate. This crystallized in the now barely remembered practice of 'Rogationtide' in Ascension Week, which continued throughout England for hundreds of years.[20] Community members took part in processions and perambulations over several days that usually ended in 'cakes and ale'.

A commons can also be created through legislation. For example, the Countryside and Rights of Way Act 2000 granted public access to land mapped as 'open country'. But laws can be overturned or amended, paradoxically providing less protection for the commons than appeals to custom.

## How the commons are lost

> Inclosure came and trampled on the grave
> Of labour's rights and left the poor a slave.
> — John Clare, 'The Mores', *c*.1815

Known during his lifetime as the Northamptonshire peasant poet, John Clare captured the plight of the commons in the nineteenth century, but he was not alone in lamenting their loss. As John Berger wrote in his 1979 novel *Pig Earth*, a 'culture of progress' was displacing 'a culture of survival'. It continues to do so. Communism, socialism and liberalism all viewed the commons as dispensable, while economic growth was sacrosanct. Progress allowed little respect for tradition and common rights.

The commons can be lost by several means, and all have figured throughout the history of the struggle to develop and retain them. In the period around the sealing of the Charter of the Forest, what most concerned commoners was simple encroachment, a confiscation by stealth, notably by just moving boundaries, fence positions or border stones. This was the stimulus for the tradition of perambulations mentioned earlier. If the whole community could share knowledge of where traditional boundaries were located, surreptitious attempts to shift them could be resisted, or so the commoners hoped.

A commons can also be lost or eroded by outright theft. Because a commons has no known value or price, it can be economically invisible to ordinary people. It may become private property without the commoners realizing or appreciating what has happened until access is needed and found to be lost. Similarly, lack of clear documentation can allow slippery practice between government representatives and private commercial interests to weaken a commons.

Historically, enclosure has been the most systemic way by which commons have been lost and is certainly the main way that natural commons have been taken away from commoners. Often land was enclosed by a formal owner who had previously accepted that commoners had beneficiary rights on at least part of the land. 'Engrossing', 'regrating' and 'forestalling' are terms that came into use in Tudor times to refer to different ways of enclosing the commons. Engrossing refers to monopolizing ownership or control; regrating means purchasing a commodity for resale; and forestalling means withholding a commodity from the market so as to push up the price. All of these methods now form the core of today's rentier capitalism, in which income and wealth are channelled to owners of property – physical, financial and intellectual.[21]

Enclosure is not the same as privatization, however, which has been the main way of plundering the commons since the late twentieth century.[22] Commercialization is another modern, creeping form of erosion, linked in particular to austerity. Commercialization played a role in the Middle Ages as well: forest law was modified to promote timber production, for instance.[23] But it is a much stronger trend today.

One insidious outcome of these trends can best be described as colonization. More and more of what used to be commons have passed not just into private commercial hands but into foreign control, with owners that have no interest in or accountability to local or national communities.

The commons have also been eroded through neglect, in recent times accelerated by budget cuts due to austerity. Often, the erosion has resulted from the deliberate neglect of stewardship, part of the strategy known as the 'micro-politics of privatization' adopted by the early Thatcherites, in which public services and nationalized industries were starved of investment and left to run down in order to induce public indifference to, and support for, their privatization.

Such a strategy is not confined to Britain. In a telling example from the United States, in January 2018 the majority of members of the US National Park System Advisory Board resigned in protest, saying that Ryan Zinke, then Secretary of the Interior (appointed by President Donald Trump), was refusing to meet them, ignoring their advice and overseeing a strategy of neglect of the parks.[24] Zinke's actions showed the US administration's intention to weaken the gatekeeping defence of the commons prior to opening up millions of acres for oil and mining operations.

Some commons have been lost by a weakened struggle by commoners to retain them. For centuries, rural smallholders and the property-less, including many urban dwellers, understood that the commons were a source of income, a means of social protection and an institution of cultural binding. The commoners placed a high value on relations of reciprocity and social solidarity, which were realized in the commons. But once the cult of progress took over – 'improvement' was the nineteenth-century term – and once the masses became an essentially urban proletariat, those that had been commoners looked to employers and the state instead to provide parts of their social income. They lost interest in defending the commons. State paternalism took over the social security functions of the commons and the class-based defence of the commons waned and almost died.

## Neo-liberalism and austerity

The commons are public wealth. But they have no price. To neo-liberals this means they have no value. So they can be used by commercial interests for free. On this view, resources only have value when they are used (depleted) to produce commodities, which define growth in conventional economics. Loss of the commons does not count.

The commons ideally are an interrelated organism that balances production, reproduction, recreation and leisure, with emphasis on reproduction and sustainability. If subject to commercialization or privatization, that balance is sacrificed; the pursuit of profit and short-term advantage rules out respect for the reproduction of resources or assets or support systems. This dislocation is even more pronounced when ownership passes to foreign capital, which by definition has no interest in being a steward of British commons. Privatization and 'colonization' are not just about a transfer of ownership; historically, many commons were on privately owned land. Privatization also transfers stewardship of the values and functions of the commons to owners whose overriding interest is to make profits.

When the global economy lurched into crisis in 2007–8 with the financial crash and the resultant 'great recession', governments reacted with policies that soon became known colloquially as 'austerity'. They claimed that people had been living beyond their means and that government had been irresponsible in splurging on public spending. This led to measures that may have seemed an appropriate response to the erroneous premise, but which deserve to be compared with what Hannah Arendt saw as the 'banality of evil' of fascism – each little step leading inexorably towards a horror of frightening proportions.

'Austerity' did evil through its twin lies: that government needs to balance its budget and reduce public debt, and that balancing the budget requires large and continuing cuts to public spending, including measures that shrink the commons. To support the first claim, the British government said high public debt slowed economic growth, an assertion based on an influential study by two American economists. Subsequently, that study was shown to be wrong; it is high *private* debt that slows economic growth. But by then the lie had been accepted.

The second fallacy was that cutting public debt required balancing the budget with big cuts in public spending. This was a disgraceful part of the austerity strategy. A deficit arises when spending exceeds revenue. Leaving aside whether a balanced budget is a worthwhile government objective, which is dubious, balance can be achieved by cutting spending or by increasing revenue. The government set about *cutting* revenue, with lower taxes and higher tax reliefs for privileged interests, and then slashed spending to fill a hole that it had artificially expanded.

It cut corporation tax from 28 per cent in 2010 to a target of 17 per cent in 2020. It cut inheritance tax, so that anybody will be able to inherit a house worth up to £1 million without paying any tax. It raised personal income tax allowances and introduced additional tax reliefs for relatively wealthy people. There is no evidence that any of these measures increased economic growth, which has lagged well below its long-term average. But by shredding vital parts of the commons, austerity has increased inequality and made our social fabric more fragile.

The commons has shrunk dramatically, not only because government has systematically cut public spending, but because local government has borne the biggest burden and is scheduled to continue to do so. It is local government that pays for the upkeep of much of the commons, in all its forms, and spending is increasingly focused on the statutory (obligatory) functions of social care and waste disposal, leaving little over for anything else.

## The Lauderdale Paradox

The commons are not inherently scarce. Land, water, air, ideas, nature, art and the public amenities that make up the social commons are potentially abundant. Though some are subject to the whims of nature and climate, it is mainly society that generates scarcity.

In 1804, James Maitland, eighth Earl of Lauderdale and an amateur political economist, wrote an essay with the splendid title, *An Inquiry into the Nature and Origin of Public Wealth; and into the Means and Causes of its Increase*. The main theme became known as the Lauderdale Paradox, which exercised the minds of several generations of economists, but which has been resolutely ignored by modern successors. The paradox is that, as private riches grow, public wealth declines. To modern neoclassical economists, that is not possible because in their way of thinking only private income and wealth count. But the commons comprise much of our public wealth. The paradox reveals an inconvenient truth. Private riches are essentially derived from commodities that have a price and can be bought and sold. But something that is infinitely abundant has no price. Thus private wealth is enhanced by generating 'contrived scarcity', turning public wealth into a commodity. This is 'the tragedy of de-commoning'.

Lauderdale wrote that 'public wealth may be accurately defined – to consist of all that man desires, as useful or delightful to him' whereas private riches depended on 'a degree of scarcity'. He then argued that 'The common sense of mankind . . . would revolt' at measures to increase private riches 'by creating a scarcity of any commodity generally useful and necessary to man'. But this is precisely what commercial interests do. Lauderdale went on to argue that only the impossibility of private owners banding together to monopolize public wealth protected it 'against the rapacity of private avarice'. Today, the noble Earl would be saddened by the ability of the plutocracy and plutocratic corporations, aided by governments, to do precisely what he thought was impossible. It is 'the tragedy of privatizing'.

## How the commons are saved

In recent years many movements across the world have emerged to defend the commons. One of the largest is the international peasant movement known as La Via Campesina that aims to protect commoners' land rights. Others are activist groups fighting to save local commons, ranging from rivers, lakes and parks to social housing, public services, libraries and museums. In Britain the Open Spaces Society campaigns to preserve common land and common rights. But any success has been against the grain of erosion. The main defence has been public protest, including through social media, such as the petitions organized by 38 Degrees in the UK and Avaaz in the United States.

Preservation of the commons depends on three groups: stewards, custodians and gatekeepers. A steward is the titular owner of a commons required or expected to uphold its integrity on behalf of the commoners. Stewardship is an ethic that embodies responsible planning and management of resources. However, if ownership becomes commercialized, the integrity of a commons becomes more fragile and uncertain; the nominal stewards are corrupted in the institutional sense of being unable to fulfil their function of preserving the commons.

A custodian is someone who takes it upon him or herself to acquire something that was in the commons and preserve it for the commons. Billionaire David Rubenstein, a prominent US philanthropist, who built up the Carlyle Group as one of the world's biggest private equity funds, bought a thirteenth-century copy of the Magna Carta in order to keep it as part of the cultural commons. He has lent it to the Smithsonian in Washington DC where any visitor can see it for free. However, he could terminate this loan at any time. There is no obligation on him to leave it in the commons, if he should choose otherwise. That is not the same as being a steward, who has a moral and constitutional duty to preserve and defend the commons.

The role of gatekeepers is to hold stewards to their

responsibilities. They are vital for the commons, as monitors tracking what happens and as intermediaries negotiating between commoners, property owners and those seeking to commodify the commons. Gatekeepers include organizations that go one step further, defending the commons by becoming their owners. The outstanding example of this is Britain's National Trust, which owns 250,000 hectares of coastline and countryside, over 500 historic buildings, parks and nature reserves, and one of the world's largest art collections. But once a gatekeeper becomes a steward, there is usually a need for a new gatekeeper to hold them to their constitutional principles. A lack of effective gatekeepers has been the bane of many commons; stewards have been allowed to depart from or abandon commons principles, by restricting commoners' rights or by drip-drip commercialization. A commons is bequeathed to the current generation of commoners, who are expected to guard it for future generations. Without strong gatekeepers, that is hard to do.

## Social memory

> Memory is the mother of all wisdom.
> — Aeschylus

> Memory is the treasury and guardian of all things.
> — Cicero

Social memory – the memory of a shared past, traditions and customs – shapes our sense of social identity. A commons derives from social memory, the collective recall of a commons and the values and informal rules governing it.[25] The commons embody values moulded by social memory and reinforce social memory as the glue of society. The richer or more widespread the commons, the stronger the networks of social memory are likely to be.

Social memory of a commons runs counter to the neo-liberal forces of commodification and individualization. Traditions of sharing and preservation stand in the way of short-term profiteering. Depleting the commons means weakening and thinning social memory, dismissing customs as matters of habit rather than a complex web of social reciprocities that reinforce community identity and solidarity. A society without a robust commons and with a fragile social memory fosters narcissistic individualism and weakens any sense of universalism, which is precisely what neo-liberalism wants.

However, neo-liberalism suffers from its own special hubris. If the commons is destroyed, and its underlying social memory is forgotten, rampant commodification will lead to a dilution of social values nurtured by the commons, including empathy, altruism, reciprocity, solidarity and tolerance of the other – of strangers. Loss of the commons leaves people unready to resist the commodification of everything and contributes to a 'plutonomy', where the economy is dominated by monopolistic corporations and where political decisions are manipulated in a pluto-populist direction by the rich and powerful. This plutocracy can pressurize governments to cut taxes, thus lowering public revenue and inducing austerity policies by government at all levels. This in turn means curbs on spending on the remaining commons and increased pressure to privatize them so as to raise windfall revenue to cover statutory spending obligations and further tax cuts.

The reverse side of social memory, 'social forgetting',

is also a threat to the commons, which depends so much on oral traditions and social norms. Forgetting can result from disuse, from memories lost by the erosion of the commons, or from state repression of what had been part of the social memory.[26] The commons can be forgotten, and thus lost. They should never be taken for granted.

## The Hartwick Rule

In 1977, the economist John Hartwick argued that to ensure inter-generational equity, society should invest enough of the rental income from extraction and use of exhaustible, and thus naturally scarce, resources so that future generations would benefit as much as today's. This became known as the Hartwick Rule of inter-generational equity. As the World Bank put it, 'The Hartwick rule holds that consumption can be maintained – the definition of sustainable development – if the rents from non-renewable resources are continuously invested rather than used for consumption.'[27]

A principle underpinning this rule is that the commons belong to all of us equally, but we are only its temporary possessors. Nobody has exclusive rights and nobody has permanent rights. As Edmund Burke wrote elegantly, we are 'temporary possessors and life renters' and we 'should not think it amongst [our] rights to cut off the entail, or commit waste on the inheritance'. Society as a whole should obtain income from the commercial use of natural resources, not only to compensate for 'externalities' such as pollution that are not reflected in the market price, but also to contribute to the welfare and living standards of all. The commons belong to the commoners, and the returns to any commercial use should go to the commoners of today and of the future. In the ongoing plunder of the commons, the Hartwick Rule has been wilfully abused. It should be used to determine what should be done in response.

However, not all commons consist of exhaustible or non-renewable resources. Many commons are renewable or non-exhaustible if properly maintained. Examples include forests and water sources in the natural commons, and just about everything in the social, civil, cultural and knowledge commons, comprising public services, institutions and amenities, where use does not lead to depletion. In these cases the Hartwick Rule need not be applied for inter-generational equity, as long as the commons themselves are bequeathed in good shape.

## Equality in the commons

A commons is a sphere of rough equality – or should be. There is a presumption that every commoner should be treated as an equal, legitimized by uncontested custom over a prolonged period, with equal access to resources and equal benefit. This prima facie principle of equality implies that if a commons is alienated, privatized or even partially commercialized, all relevant commoners should be compensated equally.

If a government sells off a commons and uses the proceeds to offset tax cuts for a rich minority, commons principles are breached in several ways. Government has no right to sell off the commons; only commoners have such a right, since it belongs to them, just as private property belongs to the property-owner. Middle-class home-owners would be up in arms if the government sold their homes and used the proceeds to cut taxes. By compensating a minority, a government would be breaching the commons equality principle. And it would be ignoring the Hartwick Rule by not ensuring future generations would benefit equally.

## The precariat: modern commoners

One group in modern Britain and elsewhere is more affected than others by changes in all forms of commons. This is the precariat, an emerging class, generated by globalization, the digital revolution and changes in economic and social policy over the past four decades. Consisting of millions of people all over the world, the precariat has distinctive patterns of labour and work, a distinctive structure of social income, and is losing citizenship rights.[28]

Those in the precariat are being forced to accept lives of unstable labour through temporary jobs, agency labour, 'tasking' via digital platforms, flexible scheduling, and on-call and zero-hour contracts. They must also do a lot of unpaid, unrecognized work, including activities they must undertake to sell themselves in the labour market, such as retraining, learning new skills, brushing up resumés, networking, form-filling, queuing and other activities they must undertake to obtain meagre benefits or services. They must work and labour outside fixed workplaces and standard labour hours as well as within them. For this reason, among others, the precariat needs a diverse commons of accessible, affordable public amenities and spaces.

The precariat exists in most occupations and at most levels within corporations. Within the legal professions, for example, there are elites with large social incomes, a squeezed salariat, and a precariat of paralegals. Similar fragmentation exists in the medical and teaching professions, with paramedics and 'fractionals' (remunerated for only a fraction of full-time). The precariat is even spreading into corporate management with 'interim managers' (as depicted by George Clooney in the film *Up in the Air*). As a consequence, the precariat finds itself frozen out of solidaristic communities, or social commons, while still needing them as an informal support system.

This group has a distinctive structure of social income, which makes access to the commons important, if not vital. It has been losing non-wage benefits and lacks the occupational benefits, including help in hard times, that come with belonging to a professional association or craft guild. Those in the precariat must rely on money wages alone, which have stagnated in real, inflation-adjusted, terms for three decades, and which have become more volatile. Income security is correspondingly low. And as the precariat must do much unpaid work, their wage rate is lower than it appears. This will intensify with the spread of 'tasking' via online platforms in the years ahead.

The precariat has also lost entitlement to rights-based state benefits. The welfare state in Britain and elsewhere was built on the presumption that the majority of men were in stable full-time employment; social and economic security could be based on social insurance involving contributions from employees and employers, providing benefits in case of 'temporary interruptions of earnings'. That model has withered.

The international trend towards means-testing and

behaviour-testing has hit the precariat hard and engulfed many in workfare regimes, forcing them to do various forms of unpaid work to obtain benefits. Means-testing creates poverty traps, since benefits are withdrawn when earned income rises. The precariat also face 'precarity traps'. Obtaining benefits takes time, during which they are without income. Once benefits are received it would be financially irrational to take a low-paying short-term job alternative, only to have to wait once again for benefits to be renewed.

Faced with the loss of non-wage employment benefits and rights-based state benefits, the precariat has had to rely on family and community support. But it has been losing access to such support, as well as to commons resources and amenities, all underestimated sources of income security for low-income groups through the ages. Instead, many in the precariat are being driven to food banks and charities.

Key to the precariat's income insecurity is uncertainty. Uncertainty differs from contingency risks, such as unemployment, maternity and sickness, which were the core concerns of welfare states. One can calculate the probability of such events and develop an insurance scheme to socialize the risks, as National Insurance in Britain was intended to do. But uncertainty cannot be insured against; it is about unknown unknowns. A different system of income support is required when most of those in need are in the precariat.

Whereas the old industrial proletariat went from having few rights to having more – cultural, civil, social, political and economic – the precariat has been losing such rights. They lack cultural rights, for instance, because they cannot belong to communities such as occupational guilds, a form of social commons, that would give them security and identity. They lack civil rights because they cannot afford legal representation and because due process is being eroded; they are being punished without a fair hearing, losing entitlement to state benefits on the whim of unaccountable bureaucrats. They are losing economic rights because they cannot work in occupations for which they are qualified. Their level of education often exceeds that required for the kind of jobs they can obtain.

Loss of rights goes with the most defining feature: the precariat are supplicants. The Latin meaning of 'precarious' was 'to obtain by prayer'. That sums up what it is to be in the precariat: having to ask for favours, help, a break, a discretionary judgement by some bureaucrat, agent, relative or friend. This intensifies uncertainty. Being in the precariat is like running on sinking sand.

In a commons, nobody is a supplicant. The precariat needs the commons and commoners' rights more than others. To have any semblance of social and economic security they need networks for mutual support and sharing, the essence of commoning. They rely on the commons for services and amenities, to supplement meagre and uncertain money incomes from work and labour. They are the most unlikely to own property and must rely on access to public spaces, such as parks. Depleting the natural, social, civil, cultural or knowledge commons hurts the precariat most of all. Sadly, this is precisely what has been happening.

## A Commons Charter

Throughout history the commons have been a vital part of social income, providing a 'right to subsistence' and lessening structural inequalities in society. Our modern commons are as important today. But they are being lost to enclosure, commercialization, privatization, colonization and neglect, increasing socio-economic inequality by more than official statistics of income and wealth inequality suggest. We need to take back the commons, revive their principles of sharing, solidarity and universality, and ensure that commoners – 'we, the people' – are properly compensated for any loss.

This book outlines a Charter of the Commons, in the spirit of the Charter of the Forest, that is the nucleus of a response to the plunder of all forms of commons in Britain. The objective should be not only to restore the commons as 'public amenities' and 'resources', to be used by commoners, but also to encourage commoning – collective, collaborative activity. The reforms demanded by a Commons Charter should aim to reduce social income inequality by ensuring a modern equivalent of the 'right to subsistence', as enshrined in the Charter of the Forest. And they should strengthen democratic management of the commons through mechanisms of responsible stewardship, gatekeeping and participation of commoners in decision-making. This should include encouraging 'communities of interest' in specific commons – such as local green spaces, hospitals or museums – to participate in communal forms of management.[29]

For many commons, these principles support a multi-stakeholder, cooperative (MSC) model of governance and ownership, perhaps better named a 'public-commons part-nership', where management of the commons would be driven by users and local community interests as well as by work-ers and, where relevant, outside investors. The MSC model – sometimes called a 'social cooperative' – has flourished in Italy, where there are over 14,000 social cooperatives deliv-ering care services.[30] The membership consists not just of workers, as in traditional worker cooperatives, or consumers, as in consumer cooperatives, but service users, volunteers, representatives of local authorities and others.

A Commons Charter should be a set of demands driven by values. Most successful charters in history have been class-based. This does not mean that they have only advanced the interests of one class. But they have been driven by the needs and aspirations of particular classes, usually those that are growing and under pressure. This applied as much to the Universal Declaration of Human Rights of 1948 – a sort of twentieth-century charter – as to the Charter of the Forest of 1217 and the great Chartist movement of the 1830s.

The Charter of the Forest reflected a momentary alli-ance between the barons and the peasantry, as commoners. The 1948 Universal Declaration reflected a momentary alli-ance between a re-emerging bourgeoisie and the industrial proletariat in the wake of the Second World War. Today, a Charter of the Commons should be driven by the needs and aspirations of the precariat, the emerging mass class. Just as the Charter of the Forest was a response to a social, economic and political crisis, when the state sought a new social con-sensus, so today there is a similar need, one that could prompt revival of the commons as the foundation of a good society.

A modern Commons Charter must pay respect to the Charter of the Forest, which, when sealed in 1217, established constitutional principles that were 'for ever'. That Charter deserves to be celebrated as the first environmental charter in history, the first to assert that previous enclosure of common land should be reversed, the first to assert that the commons should not be subject to enclosure, and the first to assert that commoners – all of us – have the right to subsistence, the right to work and the right to a home. These principles, long abused, should be renewed and respected.

Accordingly, the Commons Charter could begin with the following preamble:

> The commons are our collective heritage, our common wealth, our collective knowledge and our traditions of sharing in society. They are of most value to those on low incomes, the 'property-less' and the precariat. Shrinking the commons lowers their living standard and worsens inequality. To reduce inequality and strengthen citizenship it is vital to revive the commons.
>
> The Hartwick Rule of inter-generational equity – the principle that future generations should benefit from the commons as much as current generations – should be respected. Policies must promote and support equitable sharing, while seeking to prevent and reverse 'contrived scarcity' arising from the encroachment, enclosure and privatization of the commons, and neglect by government.
>
> To revive the ethos of the commons, we should strive to create, and bequeath to coming generations, new commons based on communities of interest and communal

forms of management that respect customs of sharing and preserving natural, social, cultural, civil and knowledge resources.

The commons can only be safe if there is strong democratic governance. All spheres of the commons should have identified stewards, responsible for their management and preservation, and adequately funded gatekeepers, without which the stewards may not be held to account.

This preamble lays out principles of sharing and indicates the need for competent stewards, monitors and gatekeepers, without which no commons can be secure. And it reminds us that the commons are spheres of sustainability, freedom and equality.

# CHAPTER 3

# The Natural Commons

> Every Free-Man from henceforth, without Danger, shall
> make in his own Wood, or in his Land, or in his Water,
> which he hath in Our Forest; Mills, Springs, Pools, Marsh-
> Pits, Dikes or Earable Ground, without inclosing that
> Earable Ground; so that it be not to the Annoyance of
> any of his Neighbours.
> — Article 12, Charter of the Forest, 1217

The Charter of the Forest focused on the natural commons
as the means of providing commoners with subsistence. This
is the commons of popular imagination. If by no means its to-
tality, the essence of the commons is nature. It is fundamentally spatial – encompassing land, the minerals and other natural
matter beneath it and on it, the forests, woods and wildlife,
the rivers and lakes, the seashores, the air we breathe, the sky
we see or should see.

In this age of environmental decay, climate change and frequent devastating natural catastrophes every part of the natural commons is under intense threat. But the threat has been
magnified many times over by deliberate action on the part
of rulers, governments and the rich and powerful to usurp
the commons for private benefit. And extensive privatization

has permitted colonization by foreigners with no interest in commoners' rights or interests.

Over the centuries, much of what was the natural commons in Britain has been lost. Throughout that time, commoners have resisted this decline, often at great cost to themselves and their families and communities. But one lesson from history is clear: once the commons are lost, they are extremely hard to revive or restore.

## Land and 'property rights'

These days, most people probably think of property and property rights as relating to private ownership and the legal rights of owners to use their property as they wish. But it is more complicated than that. In the case of land, ownership and 'property rights' mean several different things. Strictly speaking, nobody in Britain owns the land they possess. The ultimate owner is the Crown, which grants landholders tenure.[1]

The main forms of tenure in Britain today are freehold, leasehold and renting. But another widespread form of tenure – until it was abolished finally in 1925 – was known as 'copyhold'. When it was first recorded in the late fifteenth century, it referred to manorial land granted to a smallholder, either for life or as a matter of inheritance, to be used only according to the customs of the manor. Copyholders could access the commons to graze their animals, or to complement what they could produce on their individual copyholdings. But, overlapping the enclosure Acts of the nineteenth century, a series of copyhold Acts whittled away this entitlement, removing the rights of an important group of commoners.

Today, as in the past, someone may own land but have

restrictions on how they use it. In medieval times owners, including the monarch, were obliged by the Charter to allow commoners use of the commons on their land. In modern times, land transfers are often accompanied by restrictive covenants stating owners' obligations to their neighbours, such as commitments not to build on all or part of the land, or to cut down trees or erect fences. And planning controls also limit what owners can do with their land. Conversely, someone may have wide usufruct rights on a piece of land without formally owning it. Tenant farmers are one example. Allotment holders are another. And leasehold property can be held on a short or long lease, the terms of which usually specify what the leaseholder can and cannot do with the property. When the lease comes to an end the property reverts to whoever owns the freehold.

If the initial simplicity of property rights dissolves quickly on reflection, think back to the property rights principles enshrined in the Charter of the Forest, which referred to three forms of land – royal (or state) land, private land (granted to barons and the church) and common land (the commons). From the outset, the commons have never been owner-less. Rather, they impose restrictions on landowners and give designated rights to identified groups of commoners. At the time of the Charter, the idea of private property rights as conceived today was alien. Even in the case of baronial manors, the lord was expected to be a steward, observing, respecting and enforcing communal principles based on inherited custom.

Historically, many philosophers have regarded land as a natural commons. John Locke too, usually regarded as the champion of private property rights, argued that 'God gave the world to men in common'.[2] And his defence of private property came with three caveats, dubbed the 'Lockean provisos'. First, an individual may appropriate land or resources from the commons only if 'enough and as good' is left over for others. When land is scarce relative to the population, appropriation should be restricted. As Locke put it, 'where there is plenty of people under government, who have money and commerce, no one can inclose or appropriate any part, without the consent of all his fellow commoners'. The second caveat, known as the 'sustenance proviso', basically says that property owners have a moral duty to provide those without property with enough to avoid 'extreme want'. The third caveat, the 'spoilage proviso', states that a property owner should not 'ingross as much as he will' from the commons, but only as much as he can 'enjoy' or make practical use of. These provisos are rarely invoked by defenders of private property rights today.

In the centuries following the Charter, the commons evolved through farming systems operated by commoners. For generations the dominant method was open-field farming, whereby individuals or groups cultivated strips of land alongside others.[3] Much of that consisted of collaborative work. For instance, an ox-drawn plough was needed for heavy English clay soils, sometimes requiring as many as eight oxen to pull it. But few commoners could afford an ox-team of their own. So they cooperated by sharing the cost and labour of ploughing their individual strips. Dividing land into strips of higher and lower quality facilitated an egalitarian system that depended on time-honoured collective action and agreement by commoners on how the land should be managed.

In Britain, commons land can be traced back to Neolithic times and has been identified in Bronze and Iron Age settlements such as those on Bodmin Moor and in the Cotswolds. The Anglo-Saxon law code of 649 explicitly referred to common land.[4] In the Middle Ages about half the land of England could be considered commons. Today, the commons, defined as areas where commoners still have designated rights, comprises only 3 per cent of all land in England, 8 per cent in Wales and 7 per cent in Scotland, or about 5 per cent for the whole of Great Britain (Table 1).[5]

Across England, Scotland and Wales, most of what was once commons land has been enclosed, cementing one of the most concentrated land ownership structures in the world. Although the enclosures of history were mainly responsible, enclosure has continued to the present day, often aided by commercial interests.

Generations of subsidies to commercial farmers have promoted industrial farming over the needs of smallholders. The European Union's Common Agricultural Policy (CAP) has reinforced this bias. CAP subsidies amounting to about £3 billion a year have gone disproportionately to the small number of landowners who own over half the land in Britain. To put this in context, wage earners in agriculture receive in total only £2.4 billion a year. These subsidies have enabled large-scale landowners to enclose more land, wiping out hedgerows, woodlands and their wildlife, and sweeping away bits of commons along the way. Subsidies have also increased the dominance of large landowners in determining what is

| | Hectares | Percentage of land area |
|---|---|---|
| **Common grazings** | | |
| Scotland | 591,901 | 7 |
| **Registered common land** | | |
| Wales | 173,366 | 8 |
| England | 372,941 | 3 |
| **Commons exempted from registration** | | |
| New Forest | 21,995 | |
| Epping Forest | 2,458 | |
| Exempted by order | 1,020 | |
| Forest of Dean | 3,100 | |
| Total commonable land in Great Britain | 1,166,781 | 5 |

**Table 1**

Area of Common Land in Great Britain, 2017

done with agrarian land in general, forcing small-scale farmers to alter their practices or sell up. Over 33,000 small-to-medium-sized farms have closed down since the mid-2000s.[6]

The tenth Duke of Buccleuch is Britain's largest private landowner. As the descendant of an illegitimate son of Charles II he inherited 277,000 acres, for which he did not do a day's work. In 2015, the latest year for which there were published data at the time of writing, he was given £1.6 million in CAP subsidies, while twenty dukes (of the twenty-five who made their finances public) have received subsidies totalling over £8 million a year.[7] Lord Bathurst, a major donor to the Conservative Party, who owns an estate of 15,000 acres, has received over £9 million in subsidies in recent years. No doubt to obtain value for his unearned money, he transferred ownership of part of his estate to the tax haven of Bermuda.

This absurdly regressive system fosters and preserves the concentration of land ownership. It has no moral or economic justification, especially given the dubious way that much of this land was wrenched from the commons in the first place. It also damages the environment, not only by destroying hedges and woods but by encouraging monoculture and reducing biodiversity. Farming communities with small-scale plots and a commons mentality may be less 'efficient' (although this can be contested), but they tend to nurture and preserve a more diverse range of crops, seeds and breeds of animals. Industrial agriculture may maximize output in the short term but probably at the cost of long-term sustainability, creating a more fragile, less resilient productive system.[8]

While the waves of enclosure that scarred Britain never went uncontested, the first legislative moves to defend the commons came in the second half of the nineteenth century. They were primarily a response to industrialization and the expansion of cities whose growing populations needed open spaces for recreation and fresh air. In 1865 parliament set up a committee 'to inquire into the best means of preserving for the use of the public the Forests, Commons and Open Spaces in the neighbourhood of London'. This was the catalyst for the establishment the same year of the Commons Preservation Society (described by its primary founder as 'the people's watchdog')[9] and the passing in 1866 of the Metropolitan Commons Act. The Act forbade enclosure of any commons within the Metropolitan Police District – a radius of fifteen miles from Charing Cross – and allowed the London boroughs to put in place management schemes to ensure public access. It also established the exchange principle that any unavoidable loss of commons land – to widen a road, for example – should be replaced by some other equivalent space. The Commons Act of 1876 was the first piece of legislation to recognize the public amenity significance of commons land, providing for a right of access for 'inhabitants of the neighbourhood' for recreation and playing games. And, as confining access to local inhabitants was impossible to police, this essentially meant recreational access for all.

In 1895, the National Trust was established to acquire and manage open spaces for the benefit of the public, and in 1925 the Law of Property Act gave everyone free access to 'air and exercise' on all London's commons. It also protected many commons from encroachment and development, banning enclosure or building without ministerial consent.

Between 1862 and 1925 the extent to which land had been

enclosed became more transparent, following the establishment in 1862 of the Land Registry which was tasked with registering all land ownership. However, ownership was only registered when land changed hands. Large inherited estates were under-represented in the register and still are. And up to 1925 registration remained haphazard, so that many land transfers also went unregistered.

In 1925 the Land Registration Act codified and extended registration requirements, so that almost all transfers since then have been recorded. But even today land ownership registration remains incomplete. By 2018, after a concerted campaign by the Land Registry, an estimated 85 per cent of land in England and Wales had been registered. The remaining sixth is likely to be land passed through the generations.

The Countryside and Rights of Way Act of 2000 was the first legislation to give everybody the right to walk on all commons land. It also created a new category of Open Access land, to include all 'mountain, moor, heath and down' in England, plus already registered commons. Later, the Labour government added all land owned by the Forestry Commission. The 2000 Act significantly strengthened the commons, granting responsible freedom to walk on commons and open country. The Commons Act 2006 further strengthened the protection of commons land from encroachment and unauthorized development. Its predecessor, the Commons Regulation Act of 1965, had only allowed three years for commons registration, which had left many commons unprotected. The 2006 Act required commons registration authorities, normally local councils, to update and correct their registers and clarified criteria for registering town and village greens.

In addition, the Act provided for the establishment of commons councils to manage the commons, bringing together commoners and landowners, with powers to regulate grazing and other agricultural activities in ways that respected rights of public access and the conservation of nature and landscape.

However, in a reversal for defenders of the commons, in 2013 the Coalition government passed the Growth and Infrastructure Act, which outlawed registration of any land as a town or village green that was already targeted for development on the grounds that the registration procedure could be used to block new housing plans. In March 2017 the government said that it was committed 'to release enough land to build 160,000 new homes', and Prime Minister Theresa May said that Britain was 'open to business' and 'more committed than ever to creating the most business-friendly environment possible'.[10] This systemic loss of the commons was quietly unleashed by the government and was never subject to a democratic process.

The varied rights of use of the commons have also diminished as common land has dwindled. Today the most extensive right registered in the remaining commons is 'pasturage' – the right to graze domestic livestock.[11] Rights to graze sheep are registered in 53 per cent of Welsh commons and 16 per cent of English commons; rights for cattle grazing in 35 per cent of Welsh and 20 per cent of English commons; and for horses, in 27 per cent of Welsh and 13 per cent of English commons. In some commons, rights to graze goats, geese and ducks are still registered, and in a few the type of livestock is not specified.

The right to 'estover', so central to the Charter of the Forest, has been even less protected. This gives commoners permission to take limbs of trees and broken branches for minor works to buildings, for making farm implements and hurdles, and as deadwood for fuel, as well as bracken and heather for bedding. Less than 22 per cent of Welsh commons and 10 per cent of English commons have that right registered today. And gleaning as a *right* disappeared in the late eighteenth century, although it is still practised by activist groups around the country, with permission from private landholders.[12]

However, the common right to 'turbary' – to cut peat or turf for fuel – is still widely practised in Scotland, though to a lesser extent than in the past. The right, if not the practice, also exists in 12 per cent of Welsh and 8 per cent of English commons. Even less recognized today is the right of 'pannage', the right to graze pigs on acorns or beech mast in woodlands in autumn, which is listed in only 2 per cent of Welsh and English commons. The right is rarely used except in certain ancient hunting forests such as the New Forest.

'Common in the soil' gave commoners the right to extract minerals such as sand, gravel, marl (clay), walling stone and lime from common land. That right has also faded; it is now guaranteed in only 5 per cent of the Welsh and English commons, and is concentrated in a few areas, notably around Swansea. A particular form known as 'free-mining', the right of commoners to dig for coal and iron ore, persists in the Forest of Dean.

The right to 'piscary', the right to take fish, still exists in 262 commons in England and Wales, again with a cluster of areas around Swansea. Finally, there are localized rights. Over 850 commons land units in England have some additional rights, such as the right to take wild animals (*ferae naturae*), usually solely for personal use rather than for sale or for sport. In Scotland, fowling – the removal of cliff-nesting birds, fledglings and eggs – has been a traditional common right. In Norfolk some coastal areas have registered wildfowling rights. And there are rights to take reeds for thatching and seaweed, shellfish, sea lavender and samphire, all customary edibles. It seems probable that these became and remained rights simply because they were carried out over a prolonged period by commoners.

The plunder of commons land is a global phenomenon. There has been a sharp increase in the acquisition of such land by international companies worldwide, including in Europe.[13] Local people, often from indigenous communities, have been expelled from what used to be their private or common land. In Uganda, the government evicted more than 22,500 people to make way for a commercial forest plantation.[14] And when these global companies move on, they can leave behind a dead and poisoned land; in the quest for high yields and quick profits, they subject the land to excessive fertilization, pesticides and antibiotics, resulting in super-weeds, barren soil and the like. In Paraguay, 80 per cent of the country's crop land has been taken for soybean monoculture, which makes intensive use of agrichemicals. These contaminate the soil, harm human and animal health, and threaten the livelihoods of small farmers.[15] Once commodified in this way, the commons are impoverished.

## Forests under attack

Forests have always had a special place in the geopolitics of Britain, as in many other countries, and ever since the Charter of the Forest the state has been involved in their protection and exploitation. Although the traditional commoners' rights in the forest such as 'estover' and 'pannage' have shrunk, there is greater recognition of the important role forests, woods and trees play in protecting the global commons and commoners' rights. Their social and environmental benefits include the absorption of air pollution, locking up carbon to mitigate climate change, preservation of wildlife habitat and biodiversity, prevention of soil erosion and flooding, as well as recreation and enjoyment.[16]

The Forestry Commission, created in 1919, is now, with its Scottish, Welsh and Northern Irish counterparts, the single largest landowner in Britain. Initially its emphasis was on timber production and expanding the wooded area in the UK, which at 13 per cent remains one of the lowest in Europe. However, in recent years there has been a growing focus on so-called 'eco-system services'. In England, the Public Forest Estate owns a fifth of all woodland, but more than two-fifths of all publicly accessible woodland; 80 per cent of its quarter of a million hectares are accessible to the public and it is the largest provider of outdoor leisure and recreation.[17]

A proposal by the Coalition government in 2011 to privatize the Commission and sell off forest land to private operators predictably led to a huge outcry, orchestrated by the National Trust, which forced a rapid climb-down by the government. But privatization is continuing by stealth through increased

commercialization and land sales. The government's austerity programme has cut funds to the Forestry Commission and
obliged it to increase other sources of revenue. From once
being a net buyer of land, the Commission has become a net
seller, reducing its holdings from 874,000 hectares in 2013
to 863,000 in 2017. Meanwhile, commercialization has continued apace. The Commission has allowed a private company to erect luxury log cabins on its land and rent them out
at a tidy profit. The Commission itself set up Forest Holidays in the 1970s to allow people to 'enjoy the forest' in basic
cabins and tents. But by 2018 it had reduced its stake to just
14 per cent,[18] and a majority stake was acquired by Phoenix
Equity Partners, a private equity firm, in 2017.

Those basic cabins have given way to luxury accommodation, marketed by the company as 'sheer decadence'. Some
have five bedrooms, private decking, wood-burning stoves,
hot tubs, and flat-screen TVs through which guests can order
room service or book an 'in-cabin chef experience'. Forest
Holidays, which now operates 600 cabins at ten sites, has
expansion plans for at least five more sites, each with up to
ninety luxury cabins. Though the company and the Forestry Commission have refused to disclose where these future
sites are located, presumably to prevent resistance being mobilized, a list obtained by *The Times* in 2012 revealed the inclusion of some of Britain's most scenic areas, including the
Lake District, the South Downs National Park and Loch Ness.

As of 2018, the Forestry Commission expected to receive
about £200,000 a year from each new holiday park. But
while the Commission has gained £3,000 a cabin per year,
Forest Holidays is renting them out at £4,000 a week. And

the Commission has extended the company's land leases to 125 years. According to the article in *The Times*, the Commission claimed, 'This is plainly not privatization. The forests are still publicly owned and the Forestry Commission retains control of what can happen on the land through the business framework agreement and the individual site leases.' Yet the body responsible for preserving the commons has given long leases to a private commercial company to use the commons for commercial gain, blocking it from use by commoners. Besides the leased land itself, there is the impact on its surroundings. The cabins degrade the ecosystem, landscape and atmosphere and lessen the general public's enjoyment of the forest.

Forest destruction is widespread all over the world, often driven by commercial interests and aided by corrupt politicians. But it is worth singling out Poland, where the ruling Law and Justice party has deliberately allowed a massacre of the country's trees, including in the Białowieża Forest, the largest remaining primeval forest in Europe, which straddles the border between Poland and Belarus. This forest has been brought to the brink of collapse by the Polish government's decision to permit a trebling of commercial logging, removing the protection that had allowed the forest to reproduce itself and offer a safe haven to a remarkable variety of wildlife, including many species threatened with extinction.[19] It is a UNESCO natural World Heritage Site, a concept that is rapidly becoming a red flag to neo-liberals intent on 'deregulation', ostensibly in the interest of economic growth and jobs, but in reality always increasing inequality.

Citing the nationalist motto 'Poland first', the government

permitted commercial logging in more than 80 per cent of the forest, exempting only a relatively small area as a designated nature reserve. In April 2018 the European Court of Justice ruled that the logging was illegal and ordered it to stop, which could make the Polish government liable for millions of euros in fines if it ignores the order. But thousands of trees – and with them a big slice of the European commons – have already been lost.

On 6 November 2017, to celebrate the 800th anniversary of the Charter of the Forest, the Woodland Trust in the UK launched the Charter for Trees, Woods and People, which calls for stronger protection and more recognition of the benefits of trees and woodlands. In the preceding months, the Charter for Trees had been circulated online, signed by over 130,000 people and backed by hundreds of organizations, including many schools and about 300 local community groups. The Charter's ten principles are:

1. Thriving habitats for diverse species.
2. Planting for the future.
3. Celebrating the cultural impact of trees.
4. A thriving forestry sector.
5. Better protection for trees and woods.
6. Enhancing new developments with trees.
7. Understanding and using the natural health benefits of trees.
8. Access to trees for everyone.
9. Addressing threats to woods and trees through good management.
10. Strengthening landscapes with woods and trees.

These eminently reasonable principles deserve support. However, they lack the radical transformative character of the original Charter of the Forest. And the Charter for Trees lacks proposed mechanisms for stewardship and gatekeeping, accountability and enforcement, essential to restore the commons as a progressive part of social income.

## The threat to national parks

There are fifteen national parks in Great Britain, covering over 8 per cent of the land and recognized as protected areas under the 1949 National Parks and Access to the Countryside Act. They are among the country's most beautiful landscapes, home to rare wildlife, but also to rural communities for whom the national parks provide a source of livelihood, through farming and tourism. Each national park is run by its own independent authority with responsibility for safeguarding the natural and cultural heritage. But most of the land is privately owned or owned by bodies such as the National Trust. The Lake District National Park Authority, for example, owns only 4 per cent of the land it supervises.

Despite acknowledging the role of national parks in providing 'Britain's breathing space' in this overcrowded country, successive governments have cut funding to park authorities, pressurizing them to sell or commercialize land to pay for the upkeep of paths and forests. The Lake District saw its annual budget slashed by 38 per cent between 2010 and 2015, obliging the park authority to sell prized plots in this iconic part of the natural commons and resulting in further ecological degradation from commercial pressure.

George Monbiot, writer and environmental activist, has

argued forcefully that the Lake District does not deserve its World Heritage Site status, granted by UNESCO in 2017 after prolonged lobbying by large-scale commercial sheep farmers. They have converted the area into little more than a massive sheep-grazing area, denuding it of the biodiversity that had long been its character.[20]

Historically, the Lake District's 4 million hectares of uplands allowed a diversity of wildlife, a wide variety of trees and diverse sources of common food. But gradually it was effectively enclosed by sheep farmers, who consolidated swathes of land and obtained government subsidies for ranching sheep and building the necessary infrastructure. The land does not belong to the sheep farmers, but they have acquired control over it. As a result the sheep have destroyed the ecology, nibbling away tree seedlings and other sources of sustenance for anything other than sheep. The commons has ceased to be a commons in all but name.

This ecological destruction has been made possible by public money, with hill sheep farming sustained by subsidies paid for by general taxpayers. Even though the National Trust, the Royal Society for the Protection of Birds, the Lake District National Park Authority and the Cumbria Wildlife Trust all lobbied for the park to be given World Heritage Site status, it is hard to disagree with Monbiot's claim that they were supporting a travesty. They even commissioned an economic evaluation to back the lobby from a consultancy owned and run by a substantial Lake District sheep farmer. Nobody could fail to see the conflict of interest. The Commons Charter should include a demand for more diligent protection of national parks, as a statutory obligation.

In the USA an egregious plunder of the natural commons is taking place under President Donald Trump. Ever since the Antiquities Act 1906, regarded as President Theodore Roosevelt's conservationist legacy, US presidents have had unilateral authority to declare specified areas 'national monuments', effectively turning them into commons land on which commercial activity is banned. In one of his first acts as president, Trump signalled his intent to decimate areas given national monument status. By 2018, over 3 million acres of national monument area were targeted for commercialization, with more to come. Although there will surely be legal cases contesting his right to do so, in December 2017 Trump cut 2 million acres from two national monuments in Utah – over 800,000 acres from the Grand Staircase-Escalante, nearly half of the total area, and 1.1 million from Bears Ears, amounting to 85 per cent of the total area. His Secretary of the Interior also recommended that cuts be made to eight other national monuments.

In the same month, Republicans in the US Congress pushed through legislation authorizing oil drilling in the coastal plains of the Arctic National Wildlife Refuge, described by an editorial in *The New York Times* as 'an area full of wildlife, of talismanic significance to environmentalists and of great economic importance to Native Americans'.[21] Sometimes called America's Serengeti, the refuge is home to a rich diversity of wildlife, with 700 types of plants and animals, including caribou, polar bears, grizzly bears, wolves, wolverines, musk oxen, Arctic fish, and 200 species of (mainly migratory) birds. One-and-a-half million acres hitherto protected from commercial use will be lost to America's natural commons.

The removal of protection, slipped into the Republicans' big tax-cutting package, the Tax Cuts and Jobs Act of 2017, fulfilled a longstanding Republican campaign to open up the refuge for drilling, spearheaded by Lisa Murkowski, a Republican Senator for Alaska, and by her father (also a Senator) before her. The proceeds of drilling will supposedly be shared between the federal and Alaskan governments. Since Alaskan Republicans have cut state income tax to zero and rejected a sales tax, the state is dependent on oil revenue. The federal revenue from oil production in the Arctic is expected to be minimal. Nature has been sacrificed to fill a contrived fiscal hole.

In Australia, national parks are being commercialized.[22] The state government of Tasmania has launched ambitious plans for luxury tourism in its national parks that critics say will destroy the 'wilderness' experience. They include a luxury standing camp for Halls Island in Lake Malbena, a World Heritage Site, that will include helicopter access, and private lodges along charged-for hiking tracks, previously accessible only by camping. The New South Wales National Parks and Wildlife Service is hiring out buildings and locations in Sydney Harbour National Park and other national parks for weddings and functions, offering public facilities for the exclusive use of those who can afford to pay. And a luxury eco-lodge development on Christmas Island threatens to disrupt the annual crab migration, described by Sir David Attenborough as one of the ten greatest natural wonders on earth.

The depletion and commercialization of national parks and their equivalents is a global phenomenon. It is integral to globalization and resistance has been fragile. The Lake

District issue notwithstanding, UNESCO's World Heritage Site protection system is a laudable barrier. It has built up an impressive list of places considered to be of international importance. In 2014, the neo-liberal Australian government tried to delist 74,000 hectares of Tasmanian forest from protection to allow the renewal of commercial logging. UNESCO refused this 'unacceptable precedent', arguing that delisting would open the way for a rush of similar actions by other countries. But World Heritage Sites are just one small portion of the global commons under threat.

## The 'right to roam'

The 'right to roam' is the time-honoured right to walk where you will. In Britain the Law of Property Act of 1925 gave everyone the right to walk on 140,000 miles of recognized public footpaths. There are an estimated 117,000 miles of rights of way in England today, 20,600 miles in Wales, and a hazier figure in Scotland, where local authorities are not under a statutory obligation to produce definitive maps, unlike those in England and Wales.[23]

Rights of way are based on custom and customary use. The crucial test is that the path or highway must have been used 'as of right', unchallenged, 'without force, without secrecy and without permission'. The idea of permission is to protect landowners who may voluntarily grant commoners the right to use a path, but who may wish to withdraw it. Rights cannot be established if a piece of land is allowed to be used by non-owners by permission. Under the Rights of Way Act of 1932, twenty years of such use by the public constitutes adequate evidence that a right of way has been established. But it has often been hard to provide legally accepted evidence to support these claims.

The New Labour government, with the Countryside and Rights of Way Act 2000, set a deadline of 2026 for all historic rights of way not already mapped to be included on an updated register. It will be a big challenge to identify and register all these ancient rights of way in time, failing which they will be lost to the public for ever. Most people do not know what is or is not a public right of way, and few will be aware of what has been registered as such. Not only do people have to identify a path, bridleway or byway, they also have to prove it has been a commons, often in the face of costly legal objections by wealthier landowners.[24]

Open Access land gives everyone the right to wander on foot. Other commons may permit horse riding or cycling. But although larger blocks of Open Access land are marked on Ordnance Survey maps, many commons are too small to be shown on most of these maps and are hard to identify on local authority websites.

The right to roam is more than just a legal matter. In Britain, surveys suggest that in the past four decades the 'roaming range' – the area within which children are permitted to play unsupervised – has shrunk by more than 90 per cent, due to traffic growth, pressures of school, parental fears for children's safety, and a decline in green spaces. This reduction in physical activity has led to increased rates of obesity; children on average spend less time outdoors nowadays than prisoners.[25]

It has long been necessary to fight for the right to roam and use footpaths. The National Footpaths Preservation Society was formed in Victorian times, later merging with the

Commons Preservation Society in 1899 to form the Commons and Footpaths Preservation Society (now the Open Spaces Society). A National Council of Ramblers' Federations was established in 1931, becoming the more assertive Ramblers' Association (now The Ramblers) in 1935 following the famous 'mass trespass' of Kinder Scout.

In 1932, tensions came to a head over the private management of Kinder Scout, a moorland in the Peak District, where powerful landowners had effectively enclosed the land for game shooting and walkers were turned away by gamekeepers. This led to an 'occupy' movement by hundreds of walkers, after which five protestors were jailed for up to six months. The result was a surge of public sympathy and a rally of 10,000 walkers to support open access to adjoining moorland. The campaign failed in the short term, but post-war legislation, culminating in the Countryside and Rights of Way Act 2000, eventually granted public access as a legal right to common land and rights of way.

The right to roam also covers roads in every city, town and village. 'Sidewalks' and their users were considered by Jane Jacobs in her influential 1961 book, *The Death and Life of Great American Cities*, as essential combatants against disorder in the urban 'drama of civilization versus barbarism'. She argued that streets where people met and chatted, and watched what was going on, were key to keeping cities safe and reinforcing a sense of community. However, as noted later in this chapter, privatization and enclosure increasingly extend even to our city roads and pavements as privately owned public spaces or POPS have spread.

In the UK, the Conservative Party election manifesto in

2015 made a commitment to provide maps of all open-access green space freely available to the public. By 2018, that pledge was still unfulfilled. Such maps should provide detailed information on who has right of access and what activities are permitted. Farmers and other landowners also have a legal duty to maintain paths on their land so that people have access to the countryside. This should be made a condition of receiving public sector contracts or government subsidies.

## Village and town greens under pressure

> To the memory of the Rev. Herbert White, who saved
> this green from Goths and Utilitarians, 1853.
> — Plaque on cricket pavilion, Warborough Green

In England the village green is a classic open space that has been set aside for generations for recreation, sports, picnics and meandering. It breathes equality and community, something to be seen as much as to be used. Greens today are not true commons, since they are now defined as exclusively for recreation, but in the past greens and other land commons overlapped. Many were originally set aside for use by the poor, to enable them to grow food or pasture animals. Many were used by commoners to keep injured or sick animals until they could be returned to larger pastures. Greens thus had an economic function as well as a social one.

In the Middle Ages greens were typically defined on the basis that they had existed as greens since 'time immemorial' – further back than anyone could remember. Today, to qualify as a green the land must have been used for recreation for at least twenty years 'as of right', without force, without objection and without permission, as with the right to roam. Permissions can always be withdrawn, so recreational grounds provided by a local council would not normally qualify for registration, whereas areas used casually over twenty years or more without challenge may qualify.[26] As of 2018, there were about 3,650 registered greens in England and 220 in Wales, with no available estimate for the number of unregistered greens. They vary greatly in size and shape; Rosamund's Green in Frampton-on-Severn in Gloucestershire is half a mile long, while the largest is Duncan Down in Whitstable, covering 52 acres. However, the number of greens today is a fraction of the number that existed in medieval times.

Many village greens were lost in the commons enclosure movements over subsequent centuries. Their collective defence began in 1865 with the formation of the Commons Preservation Society (CPS), which organized the first major action against their further erosion in 1866, the same year as the Metropolitan Commons Act that blocked further enclosure of commons around London. Village greens were given formal protection in the Commons Registration Act of 1965, after which some 3,000 greens were successfully registered. But many were still unregistered by the cut-off date and were subsequently lost. In 1990 greens registration was reopened and the successor to the CPS, now named the Open Spaces Society, successfully promoted registration of land traditionally used for recreation and sports, protecting it from development.

The Commons Act of 2006 revised and clarified the procedures for registering greens, which helped stop further erosion. To be registered as a town or village green, 'a significant number of the inhabitants of any locality, or of any neighbourhood within a locality, have indulged as of right in lawful sports and pastimes on the land for a period of at least twenty years'. The Act also made it an offence to enclose or encroach on a registered green, which prompted an increase in applications to register greens as a defence against development. Consequently, the Conservatives, continuing their historical role as supporters of enclosure and privatization, passed the Growth and Infrastructure Act in 2013, which refused registration to land already the subject of development proposals.

Village greens as gathering places have also played an important role historically in social protest, going back to the Peasants Revolt of 1381 against high taxes and serfdom. There is now a Wat Tyler Green in Essex, commemorating its leader. Greens are also associated with the famous Tolpuddle Martyrs. After calling for the formation of a trade union on Tolpuddle village green in 1834, six labourers were sentenced to seven years of hard labour in Australia, an injustice that led to a series of protests and eventual pardons in 1836.

Village and town greens have always been of more value to lower-income groups than to the wealthy, who typically have their gardens and second homes in leafy places. This was recognized in some cases of enclosure of what were greens or commons, when small parcels of land were excluded from enclosure for the subsistence needs of the poor. A classic example is Twickenham Green in London, all that is left of a large tract of commons after enclosures in 1800 and 1818. A small triangle of land was left for the destitute, in compensation for loss of their fuel rights on the common, and for allotments for use by an adjoining workhouse.

In recent years village and town greens have been under almost constant attack, led by a government that favours land-owners over commoners and sees the preservation of some greens as hampering housing development and econom-ic growth. Still, the fight to preserve our greens continues, based on the simple ancient concept that customary use is the foundation for establishing rights.[27]

## Public parks in decline

The origins of the modern park are similar to those of common land appropriated by enclosure: the old term 'imparked' im-plied that an area of common land had been taken over by a landlord or manor.[28] In a sense the park is the antithesis of the forest, as its sculpted form is a man-made creation. Unlike traditional forests, which were used for subsistence, parks are tamed nature, orderly, rule-governed and primarily intended for recreation.

Still, to the modern mind the public park is part of the commons. In Britain the creation of public parks has run in parallel with moves to recognize and protect the commons, especially in urban areas. The eight Royal Parks in London, given to the nation by Queen Victoria in 1851 for the pub-lic's 'quiet enjoyment', were intended as green spaces for the free use of all, rich and poor. Distinguished parks have also been bequeathed to other cities. Graves Park in Shef-field, an 83-acre expanse of woodland, hills and playing fields, was gifted as a commons in the 1920s by one-time Alderman

John Graves, in an act representing a rare redistribution of private riches to public wealth.

Public parks, of which there are perhaps 27,000 in the UK,[29] are vital for healthy living in cities. Men, women and children of all ages are to be found in a park – strolling lovers, playing children, joggers and walkers, the elderly out for a constitutional. All these free activities are worth a great deal. Living near a park improves physical and mental health and promotes a sense of well-being. By one estimate, parks save the National Health Service £113 million a year as a result of fewer visits to the doctor.[30] Parks also reduce heat in built-up areas and help manage run-off from heavy storms.

Yet today in Britain public parks are threatened as never before. A survey of park managers in 2016 (Table 2) showed that nearly all had experienced budget cuts in the previous three years, with more reductions expected in the next three years. Only half of parks were reported to be in good condition. The survey also showed that staff cuts were leading to a severe decline in horticultural, landscape design and wildlife management skills.

Spending on public parks has been disproportionately hit by cuts in local council funding by central government. In 2017 the London Councils' Transport and Environment Committee warned that budget cuts could mean the piecemeal sale of London's parks to private firms, as councils were obliged to prioritize spending on the rising number of homeless and those requiring social care.

The same year Bristol City council announced that its spending on parks would be cut to zero in 2019, though it was forced to backtrack after a public outcry; Newcastle had cut

| Public Park Use | Percentage | Change since 2014 |
|---|---|---|
| Adults using their local park once a week or more | 35 | Same |
| Adults using park once a month or more | 57 | +3 |
| Households with child under age 5 using local park at least once a month | 90 | +7 |
| **Park Condition** | | |
| Park managers reporting park in good condition | 53 | -7 |
| Managers reporting park improved in past 3 years | 27 | -14 |
| Managers expecting park to improve over next 3 years | 20 | -1 |
| Managers reporting park had deteriorated in past 3 years | 18 | -1 |
| Managers expecting park to decline over next 3 years | 39 | +2 |
| **Park Budgets** | | |
| Park managers reporting cuts to budgets over past 3 years | 92 | +6 |
| Managers expecting cuts over next 3 years | 95 | +8 |
| Managers expecting cuts of between 10 and 20 per cent | 55 | +17 |
| Managers expecting cuts of over 20 per cent | 21 | -11 |
| Reporting cut in management staff over past 3 years | 75 | -6 |
| Reporting cut in operational staff over past 3 years | 71 | -6 |
| **Expected changes** | | |
| Local authorities considering sale or transfer of parks/greens | 50 | +5 |

**Table 2**

The State of UK Public Parks, 2016

Source: Heritage Lottery Fund, *State of UK Public Parks 2016*

its parks budget by 90 per cent in the previous seven years; and Stockport had decided to allow the building of seventy houses on its country park. Meanwhile, Liverpool was considering privatizing the management of its parks; it had already cut spending on maintenance and allowed the building of luxury houses on Calderstones Park, which contains Neolithic remains and a 1,000-year-old oak tree, the Allerton oak.

Budget cuts have been accompanied by the commercialization of parks to raise revenue, a further erosion of the commons, which has adversely affected the quality of parks and altered their character. 'Eventeeism', the renting out of parks for commercial events, brings noise and crowds in place of peace and quiet. In 2016 London's Battersea Park hosted more than 600 events, compared with about 100 in 1991, while in the summer of 2018 Finsbury Park in north London was almost continuously occupied by festivals, restricting access for residents, trampling the ground and scaring birdlife away.[31]

Financial stringency has also forced commercialization on London's Royal Parks. Between 2009 and 2014, the government cut funds for their maintenance by a quarter and obliged them to raise 60 per cent of their income themselves. Hyde Park's Winter Wonderland, Proms in the Park and rock concerts eat into quality space and the public's 'quiet enjoyment', blocking off large areas of the park not only during the events but long after them as well, to allow the grass to recover. Just because events such as rock concerts are popular does not justify converting the commons into sites for them. You might as well say that lifeboats would bring in more money and give more pleasure if used for cruising tourists. That is not what they are for.

Once one form of commercialization is allowed, others will follow. And charging for entry puts more events, and areas of the park, out of reach of the precariat and others. Commercialization erodes respect for traditional commons and weakens the citizens' resolve to defend them – though it has not gone unchallenged. A proposal to licence part of London's Victoria Embankment Gardens to an events company was withdrawn after objections from locals. The London Borough of Haringey faces a lawsuit demanding restrictions on the commercial renting out of Finsbury Park. But opposition to licences for events in public parks inevitably runs up against the fact that the same authority responsible for licensing stands to gain financially from granting them.

Meanwhile, as eventeeism spreads and austerity bites, our parks are becoming shabbier and uglier, increasing the risk of anti-social behaviour. If people become hesitant to use local parks because they are no longer seen as attractive and safe, they will be less inclined to defend them. At present, they remain much loved and an important source of social income. But their degradation is lowering social income, especially for low-income people and communities lacking private gardens and green spaces of their own, who rely on parks for fresh air, open space, exercise and experience of the beauty of nature.

## POPS: privatization of public spaces

Successive governments have orchestrated an unheralded and almost unnoticed privatization of what was formerly public land, starting in 1979 with the election of the Thatcher government and continued by Conservative, New Labour and Coalition governments. Land of all types has been sold by local and central government, including by the National Health Service and other public bodies. Privatization of the former nationalized industries – telephone, water, electricity, gas, railways and the Royal Mail – has also resulted in the transfer of large tracts of land to private companies. About 2 million hectares of public land have been privatized since 1979 – an astonishing 10 per cent of all British land and about half of all the land owned by public bodies four decades ago. This sold land is worth an estimated £400 billion in today's prices, a spectacular plunder.[32] It has been accompanied by creeping privatization and commercialization of the urban commons – roads and squares, as well as whole areas of residential and non-residential public property. All over the world, cities' public places are being transferred into private ownership, often as part of 'regeneration' or redevelopment plans.[33]

The Turkish government's intention to build a shopping mall on Istanbul's Taksim Gezi Park sparked a huge protest movement in which an estimated 3.5 million people took part. It became the catalyst for the expression of much broader discontent with government policies. The proposed development would have annihilated the small park, one of very few recreational spaces in the city. Parks and gardens cover only 2 per cent of Istanbul's total area, compared with 33 per cent in London. Among the thirty-four cities surveyed, only Dubai has less.[34]

In Britain, and especially in London, encroachment on the urban commons by private, often foreign, capital has become endemic.[35] In 2007, the Royal Institution of Chartered Surveyors described the privatization of public spaces as 'a revolution in land ownership'. It is nothing less than enclosure.

London is losing its distinctive character and the spaces that ordinary Londoners can use freely are shrinking. Privatization of the urban commons now has an informal acronym, POPS (privately owned public spaces), to signify the growing number of squares, gardens and parks that look public – but are not. Newly created Granary Square near London's King's Cross station, one of Europe's biggest open spaces, fringed by fashionable cafés and restaurants, is a private estate that can be hired for commercial events. Bishops Square, which includes Spitalfields market and historic streets in east London, is now owned by J. P. Morgan Asset Management. The £15 billion redevelopment of the 561-acre Nine Elms site along the south bank of the Thames will leave the area's squares and green spaces in the hands of its Malaysian developers. And the conversion of Battersea Power Station into shops, offices and luxury flats – as well as Apple's UK headquarters – will have as a centrepiece Malaysia Square, plans for which take their inspiration from Malaysia's landscape and geology.

In 2009, Boris Johnson, then London's Mayor, bemoaned the 'corporatization' of streets and public spaces that, he said, made Londoners feel like trespassers in their own city. Even the Mayor's headquarters, City Hall, and its 13-acre site are owned by More London, an estate management company bought in 2013 by a Kuwaiti property group, St Martins, which owns swathes of prime London property. Yet, despite his fine words, Johnson extended privatization and corporatization to an unprecedented degree. His watch included the Nine Elms development and expensive preparation of the proposed private Garden Bridge across the Thames (scrapped by his successor), which would not have been a public right of way and would have been closed to the public for corporate events.

Elsewhere in Britain, Brindleyplace in Birmingham, Gunwharf Quays in Portsmouth, and Liverpool ONE, owned by the Duke of Westminster's Grosvenor estate, are all privatized public zones. Exeter's Princesshay is owned by US property group Nuveen Real Estate and the Crown Estate, which manages the monarch's property portfolio. While developers often claim they are creating new public spaces – for example, by reclaiming derelict land – these areas are being reshaped by commercial interests to maximize rental income from property and retail outlets.

Since the 1980s almost every major property redevelopment in London has involved privatization of hitherto public space or publicly owned land.[36] The austerity regime has made matters much worse. Local councils around the country, desperate to cut maintenance costs and their liabilities, have released a lot more land,[37] yet many apparently do not know what land they own nor what has been sold to private developers.[38]

One unique anomaly is the land of the Crown Estate, land and property nominally owned by the monarchy. A principle of the Charter of the Forest was that the monarch's land could not be commercialized. Yet the Crown Estate has become a highly profitable property management company, generating £329 million in net profits on its £12.4 billion portfolio in 2017.

In recent years, as brilliantly documented by investigative journalists on *Private Eye*, and by Guy Shrubsole and Anna Powell-Smith on WhoOwnsEngland.org, leases on Crown Estate properties in prime areas of London have been sold to offshore companies based in tax havens and controlled by oligarchs and plutocrats.[39] Examples include a 125-year lease on part of Carlton House Terrace overlooking St James's Park, sold in 2006 to the billionaire Hinduja brothers via a company based in the tax haven of Guernsey and later transferred for £150 million to a company based in the British Virgin Islands, another tax haven. In 2012 a former Crown property on the edge of Regent's Park was sold to Russian financier Vladimir Chernukhin for £18 million, again via a company based in the British Virgin Islands. In all, over 40,000 London properties are owned by overseas firms, a quarter of them registered in the British Virgin Islands.[40]

Privatizing public spaces erases local traditions and character in favour of corporate sterility and erects a barrier to creativity and expression in the form of what are sometimes called street politics and street art. Commercial mega-projects kill the urban tissue and de-urbanize city life.[41] Private owners of public space can prohibit or restrict what people can do – eating and drinking, cycling or skate-boarding, busking, snoozing, even taking photographs – and can deny access altogether if they choose. They are not subject to local authority by-laws, and apply their own restrictions, usually enforced by private security firms.

Inevitably, the privatization restricts social and political

activity. In 2011 (and subsequently) Occupy London protesters were prevented from demonstrating in front of the
Stock Exchange in Paternoster Square because, as the court
injunction stated, 'The protestors have no right to conduct
a demonstration or protest on the Square, which is entirely
private property.'[42] Paternoster Square, close to St Paul's
Cathedral, is owned by Japan's Mitsubishi Estate Company,
which is making a substantial rental income from properties
there, including offices of investment banks Goldman Sachs,
Merrill Lynch and Nomura Securities. Much of the City of
London is now in private hands and thus off-limits for legitimate protest. Protest is banned outside City Hall, managed
by More London.

Elsewhere in London, a witness statement in support
of another injunction barring protestors from the Broad-
gate estate around Bishopsgate and Liverpool Street stated:
'There are no public rights over the common parts. The gates
to the Estate are ritually closed, once a year, to ensure that
no such rights can arise by prescription.'[43] In other words, the
time-honoured rights to demonstrate and to strike, and to
participate in public life in what the ancient Greeks called
the *agora*, a central gathering place for citizens, are being
taken away by commodification of the commons. It is the
ultimate phase of the neo-liberal project.

Bradley Garrett, a geographer and POPS activist, has
proposed an echo of the mass trespass of the Kinder Scout
in 1932, once described by Roy Hattersley as 'the most successful direct action in British history'. While that might be
hyperbole and unfair to other, more painful episodes in earlier times, the trespass led to a heart-warming achievement.

Something comparable in terms of direct action may be needed to arrest the creeping enclosure and privatization of urban public spaces today.

## The massacre of urban trees

There is a tendency to think of the natural commons as mainly rural, but cities and towns are increasingly part of the contested terrain. Besides parks, think of streets and squares; street-side trees are part of our commons. They add to the aesthetic of our streets and have been shown to improve physical and mental health. In Toronto, research concluded that living in a tree-lined street made people feel younger and more affluent, and improved mental health.[44] Trees also help clean the air by absorbing pollutants; they lower ambient temperatures in summer and aid flood alleviation. And they have always had a symbolism that has influenced our imagination and sense of identity.[45]

Yet in the neo-liberal era millions of urban trees are being sacrificed in the plunder of the commons. In the USA, a 2018 study by the Forest Service estimated that about 36 million trees in towns and cities were being lost each year, with an annual decline in 'urban forests' of 175,000 acres, much of that land being covered by concrete.[46] The benefits derived from those urban forests have been estimated at $18 billion annually in terms of less pollution and lower energy use in buildings.[47]

In Britain too, street trees are imperilled. More than 110,000 trees were lost between 2015 and 2018 and felling continues.[48] There is no government department or agency responsible for maintaining urban trees, unlike government-owned woodlands, which are managed by the Forestry Commission. Instead, they are the responsibility of local authorities, which have drastically cut back on spending to maintain, preserve and replant trees, a consequence of the austerity regime imposed by central government after 2010.

Although Newcastle upon Tyne has cut down more trees, the most notorious example is Sheffield, where budget cuts were followed in 2012 by a partial privatization of tree care. The council entered a public-private partnership, signing a twenty-five-year private finance initiative (PFI) contract with Amey, a subsidiary of a Spanish multinational, to manage its roads, including the city's 36,000 street trees. Amey immediately started to remove mature trees, felling about 5,500 between 2012 and March 2018, when the council called a temporary halt following protests by residents. A foreign firm cutting down British trees has a whiff of colonization; the defenders were reduced to tree-hugging.

While Amey and the council claimed the trees were dying, dangerous or obstructive, critics noted that Amey was taking the cheapest, most profitable option that minimized pruning costs and damage to pavements. More of the commons was lost. It included a row of rare English Chelsea Road elms on which lived equally rare White-letter Hairstreak butterflies.[49] As Save Sheffield Trees, a campaigning group, said bitterly: 'If they blitz the city's trees in the first five years of their twenty-five-year contract, they can spend the next twenty years with much lower maintenance costs.'[50] Under the PFI contract, pollarding a tree, the best way of rejuvenating an old tree and making it safe, was not allowed as a 'free' option. The council would have had to pay extra, as it would if any particular tree was 'saved' by its intervention. The council hid behind the consequences of its own incompetence, saying that 'alternative engineering solutions . . . are not funded within the contract'.[51]

In Wandsworth, south London, the council used cash from the Heritage Lottery Fund intended for 'rejuvenating' Tooting Common to replace well-established chestnut trees in Chestnut Avenue with young lime trees that are much cheaper to maintain. This was in spite of a petition of protest signed by over 5,000 people. Although the council claimed that the chestnut trees were unsafe, an independent tree consultant said that only a couple were of concern and the remainder could just be trimmed. His expertise was to no avail.

Significantly for a future counter-attack on councils and contractors wanting to fell well-established trees, the value of an urban tree can be calculated using a method developed by arborists known as CAVAT (Capital Asset Valuation of Amenity Trees). This estimates how much it would cost to replace the tree with one of similar age and condition. According to CAVAT, Chestnut Avenue was worth £2.6 million, while the young lime trees set to replace the chestnut trees had an estimated value of under £100,000. Using the same method, the Sheffield trees cut down between 2012 and 2017 were worth £66 million. Felling such trees so wantonly is an act of urban vandalism stemming from austerity and the privatization of tree services.

# The 'colonization' of water

> What opinion would be entertained of the
> understanding of a man, who, as the means of
> increasing the wealth of . . . a country, should propose
> to create a scarcity of water, the abundance of which
> was deservedly considered one of the greatest blessings
> incident to the community? It is certain, however,
> that such a projector would, by this means, succeed in
> increasing the mass of individual riches.
> — Earl of Lauderdale, 1804[52]

Few aspects of the ongoing plunder of the commons excite as much controversy as the enclosure and privatization of the world's water. It is a frontline issue. Water has been a public service since antiquity. The principle of water as a public good goes back to the ancient world, back even to 3000 BC in what is now Pakistan and India. The Romans built public aqueducts and sanitation services; access to water was regarded as a civic right. Yet in recent decades water has been turned into a scarce commodity from which corporate capital can make profits.

Privatization of water took off in the 1980s around the world. Numerous cities in the United States privatized their municipal water supplies, and the World Bank put pressure on developing countries to privatize theirs. Notoriously, the Bank insisted that the city of Cochabamba in Bolivia privatize its water system as a condition of continuing development loans to the Bolivian government. In 1999 the tripling of water prices by the private owner, an international consortium involving

US, British and Spanish companies, triggered violent protests later dubbed the 'water wars'. Months of street demonstrations, road blocks and a general strike led to the declaration by the government of a 'state of siege'. The army and police were mobilized to put down the protests by force, resulting in several deaths. In April 2000, the privatization was reversed.

The 1989 privatization of the water supply in England and Wales transferred not only the provision of clean water and sewerage but also vast swathes of land to ten regional monopolies. These water corporations owned 424,000 acres as of 2017, putting eight of them among the largest fifty landowning companies in England and Wales. Several have refused to release maps of their landholdings.[53] Those that have reveal that much of the land they own is scattered and some is not adjoining water sources at all.

In what should be a national scandal, the government gave the water companies huge subsidies at the time of privatization, writing off all the £4.9 billion debt owed by their predecessors and adding what was coyly called a 'green dowry' of £1.5 billion. Investors paid £7.6 billion for the shares but the subsidies in effect reduced the net amount to little more than a billion.[54]

Monopoly control of water provision enables commercial companies to contrive scarcity by restricting water supply, divert it to where profits are greatest, and raise its price. They can take short-term profits at the cost of creating a long-term shortage. Most European countries have wisely kept water supply in the hands of public utilities. The English experience of privatization – Welsh Water became a not-for-profit organization in 2001 – is unlikely to change their mind.

The Thatcher government claimed that private water companies would be more efficient than public utilities and would raise more money for investment in infrastructure, needed to replace old, often Victorian-era distribution pipes and improve storage facilities. Neither claim has proved to be true.[55] And converting a nationally integrated public system into private regional monopolies killed off a complex plan that had been developed in the years beforehand to transfer water from the flood-prone north to the drought-prone south through a series of aqueducts and reservoirs.

Scottish Water, which remains a public utility, has invested more and charges consumers less than any of the privatized companies in England. Although the English companies could have afforded to finance their operations and investments from current revenue,[56] they loaded themselves up with debt, partly to reduce tax bills, and used the money to finance huge bonuses for their executives and generous dividends to their shareholders, who are increasingly private equity groups. In the ten years to 2017, the nine English regional water companies made £18.8 billion in post-tax profits, of which £18.1 billion was paid out as dividends.[57] Dividends exceeded the companies' cash balance in every year except one since privatization.[58]

Ironically, foreign state capital has been a major beneficiary of English water privatization, with a heavy presence of sovereign wealth funds from China, Singapore, the Middle East and elsewhere. These foreign investors have no interest in preserving the commons; their interest is purely speculative. Indeed, privatization created the groundwork for colonization. By 2010, taking regional and the remaining local corporations together, ten of the twenty-three water companies in England and Wales were under foreign ownership and a further eight were owned by private equity groups with substantial foreign involvement.[59]

Permitting private equity groups to acquire public utilities like water was one of the most irresponsible aspects of privatization. Private equity funds are buy-out funds with a seven- to ten-year lifespan, after which they liquidate and pay out the profits to their investors. The British government has allowed public utilities, which necessarily have long-term time horizons, to be acquired by entities explicitly set up to make short-term profits. It has been a recipe for chaos and eventual public bail-outs, at taxpayers' expense.

Thames Water, which supplies water to London, is owned by a private equity consortium and, despite steadily raising bills to customers, is so indebted that it has asked for government help for infrastructure improvements to overcome chronic supply and leakage problems. Meanwhile, South West Water raised their charges to customers to such a high level that the government felt obliged to pay the company to reduce household bills, a subsidy paid for by taxpayers that ultimately enriched the company and its shareholders.

In March 2017 Thames Water was fined £20.3 million for pumping 1.4 billion tonnes (4.2 billion litres) of untreated sewage into the upper reaches of the River Thames. The judge said it was 'shocking and disgraceful' and was 'borderline deliberate'. People using the river went down with stomach bugs, and fish and birds died from pollution after tampons, condoms and sanitary towels were left floating in the river. For dumping sewage, endangering the lives and health of people, fish and wildlife, the fine imposed was just a slap on the wrist. Those responsible for poisoning the river should have been prosecuted.

Later the same year, Thames Water was fined a further £8.5 million for failing to reduce leaks so great that, for every property the company was supplying, about 180 litres were being lost every day.[60] Then in 2018 it was fined a further £120 million and told to return that sum to customers for its continued failure to tackle leakages that the company admitted amount to a quarter of all the water it treats and puts into its own network of pipes. Still, the corporation can easily afford such fines. The highly profitable corporation paid about £1.6 billion in dividends to its shareholders over the decade to 2016.

The dirty practices of Thames Water are not isolated incidents. In 2016 Yorkshire Water was fined £1.7 million for polluting a lake near Wakefield and a section of the River Ouse. Yet in the wake of the sewage dumping, the CEO of Thames Water was given a 60 per cent pay rise, receiving £2 million in 2015, and the CEO of Yorkshire Water received £1.2 million.[61]

As of 2017 London's elderly sewer system was pouring an estimated 40 billion litres or more of water and raw sewage into the Thames each year.[62] Meanwhile, Thames Water has offloaded its responsibility for curbing sewage pollution by setting up a separate company to design, finance, build and maintain a new 'super sewer', the Thames Tideway Tunnel. This should have been a capital cost, set against Thames Water's profits. Instead, Londoners will pay for the sewage project through higher water bills while the new company is covered by government guarantees to provide additional money if cost overruns exceed 30 per cent.[63]

A final irony is that Thames Water was given ownership of what is reputedly the biggest urban wetland in Europe, in the Lea Valley in east London. With funding from the London Wildlife Trust, Waltham Forest Council and the Heritage Lottery Fund, Thames Water has overseen the conversion of the area into the Walthamstow Wetlands, now free for visitors. It is a beautiful creation. But should it not belong to the commons?

Some water corporations have allowed what were long regarded as commons to be left unmanaged. After pressure, Southern Water, which owns a former allotment area, has allowed a community group to use the land for community food-growing and for a community apiary. While this can be applauded, such decisions should not be a matter of corporate discretion by a private company; the land should be restored as a commons right. Water companies have failed in their responsibility to be stewards of the water commons while regulatory oversight by gatekeepers has signally failed. Commons ownership should be restored and private owners compensated only for their equity investment, which has been minimal. However, a new governance system is needed that would restore the commons character of water while overcoming the drawbacks of both old-style nationalization and privatization. A community-based form of ownership is required.[64]

For instance, since the 1600s in former Spanish colonies in the Americas, including New Mexico in the USA, native Hispanic Americans have retained commons control over water through community-based irrigation channels known as *acequias*.[65] This has worked well even in arid regions, showing how a commons can align community usage of water with ecological limits. The *acequias* are recognized by Mexican state law, and all *acequias* members are expected to share maintenance responsibilities. The community itself manages and protects the water supply.

A similar and even older system still operates in a number of communes in the Swiss canton of Valais.[66] If imported into Britain, this would be a wonderful way of engaging the whole community in efforts to improve the quality and availability of fresh water, with a bias in favour of conservation. Unlike the existing privatization model, nobody would have an interest in creating real or artificial scarcity.

## Seashores endangered

Cruise liners are a global menace. These mega-vessels, carrying many thousands of passengers, enter iconic waterways like Venice's lagoon, bringing short-term revenue for corporations and public agencies, but at huge ecological cost. Venice is part of our global heritage; already under threat from rising sea levels, it is being further damaged by liner backwash and oil pollution, not to mention the ruin of the skyline by ships that tower above the churches and palaces that line the canals.

Southampton, a favoured stopping point for cruise ships, while no Venice, epitomizes the problem. Each ocean liner uses as much fuel as a whole town while in port, since they keep their engines running and use the most polluting form of diesel, which contains higher sulphur levels than road fuel. The resultant air quality is so poor that it breaches international guidelines, and while the British government is now taking measures to curb the use of diesel in motor vehicles, it has done nothing to regulate visiting cruise liners.[67] In Marseilles on France's Mediterranean coast, the increase in luxury cruise liners has been linked to a rise in the incidence of throat cancer.[68] And other research suggests that about 50,000 people in Europe die prematurely each year due to pollution from ships.[69]

The seashore around Britain should be a permanent part of the country's natural commons, along with rivers, riverbanks and its natural lakes. In some countries, they cannot be privately owned. But in the UK a growing number of private marinas block off and pollute parts of the shoreline and riverbanks, some of which have been colonized by global finance. In 2005, the US financial giant Blackrock bought Premier Marinas, which operates a number of marinas along the south coast. After making good profits, in 2015 Blackrock sold Premier Marinas to the Wellcome Trust, a global health charity, for £200 million. Wales uniquely has a public coastal path covering the whole of its coast. England should do the same.

Around the world, natural sand beaches are disappearing, due partly to rising sea levels and more violent storms, but also to massive erosion caused by development. And the demand for sand to make concrete has spurred a global boom in sand-mining, despoiling remaining beaches, especially in poor countries, and threatening an impending shortage of sand.[70]

## The air, sky and wind

The air we breathe and peer through is part of the natural commons. In recent years, it too has been depleted by the

familiar processes of encroachment, enclosure, commercialization and commodification, as well as by neglect.

The sky, particularly the night sky, is being privatized.
After dark we are bombarded with neon-lit commercial messages, seeking to condition our minds.[71] By day, to see the
worst excesses, go to Warsaw, where underwear advertising
on 30-metre-square billboards on high-rise buildings might
amuse at first sight, but is culturally impoverishing and an
encroachment on the skyline. Meanwhile, light pollution
means we can no longer see the stars in many of our towns
and cities.

Historically, the air and sky did not figure in the commons,
as times past were not disfigured by commercial sounds and
sights. However, Hugo Grotius, a seminal early seventeenth-
century defender of the global commons, did regard the air
as the primal natural commons. He argued this was the case
because it could not be 'occupied' and it was constituted by
nature for the use of all humans. But few worried about the
air as a commons resource. Then came the Industrial Revolution and the realization that the air was being poisoned,
imperilling life and health. In many places today the air has
become toxic. Air pollution causes cancers and lung dis-
eases and globally is directly responsible for the premature
deaths of millions of people each year, including an estimated 40,000 people in Britain.

Regulations have not kept pace. In 2018, for the third
time, the British government was condemned by the courts
for failing to tackle illegal levels of air pollution. The air
breathed by every Londoner is far above the safety limit set by
the World Health Organization;[72] in 2017 nearly 95 per cent of

the capital had a level of toxicity 50 per cent above the limit. Over 4.5 million children in the UK, most living in low-income areas, are exposed to unsafe pollution levels.[73] This not only affects their physical health but also brain development and educational attainment, another source of inequality.[74] And at the other end of the age spectrum, the over-fifties living in high-pollution areas have a 40 per cent greater risk of developing dementia than those in low-pollution areas.[75] For all age groups, high levels of air pollution reduce intelligence.[76] In Britain and around the world, exposure to toxic air pollution is more unequal than money income,[77] another example of how corrosion of the commons worsens 'social income' inequality.

Surely the ultimate commodification of the natural commons, beyond all parody, occurred in 2015 in China. Chinese cities are on the frontier of rentier capitalism, spawning a rapidly growing plutocracy of billionaires as well as the world's largest precariat. They are also so heavily polluted with toxic smog that on many days of the year it is dangerous to breathe the air outside. Fresh air has become a scarce commodity, a situation happily exploited by an enterprising Canadian start-up, which bottles fresh mountain air from the Rockies to sell in China's smog-affected cities. At $24 a bottle, market demand has far outstripped supply. The company now has India in its sights. Companies from Australia and Switzerland have also got in on the act.

The wind that blows in and around a country is part of our natural commons. In Britain it has become a vital new commons resource with the development of wind power as renewable energy. By 2017, the UK was generating more energy from wind than any other country, with about 40 per cent of Europe's total installation of wind farms. Offshore wind turbines were then generating nearly 6 per cent of the country's electricity, a figure expected to double by 2021. Proponents claim that, potentially, offshore wind farms could power the country's electricity needs six times over.[78]

Yet all but 7 per cent of Britain's wind generating capacity is foreign-owned.[79] Foreign capital is profiting from British wind. The single biggest foreign owner, accounting for 31.5 per cent of UK offshore wind energy, is Ørsted (formerly DONG Energy), a Danish enterprise that is 50.1 per cent state-owned and 18 per cent owned by the ubiquitous Goldman Sachs. British wind has been privatized and colonized.

The air as commons also includes the gem of silence, or silence interspersed with the gentle sounds of nature: the dawn chorus, the rustling of leaves, the patter of rain. We are in danger of losing the therapeutic 'sound of silence', instead being bombarded by alien and alienating noise, driven mostly by commercial interests, ranging from traffic noise to 'muzak' pumped into shopping arcades to entice people to spend more. Noise is not just unwelcome to those who do not like it. This invasion of our air harms people's health.[80] Again, those on low incomes are most affected, as they are more likely to live near busy roads, under flight paths, near noisy industrial factories or construction sites. Noise triggers the release of the stress hormone cortisol, which damages blood vessels. Long-term exposure to road traffic noise raises the risk of heart attacks and has been linked to the rise in Type-2 diabetes.

# The commons underground: colonization in prospect

The Charter of the Forest confirmed commoners' rights to extract usable materials from the ground, but this principle has been much abused. Today the plunder of the natural commons has taken on global proportions. Neo-liberal governments in many countries have privatized not just 'the people's land' but the resources underneath or on it. Soaring world demand for gold, copper and other minerals used by the electronics industry in devices such as smartphones has spurred a huge increase in mining operations, often through confiscation or usurpation of native land, leaving environmental devastation in their wake. One study has identified more than 1,500 conflicts involving international mining and oil companies over water, land, spills, pollution, ill-health, relocations, waste, land grabs and floods.[81] Plans to exploit the Tampakan copper and gold deposits in the Philippines may force 5,000 people to move and resistance by local tribes has been met with military force, resulting in many deaths.

In the UK, the most egregious case concerns North Sea oil. Leaving aside the contentious issue of whether this is British or Scottish oil, it should have been exploited for the benefit of the whole of society. Applying the Hartwick Rule, future generations should also have benefited. Instead, there was a huge rental transfer to an elite and windfall gains for middle-income earners in the form of tax cuts.

Unlike Norway, which set up a sovereign wealth fund with the proceeds of oil sales and did apply the Hartwick Rule, the Thatcher government licensed drilling areas at fire-sale prices to a few multinationals. Those rich corporations received further subsidies to help them expand production, with much of the profits flowing abroad. Ironically, many years later, a large chunk of North Sea oil production ended up in the hands of Chinese state corporations. And in a final twist the British government is now subsidizing the cost of dismantling redundant oil rigs with which the oil corporations had made their ample profits.

As if nothing had been learned from the oil giveaway, another manifestation of the plunder of the commons concerns 'fracking'. Recent British governments, as in other countries, in response to systematic lobbying by powerful interests, have given selected corporations ownership and commercial usufruct rights to common land to earn rental income from extracting gas from shale rock. Scotland, which has imposed a moratorium on fracking, is an exception. David Cameron, when Prime Minister, said his government was going 'all out for shale'. The British Geological Survey estimated that Britain possessed shale gas deposits that could supply the country for fifty years or more. If so, those deposits are a significant part of the natural commons from which all commoners are entitled to benefit.

However, nobody can sensibly deny the environmental and social costs of fracking, which include blighting the landscape, noise and disruption from construction and traffic, air and water pollution, and the risk of earth tremors.[82] These costs are borne by commoners, and not just in the areas of mining. In reality, profits are likely to be privatized, while the costs of the depletion of common resources will be socialized.

Yet, despite the concerns, landowners and local authorities are receiving extensive subsidies to allow fracking on their land.

In 2014 the Coalition government of Conservatives and Liberal Democrats altered the time-honoured trespass law to allow shale gas corporations to mine under the ground of landowners. This went ahead in spite of a public consultation which received over 40,000 objections, comprising 99 per cent of all responses. It was clear the government had made up its mind beforehand. Henceforth, a fracking company could gain underground access without needing to seek landowners' permission, as long as it had government approval. The government issued a statement that 'no issues have been identified that would mean that our overall policy approach is not the best available solution'. The change gave automatic access for gas and oil development at depths below 300 metres, with a voluntary scheme for notification and compensation. At the time, the chief executive of the industry's trade body, UK Onshore Oil and Gas, said, 'Landowners on the surface will not notice this underground activity [usually a mile deep], it will have no impact on their day-to-day lives.' The loss of traditional land-ownership rights and the rights of the commons was a silent victim.

Ineos, the largest owner of shale-gas licences in the UK, argued in a legal case intended to stop protestors occupying fracking land that they would be putting themselves at risk from dangerous carcinogens. Yet in all their PR the companies have claimed that fracking is safe. The CEO of Ineos, Jim Ratcliffe (in 2018 named by *The Sunday Times* as the richest person in Britain), has maintained that 'a lot of the opposition is based on hearsay and rumour'. But of nearly 7,000 academic articles published between 2009 and the end of 2015, the overwhelming majority contained field data showing contamination of water or air and thirty-one indicated public-health hazards and outcomes.[83] A study in heavily drilled counties in Pennsylvania in the USA found evidence linking fracking to low birthweight in babies, which the authors attributed to air pollution.[84]

In 2015, the British government's Air Quality Expert Group gave ministers a report showing that shale gas extraction increases air pollution. But this was suppressed until July 2018 when it was quietly slipped out three days after the government gave the go-ahead for the first fracking operation to start. An earlier report showing fracking's likely effects on pollution and local house prices was also delayed until after local council approval had been secured.

Companies are being allowed to drill around and under Britain's national parks, precious wild spaces, despite a pledge by the then Energy Secretary Amber Rudd before the 2015 General Election that they would be protected. 'We have agreed an outright ban on fracking in national parks [and] sites of special scientific interest,' she said. Immediately after the election, the same minister announced that fracking would be allowed around them and that companies could dig under them.

The government subsequently decided that the Communities Minister would have the final say on fracking plans, removing local democratic control. Local authorities must now fast-track fracking applications, giving councils less time to build their case and forcing them to cut corners. If the minister deems the grounds for refusal inadequate, he can overrule the council's decision, as he did in the case of drilling near Blackpool. And any company appeals against refusal are to be determined by the minister, that is, on political not technical grounds. As the Department of Communities put it, 'The Secretary of State hereby directs that he shall determine these appeals instead of an inspector.' There is no statutory direction stating that technical or environmental considerations should prevail.

Because of fuzzy property rules, corporations can bribe local landowners to support fracking. Cuadrilla, the first to gain government consent to frack at its Lancashire site in 2018, has paid £2,070 to twenty-nine households within a 1km radius of the site and is paying £150 to another 259 households living between 1km and 1.5km away, from what was called a community benefit fund.[85] The bribe may have worked as the company intended, but it is far from clear that a few local landowners are the rightful commoners or that they have the right to alienate the land in this way. The costs of fracking are not borne just by landowners; they are not the only commoners affected.

Some local landowners made their moral position clear in refusing to take the money. As a farmer who turned down £2,070 put it, 'It is absolutely the most appalling thing. How can you give money to compensate for affecting people's health and spoiling their environment? What we want is our health. It's just blood money really.' The company's bribe was being paid in addition to the promise by the government to give 'frackpot' payments of up to £10,000 to households living near a shale well, if the company moves from exploration to full commercial production. This amounts to a huge subsidy not only to the households but to the company, making it easier for it to gain agreement from the local landowning community. But why should only local households receive a compensatory payment?

To enclose the commons in this way is to go against the ethos of the commons and ignore the risks and impact for all non-landowners and for future generations. It is shabby policy to treat our inherited assets as a windfall gain for a tiny minority. And the inequity will be intensified by the revised National Planning Policy Framework introduced by the government in 2018. Despite overwhelming opposition during the consultation process, the framework requires councils in England to 'recognize the benefits of on-shore oil and gas development' in the interests of 'energy security' and to facilitate exploration and extraction. In other words, councils are being instructed to say 'yes' to fracking, whatever the cost.

It is not just fracking. In 2015, the North York Moors National Park Authority narrowly gave the go-ahead for plans by a mining corporation, Sirius Minerals, to create one of the world's largest mines for potash, used for fertilizer. This involves drilling a 1.5km-deep shaft under the moors and a 37km-long tunnel to transport the deposits, with infrastructure within the park as well as outside it. Officials prepared a report that stated, 'The economic benefits . . . and extent of the mitigation/compensation offered . . . do not outweigh the extent of the harm,' and noted the park authority's 'statutory responsibility to conserve and enhance the North York Moors for the enjoyment of present and future generations'.[86] Strangely, in the circumstances, they did not recommend rejection.

This may have been because there was local support for the multibillion-pound project, which Sirius claimed – on dubious assumptions – would create a thousand jobs, boost exports and transform the economy of the depressed region around Scarborough. A few local farmers and other landowners also stood to gain substantial sums for potash mined under their land. So perhaps it is not surprising that, despite pleas by conservation organizations, the government refused to hold a public inquiry. The commercial juggernaut was allowed to plough on by the very authorities charged with safeguarding the commons on behalf of the public.

No doubt chief executive Chris Fraser and his associates behind Sirius took a financial risk in developing the project, described as the largest mine ever dug in Britain.[87] But the national park and the polyhalite deposit to be mined, 70 metres thick and extending over 775 square kilometres, are part of the national commons. The deposit does not belong to the landowners, who did not know it was there, and they have taken no financial risk. Yet local landowners (including the Crown Estate and the Duchy of Lancaster) will reportedly receive a windfall of over £4 billion over ten years. Meanwhile, Sirius is seeking £2 billion in government guarantees to back the mountain of debt incurred in the exploration stage, representing a risk subsidy funded by taxpayers. And there is the environmental cost to the national park and its surroundings, the heritage not just of local residents but of commoners across the country, those living today and those of future generations. The issues go to the heart of the debate on the commons.

In Britain, minerals (other than gold, silver, oil and other petrochemicals, which belong to the Crown) belong to whoever owns the land above or around them.[88] This compounds the extreme inequality in land ownership. Britain's natural resources, and income from their exploitation, should belong to the citizenry. As it is, the biggest beneficiaries from the potash mine, apart from Sirius's shareholders, will be the descendants of people who took the land from the commons in the first place.

Mineral assets are part of society's general wealth. They are inheritable and so, if depleted, must meet the Hartwick Rule of inter-generational equity. Government should be the steward, or trustee, of resources for the country's present and future citizens. Subject to the Hartwick Rule, the governance of natural resources must involve all 'stakeholders', including those in surrounding local communities.

## The Natural Capital Committee

The commodification and privatization of our natural commons is being shaped by an official vocabulary that treats nature as yet another economic resource to be exploited. The New Labour government began this by giving a commercial research company £100,000 to calculate the 'annual price of England's ecosystem',[89] a meaningless exercise. Sure enough, the company, having pocketed the money, concluded that 'some of the ecosystem may have an infinite value'. This did not deter the Coalition government from setting up an 'independent business-led' Ecosystem Markets Task Force, headed by Ian Cheshire, chair of Kingfisher, a multinational retailer that owns the B&Q chain of DIY stores.

In its final report in March 2013, the Task Force claimed to have identified 'substantial potential growth in nature-related markets – in the order of billions of pounds annually'.

The report refers to 'natural capital', 'ecosystem services', 'green infrastructure', 'asset classes' (a.k.a habitats), all within an 'ecosystem market'. In its response, the government referred to landowners as 'providers of ecosystem services', who could presumably expect to be paid or subsidized for providing the 'services'. The Task Force also recommended reaching out to the ultimate rentiers, talking of 'harnessing City financial expertise to assess the ways that these blended revenue streams and securitizations enhance the return on investment of an environmental bond'.

The institutional derivative of this Task Force, the Natural Capital Committee, is trying to put a value on all the nature in Britain by developing 'national natural capital accounts'. According to one definition, '"Natural capital" refers to the living and non-living components of ecosystems – other than people and what they manufacture – that contribute to the generation of goods and services of value for people.'[90] But nature is not capital, unless turned to commercial use. To call it natural capital is to imply it is no longer part of the commons. Describing the world's mountains as natural capital, as one member of the committee did,[91] is meaningless. Capital is about a relationship of production, about making profits. The committee is looking for ways of commodifying nature, without any democratic decision to do so or any system of accountability to commoners.

The government claims that unless a price is put on every bit of nature, it will not be treated as having value. But a price only comes when something is for sale, when it becomes a commodity. The Natural Capital Committee, whose remit runs until 2020, should be mocked out of existence, along with the ideological pretensions it conveys. As it is, the Committee reported in 2017: 'At present UK natural capital is not even maintaining its current condition; it is declining.'

## The tragedy of the global commons

Areas outside national jurisdiction – the oceans, the atmosphere, Antarctica and outer space – are our global commons, recognized in international law. All are under threat. Only about 3.5 per cent of the world's oceans are what might be called sea commons, protected by national ownership on behalf of citizens. The remainder are essentially a free-for-all, unregulated by stewards and open to uncontrolled exploitation and blatant disregard for reproduction. Over 140 countries have agreed in principle to draw up by 2020 a High Seas Treaty, more than the two-thirds needed for passage of an international accord.[92] But neither the USA nor Russia has agreed, while it is unclear how such a treaty would be enforced.

The atmosphere too is part of our global commons, threatened by neglect and commodification. The response to climate change has not only been dilatory; the limited action to curb greenhouse gas emissions that has been taken has tended to harness market mechanisms such as 'cap-and-trade' schemes, allowing corporations to buy permits giving them a 'right to pollute' rather than penalizing them or obliging them to reduce emissions through regulation. Even our atmosphere has been converted into a commodity. The citizenry pays the price. And the permits are being sold so cheaply that there is little incentive to cut pollution.[93]

In the 1990s, international initiatives to combat climate

change included proposals to fine companies for exceeding limits on carbon emissions that cause global warming. This made sense. Paying a fine is not just paying a price for breaking social rules; it damages the reputation of the company, and it implies harsher penalties if the offence is repeated. A system of fines would have stigmatized destruction of the global commons.

However, in the negotiations leading up to the Kyoto Protocol in 1997, the US administration, influenced by corporate lobbyists, managed to transform the proposed fines, which were to be paid into a new Clean Development Fund, into a system of prices for carbon emission permits.[94] This effectively converted emissions into predictable costs, which could be passed on to consumers in higher prices.

In Britain, the 2017 Conservative election manifesto included a target of imposing the lowest energy bills on households in Europe. This implicitly sacrificed environmental protection and the global commons. Taking account of the full cost of burning fossil fuels requires a proper carbon tax to penalize emissions that cause global warming. A carbon tax should be extended to all users of energy, not just power generators to which the present carbon price support mechanism applies.

By itself a carbon tax would be inequitable. It should be coupled with measures to compensate those on lower incomes, who use less energy and consume fewer goods and services that use fossil fuels, but who would be hurt most by higher prices due to the tax.[95] How this might be done is the subject of Chapter 8.

In 1967, the United Nations passed the Outer Space Treaty, which declared that the moon and other celestial bodies 'shall be the province of mankind' and 'not subject to national appropriation by claim of sovereignty, by means of use or occupation, or by any other means'. This was reiterated by the Moon Agreement of 1979, which stated that 'the moon and its natural resources are the common heritage of mankind'. Yet in December 2017, Scott Pace, executive director of the US National Space Council, said:

> It bears repeating: Outer space is not a 'global commons', not the 'common heritage of mankind', not 'res communis', nor is it a public good. These concepts are not part of the Outer Space Treaty, and the United States has consistently taken the position that these ideas do not describe the legal status of outer space . . . To unlock the promise of space, to expand the economic sphere of human activity beyond the Earth, requires that we not constrain ourselves with legal constructs that do not apply to space.[96]

This was a strident rejection of common collaboration for the benefit of the world. Pace went on to assert that US citizens were 'entitled to own, as private property, asteroid and space resources'. Other countries, including Russia, have contended that outer space should not be a zone of private property. But the world has been warned that commercial rivalry, and with it the possibility of military hostilities, are closer to reality as a result of American posturing.

*

## Where do we stand?

> As nature thins, so does our memory of it.
> — Robert Macfarlane, 2017

The modern plunder of the natural commons was started by the mania for privatization that Margaret Thatcher unleashed in the 1980s. When she was given a state funeral in 2013, with all the elite in attendance, everyone in the land should have paused to reflect on what commoners had lost.

Privatization has paved the way for a pervasive colonization of what had been commons. More and more land and property, including public spaces in towns and cities, have been sold to foreign property developers and financial capital, and much has been bought by dubious oligarchs. Water supply and wind power have been colonized, as has North Sea oil. Mineral resources are going the same way. And this has happened without any democratic process involving consultation with the commoners. Instead, the loss of sovereignty over what were commons resources has been facilitated by politicians, some of whom campaigned for Brexit to 'restore national sovereignty'. The hypocrisy was breath-taking.

Subtle losses to society come with the erosion of the natural commons. Access to nature teaches children to learn about and appreciate it. Many more children in Britain today have little 'natural literacy'. One survey linked 'loss of knowledge about the natural world to growing isolation from it'.[97] The ignorance is not restricted to children. In a 'Birdwatch' survey in 2017, the Royal Society for the Protection of Birds found that half the sample of 2,000 adults could not identify a house sparrow. Two-thirds of adults in another survey the same year said they felt they had lost touch with nature. Let the wretched Natural Capital Committee put a price on that.

Meanwhile, there are some heart-warming stories of commoners defending the natural commons. In West Yorkshire, a group of residents of Todmorden, an old mill town, stumbled into setting up the Incredible Edible Todmorden (IET). Since 2008 they have been identifying bits of public land in and around the town, some seventy sites in all, to plant food to feed the community. Their model is now being copied in several other places and has led to a surge in purchases of local food. While such initiatives flourish, the natural commons, though sadly weakened, are certainly not lost.

## The Charter: the natural commons

This assessment of the state of the natural commons leads to the following suggested articles for the draft Charter of the Commons:

Article 1: Ownership of all land in Britain should be registered with the Land Registry within a year of the order being made, with penalties for non-registration that could include taking land back into common ownership.

Article 2: A new Domesday book should compile a comprehensive record of the public and private ownership of land, including a map showing all commons and Open Access land.

Article 3: Farm subsidies based on the amount of land owned should be abolished.

Article 4: Local authorities should be re-empowered to acquire land for rent to small-scale farmers.

Article 5: In keeping with the spirit of the Charter of the Forest, the Forestry Commission should be obliged to preserve the nation's forests as commons. This means halting and reversing privatization and commercialization, and maximizing public access consistent with conserving the environment.

Article 6: The Charter for Trees, Woods and People, as drawn up by the Woodland Trust in 2017, should be supported by all levels of government.

Article 7: National parks should be preserved as zones of biodiversity, and commercialization should be reversed.

Article 8: The time-honoured right to roam must be preserved. The period for registration of paths and footways should be extended beyond the existing 2026 cut-off. Maps of all open-access green space should be freely available to the public.

Article 9: Public parks must be protected and properly funded.

Article 10: The privatization of roads and squares in cities and towns should be stopped. Privately owned public spaces (POPS) should be rolled back and common rights of use restored. All urban public spaces, including POPS, should be mapped and made publicly available.

Article 11: Urban trees must be preserved and increased in number. Mature trees should not be felled unless they endanger people or property. Privatization of tree maintenance should be reversed.

Article 12: Privatized water companies must be restored to common ownership.

Article 13: The skyline is part of our commons. Those who block or blight the urban skyline with billboards and advertisements should pay a commons levy, as should factories, mass distribution sheds, supermarkets and other non-agricultural constructions that scar our open countryside.

Article 14: Air pollution is a severe subtraction from the commons. It must be regulated and taxed.

Article 15: Wind power is a natural commons that should be converted to common ownership.

Article 16: All resources in or under the ground or sea should belong to the commons and be exploited according to commons principles for the benefit of all commoners.

Article 17: No fracking or other resource extraction should take place in or under any public commons such as national parks.

Article 18: A carbon tax should be imposed to slash greenhouse gas emissions, at a level that will enable the UK to fulfil its pledges to combat climate change. Those on lower incomes should be compensated for the higher energy prices.

Article 19: The Natural Capital Committee must be abolished. Nature is not capital.

CHAPTER 4
# The Social Commons

> Every Free-Man . . . shall also have the Honey that is found
> within his Woods.
> — Article 13, The Charter of the Forest

The social commons includes the facilities and amenities essential to normal living that are provided outside the private market, built over the generations and paid for through
taxes, donations and, often, voluntary commoning in their
construction and maintenance. They include the many services of the welfare state – public housing, child and elder
care, healthcare and social services – as well as security services, mail services, public transport, and basic infrastructure such as roads, sewerage systems, flood defences and
public parks.

The social commons contribute to a person's social
income by lowering the cost of attaining or maintaining a
standard of living and raising the quality of life. Public social
amenities are as much part of the 'poor's overcoat' as the
forest was at the time when the Charter of the Forest was
drawn up. Yet the social commons are under attack from
all sides. The effects of austerity have been particularly
pernicious.

## Home, homes and homelessness

> Housing has lost its social function and is seen instead
> as a vehicle for wealth and asset growth. It has become
> a financial commodity, robbed of its connection to
> community, dignity and the idea of home.
> — Leilani Farha, UN Special Rapporteur
>   on the Right to Housing, 2017

Home is where the heart is, goes the saying. If so, a large and growing number of people in many countries, including Britain, are feeling homeless, even if they have somewhere to live or sleep at any particular moment. The commons and the idea of home are intimately linked. A core claim of the Charter of the Forest was that everybody had a right to a home, and for many people the commons was where that right was ensured. Yet the idea of home has a double meaning, implying both a place to live and a place to which one has a strong attachment and sustainable sense of belonging.

Lack of a home is linked to being a 'denizen', a term applied in the Middle Ages to someone, an outsider, who entered a town and wished to ply a trade. On proper application, the person could be given permission to stay and do business but without the full range of rights possessed by citizens of the town. As denizens, they continued to have outsider status, blocked from feeling completely 'at home'.

This situation applies to those in the precariat today.[1] Many feel they are not 'at home' anywhere. The feeling of psychological homelessness while having a place to stay is not new, but we should recognize that the stronger the social commons, the stronger the sense of home and belonging is likely to be. If the neighbourhood commons is degraded, people start to lose commoners' rights and become denizens rather than citizens.

However, the most visible problem today is rising homelessness in the literal sense. As a mass phenomenon, this is a modern malaise. Robin Hood and his merry men were not homeless in either the literal or anthropological sense. Not only did they have places to lay their heads; they felt they belonged to Sherwood Forest and that the forest belonged to them. Homelessness as a mass phenomenon came with urbanization and industrialization. As the modern British state developed in the nineteenth century, it first relied on the dreaded workhouse as a cruel and deliberately demeaning substitute for home for those victimized by land enclosure and surplus industrial labour markets. Then, in the early decades of the twentieth century, the state tried to provide certain commoners – the proletariat – with a right to a home through provision of local council housing. This has evolved into fuzzier concepts of social housing and affordable housing.

In recent years, the social right to a home has been lost, due in part to falling incomes and social protection support for the most vulnerable and in part to government policies that have resulted in a cut in the supply of low-cost housing. In 1981, nearly a third of households in England were renting social housing, most provided by local authorities. Since then, that proportion has halved, while the proportion in private rented accommodation has doubled. Meanwhile the charity Shelter estimated that in 2018 a record 320,000 people in Britain were homeless or lacked a permanent place to live, while the number of rough sleepers had more than doubled since 2010. It expected the numbers to go on rising as fresh cuts to local authority housing support began to bite.

Homelessness is a result of a shrinking social commons. Britain has never been richer, yet in addition to a record number of homeless, there is a record number of food banks, with at least 2,000 operating in 2017.[2] Although they do not only serve the homeless, the growth of the two has gone together. The Trussell Trust, Britain's biggest food bank chain, reported that it gave out a record 1.2 million food parcels in 2016–17, the ninth successive year of rising demand. There are over 650 other food bank institutions in Britain, all facing rising demand for help.

A report by the House of Commons Public Accounts Committee in December 2017 noted that at any one time in England over 78,000 families, including 120,000 children, were homeless and living in temporary accommodation, a rise of more than 60 per cent since 2010. As the report pointed out, these figures are likely to be a considerable underestimate as they do not count the 'hidden homeless' lodging with family or friends. In addition, as many as 9,100 people were sleeping rough on the streets or bedding down in hostels or shelters.

Homelessness has dire effects on individuals and families. Children are more likely to miss school and fall behind; rough sleepers die on average at age forty-seven, thirty years before their contemporaries with homes. And, contrary to the common perception, homelessness is not restricted to people with character faults or mental and physical impairments. 'Increasingly, [homeless people] are normal families who would not have expected to be in this situation,' the Local Government Ombudsman said in a report in December 2017.

Homelessness has been growing fast among groups with full-time jobs, such as nurses, hospital staff, council workers and taxi drivers, evicted by private-sector landlords seeking higher rents.[3] The end of a private tenancy is now the most common cause of homelessness;[4] according to Shelter, 78 per cent of the rise in homelessness between 2011 and 2017 was due to evictions from privately rented accommodation.[5]

In 2017 the government, which earlier made a commitment to eliminate rough sleeping by 2027, passed the Homelessness Reduction Act, obliging local councils to do more for the homeless in their areas. Yet at the same time it cut the funds made available for housing support services for vulnerable groups – by almost 70 per cent between 2010–11 and 2016–17.[6] And while homelessness and rough sleeping is concentrated in the big cities, especially London, it has been rising in rural areas as well, where there is even less help on offer.[7]

One vital part of the social commons has been the network of refuges for women and children fleeing domestic violence, of which there are some 270 in England. They too have been victims of austerity, losing funding and thus the means of providing social support. In January 2018 the government announced that it would withdraw direct support, in the form of housing benefit paid to the women, and instead channel funds to local authorities to decide on how the money should be spent.[8] Refuges would have had to compete with other services in a context of an overall cut in funds. Women's Aid also pointed out that women often move from the local authority area where they have lived and been abused, to be further away from their attackers. It predicted that thousands of women and children would end up homeless as refuges shrank or closed. Fortunately, concerted opposition forced the government to backtrack on housing benefit. But spending on refuges by cash-strapped local councils has fallen sharply.

Although women make up a majority of those abused, of the 1.9 million adults in England and Wales who said in 2017 that they had been victims of domestic abuse, nearly 40 per cent or 700,000 were men, including men in same-sex relationships. There has been virtually no help in the form of refuges for them.

In the neo-liberal era, the stock of council housing was slashed and the subsequent notion of affordable housing was easily perverted. The first blow came with Margaret Thatcher's decision to give council house tenants the right to buy their homes, at a discount. Instantly, a major part of the social commons – created by and for commoners in general – became a privatized commodity. While a fortunate minority made short-term gains with the aid of a big and inequitable subsidy from government, the stock of social housing was drastically reduced. As of early 2018, just under 2 million council properties in England had been sold since the right-to-buy was introduced in October 1980.[9] The council housing stock has fallen by two-thirds to its lowest on record, from 5 million in 1981 to 1.6 million in 2017, though the drop also reflects homes transferred to social housing associations.[10]

The Coalition government reinforced Thatcher's original right-to-buy policy by increasing the discount to council tenants wishing to buy their homes, giving a further boost to council house sales. Sales in England rose five-fold from 2,638 in 2011–12 to 13,416 in 2016–17.[11] Meanwhile, just one council house was being built for every five sold and these must now be let at 'affordable' rents (80 per cent of market rents) rather than 'social' rents (typically 50 per cent of market rents). In some cases, tenants have been able to buy their homes for less than half the market value. The inevitable consequence has been the purchase of council homes for private letting at much higher rents. Four in ten properties sold under the right-to-buy are now owned by private landlords. And to add insult to injury, local councils are paying tens of millions of pounds a year to rent back former council homes to house the growing number of homeless families.[12]

The subsequent proposal by the incoming Conservative government to permit all 1.3 million housing association tenants in England to buy their homes, at the same enticing discount, marked a further step in the planned privatization of the social commons. After running into sustained opposition, it later agreed to a voluntary scheme, due to start in 2019 at the earliest, to be financed by a new requirement on local councils to sell the top third of their most valuable properties. As many councils have argued, this would mean selling all the new council homes they build, an obvious disincentive to building more.

The stock of social housing – the social commons – is being deliberately run down, contriving yet more scarcity and forcing more families into expensive privately rented accommodation or into a downward spiral to homelessness. For just these reasons, the Scottish and Welsh governments have decided to scrap right-to-buy, effective in Scotland from

2016 and in Wales from January 2019. But the Conservative government in London has shown no sign of following suit.

Policies such as the so-called 'bedroom tax', which reduces housing benefit if someone in social housing has any room 'spare' above the minimal number deemed adequate, have added to the homelessness crisis. You cannot retreat to Mum's place if she has been forced to give up her second bedroom.

The shrinkage of the housing commons has been accentuated by the changing nature of the labour market and the growth of the precariat. Private landlords and private housing agencies have been refusing to give tenancies to those on short-term or zero-hour contracts and have been even more averse to giving them to recipients of housing benefit or the so-called Universal Credit, both of which are not only inadequate but can be withdrawn at almost any time. Precarious benefits intensify the loss of the social commons.

Social housing in cities is integral to the preservation of structured communities. With rising property prices and stagnant real wages, more workers depend on social housing to live in inner cities where the jobs are. But the quality and availability of social housing provided by local councils and housing associations have been declining as they sell off properties in expensive areas to raise funds. And because local authorities gain from gentrification and rising property prices in the private sector, they have tended to give even lower priority to those in social housing, thus increasing their marginalization.

One tragic consequence was the Grenfell Tower fire in the Royal Borough of Kensington and Chelsea in June 2017. Over seventy people perished as the high-rise building was engulfed in flames and smoke. It turned out that the local authority had approved cheap inflammable exterior cladding, one objective being to make the building less of an eyesore for more affluent residents living nearby.[13] Grenfell tenants had warned the authorities repeatedly – most notably, the Kafkaesque-sounding Tenant Management Association – that the building was unsafe. They had been ignored with disdain. Indeed, two words summed up their feelings at their treatment: 'invisibility' and 'contempt'. Far from having a right to a home, the tenants had been 'housed'. As one resident told the *Financial Times*, 'It was not that we stayed silent, but that they never responded. It was not just that they ignored us, but that they viewed us with contempt.'[14] It was later revealed that 1,652 properties in the borough were owned by oligarchs, foreign royalty and very rich business folk who were keeping them unoccupied, mostly because they were using them as speculative investments.[15] More than a third had been empty for over two years.

The decline in social housing is also due to what has been termed 'state-led gentrification'. Again, London is an extreme case. Many London boroughs have initiated 'regeneration' schemes, inviting commercial developers to overhaul public housing estates – including 195 council estates in the twenty-one Labour-run boroughs – and to build anew.[16] The developers have typically erected a lot of expensive properties and a risible number of 'affordable' homes. The Heygate Estate in London's Elephant and Castle area, which once housed 3,000 low-income people, was demolished and sold to a property company to create 2,500 homes, of which only seventy-nine were social housing.

One high-profile scheme of this type, now scrapped after

massive opposition by local people, would have redeveloped the Northumberland Park estate in Tottenham through the establishment of a 50–50 joint venture between the developers LendLease and the London Borough of Haringey. This would have involved the transfer of land and property to a new private company, which would also have paid LendLease handsomely for managing Haringey's commercial portfolio as well as the development project itself.

Meanwhile, large parts of the property market in London have been handed to foreign investors. By 2015, sites for about 30,000 homes were owned by ten investors from China, Hong Kong, Malaysia, Australia, Singapore and Sweden.[17] Most of the planned building was for luxury housing, well out of reach of the average Londoner. The Crown Estate has joined in the sell-off, transferring valuable properties to known Russian (and other) oligarchs with dubious pasts. Many properties acquired by foreign interests are left empty for years, even though local councils have legal powers to take them over using Empty Dwelling Management Orders (EDMOs).

In addition, central government has embarked on a massive sale of public land for private housing, with apparently little analysis or oversight. A report by the House of Commons Public Accounts Committee (PAC) on the sale of nearly 950 sites between 2011 and 2015, intended for 100,000 homes, revealed that the government did not know how much the land was sold for, whether or not it was sold below its market value, or how many houses had actually been built.[18] As the report concluded, 'There is no means of knowing whether taxpayers are getting a good deal from the sale of their land.' Nevertheless, yet more sales of public land were being lined up, supposedly for building 150,000 homes between 2015 and 2020. The PAC expressed understandable concern that, in a rush to meet arbitrary government targets, land would be sold at knock-down prices, enriching property developers at public expense.

Another peculiarly modern factor in the shrinkage of the housing commons is the Airbnb phenomenon. In 2016–17 alone, the number of users in the UK of the online short-term lettings platform grew by 81 per cent. This is really a continuation of the trend to commodification of the commons. Successive governments gave generous subsidies to relatively affluent people to purchase 'buy-to-let' properties, aimed at increasing the supply of privately rented housing. Besides inflating property prices, it was blatantly regressive. By 2017, there were some 2 million 'landlords' across the country, renting out over 5 million housing units.[19] However, six in ten landlords owned only one property and nearly 30 per cent of privately rented homes were classified as failing to meet basic standards, twice the proportion for social housing.[20]

Although buy-to-let subsidies were largely withdrawn by the 2016 budget, landlords are still finding a potentially lucrative source of income through Airbnb. In 2017, one so-called Airbnb 'host' gained £12 million from nearly 900 different 'listings'. Instead of letting to the precariat and those relying on state benefits, with their doubtful ability to pay rents, landlords can let to short-term guests, as quasi-hotels, to 'tourists', for a few days at a time. This has turned many more houses and apartments into commodities, rather than homes, while chipping away at the very idea of neighbourhoods and community. Consider a house with rented apartments on three floors. If the landlord converts the second floor into an Airbnb rental, the remaining tenants will find themselves in a lodging house, subject to the whims of people coming and going without any sense of responsibility to those who see the house as their home.

Although the Charter of the Forest's commitment to a right to a home in the commons has fared badly over the ages, now may be among the worst of times, at least since the era of the workhouse in the nineteenth century. But even worse is to come: homelessness is increasingly being treated as a crime. Since the Vagrancy Act of 1824, it has been a criminal offence to sleep rough or to beg in the streets, but convictions were few until fairly recently. The Anti-Social Behaviour Orders (ASBOs) introduced under the Blair government intensified the legal hounding of the homeless, which was further reinforced by the Anti-Social Behaviour, Crime and Policing Act of 2014. This replaced ASBOs with a still harsher instrument, Criminal Behaviour Orders.

Under the 2014 Act, local councils can target rough sleepers with Public Spaces Protection Orders (PSPOs), which ban them from doing anything deemed by the authorities as having a detrimental effect on the quality of life of the locality. Anyone alleged to be in breach of a PSPO must pay a £100 penalty; if they do not pay they are subject to a £1,000 fine and given a criminal record. For breaching a Criminal Behaviour Order (for instance, for repeated begging) they can be sent to prison for up to five years. As of 2018 more than fifty local authorities in England and Wales were reportedly using PSPOs, with hundreds of fixed-penalty notices issued since the 2014 Act came into force.[21]

Highlighting the tougher line, in January 2018 while on a skiing holiday in the United States, the Conservative council leader of the Royal Borough of Windsor and Maidenhead wrote to the Windsor police asking it to clear the town of beggars and the homeless by the time of the wedding of Prince Harry and Meghan Markle in May, using the Vagrancy Act and the powers given under the 2014 Act. Despite some softening of the rhetoric after criticism from homelessness charities and even Prime Minister Theresa May, the council went ahead with what it called a 'homelessness support strategy', using PSPOs to prohibit 'aggressive' begging and leaving 'unattended' bedding on the street. The plan had a moralistic rationale that many local residents would probably support. The homeless were to be offered housing, medical and addiction services. But if they did not accept the offer within a fifty-six-day window they faced prosecution.

The creeping criminalization of homelessness in cities and towns is an international trend. Hungary made homelessness a criminal offence in 2013 and in 2018 wrote that into the country's constitution. In 2014, in Fort Lauderdale, Florida, ninety-year-old Arnold Abbott was arrested and threatened with jail and a $500 fine for attempting to feed the homeless. The Mayor said the arrest was justified because feeding the homeless annoyed local property owners. Today, the action is a crime in at least thirty-four US cities.

In 2017 in Melbourne, Australia – where there has been a steep growth in homelessness in recent years – the city council proposed amending a local law to ban 'camping' in all public spaces. Again, the UN Special Rapporteur on the Right to Housing spoke up:

While homeless people are not specifically referenced, it is clear they are the target; the amendment was put forward following the forcible removal of a homeless camp in the city centre last month. The criminalization of homelessness is deeply concerning and violates international human rights law. It's bad enough that homeless people are being swept off the streets by city officials. The proposed law goes further and is discriminatory – stopping people from engaging in life-sustaining activities and penalizing them because they are poor and have no place to live.[22]

The proposed amendment was later abandoned, but only after the council decided it could use existing local by-laws instead, to much the same effect.

The right to a home has been gravely weakened by neo-liberal policies and austerity. Homelessness has become a modern nightmare for many and a reality for an alarming number of others. In the spirit of the Charter of the Forest, the housing crisis must be tackled by policies that prioritize social housing at a genuinely affordable rent, clamp down on exploitative private landlords and end subsidies that bene-fit the more affluent most. Provision of housing should be recaptured for local communities, by involving community groups and small-scale local builders, ideally those steeped in their community traditions and landscape. And there should be more scope for community land trusts, co-housing schemes and cooperatives.[23]

## Student accommodation: from commons to commerce

Student housing represents another form of social income inequality that has grown alarmingly. There has been a dualistic development, with shabby but over-priced accommodation for low-income students and increasingly luxurious accommodation for those from wealthy backgrounds.

Purpose-built student accommodation has become one of the fastest growing and most lucrative sectors in the UK property market and has provided plenty of candidates for the ugliest building in Britain.[24] Meanwhile, keen to maximize profits or to overcome cost pressures, universities have been selling their previously low-rent student dwellings to private investors. By 2013 over 80 per cent of student accommodation was being provided by profit-making firms and rents have soared. The student accommodation 'industry' has become a favourite for global finance, attracted by the high returns that look set to continue as demand far outstrips supply. Much of the investment comes from overseas, notably from North America, Russia and Middle Eastern countries. Meanwhile Goldman Sachs and the Wellcome Trust have combined to set up a student housing venture called Vero Group, which aims to become the UK's leading student accommodation provider. The biggest current operator, Unite Group, has 50,000 beds across the UK.

Student housing is not covered by official housing regulations. Property developers do not have to adhere to safety, lighting, acoustics and space standards of ordinary housing. Over sixty tower blocks for student accommodation have cladding that has failed fire safety tests following the Grenfell Tower disaster.[25] (In October 2018 the government said it would ban inflammable cladding for all high-rise buildings, including student housing.) Universities do not have responsibility for ensuring the quality of their students' accommodation, while the overseas investors that are backing and gaining from these ugly intrusions into the housing landscape do not have to see what their money produces.

## The National Health Service: privatization drip by drip

The NHS became part of the British social commons in 1968, after it passed the critical twenty-year threshold of existence as a virtually uncontested part of the social landscape. It has remained the most popular public service in the country: in 2017, 83 per cent of the electorate said they wanted more money spent on it.[26] Yet since the 1980s, despite professing commitment to its preservation, successive governments have whittled away at its commons character. By 2018, the NHS could no longer be described honestly as a nationalized public service.

Reforms since the early 1990s have seen the NHS in England (the NHS is run separately in Scotland and in Wales) devolved and fragmented into an extraordinary number of quasi-independent competing sections, with 7,500 general practices, 233 'trusts' (covering hospitals and other direct providers), and some 850 companies and charities that provide care on its behalf.[27]

Although NHS privatization started under Margaret Thatcher, the decisive changes were made in 2007 by the

Blair government. The reforms ushered in privatization by stealth, mainly by inducing NHS hospitals to contract out services.[28] Under the Coalition government, privatization was accelerated by the Health and Social Care Act of 2012, which in all but name abolished the government's responsibility to provide a national health service. There was henceforth no legal guarantee to provide comprehensive health services, beyond emergency care and ambulances, while NHS contracts were opened up to unlimited privatization.[29]

By 2018 non-NHS providers accounted for almost half NHS spending on community services such as community nursing, health visiting and occupational therapy.[30] Private service contractors, often with links to those commissioning their services, are making large profits from contracts paid by an increasingly cash-strapped (tax-funded) NHS. And contractual conditions stipulate that they have first call on limited NHS budgets, even at the expense of medical services.

The most outrageous example relates to private finance initiative (PFI) hospitals under deals signed by over 100 NHS hospital trusts in England, which committed those trusts to repay private investors for building and maintaining their hospitals. Although conceived by John Major's Conservative government in 1992, the vast majority of these PFI arrangements were made between 1997 and 2010 under New Labour, which wanted to shift the cost of projects off government borrowing requirements. Succeeding Conservative-led governments continued to support them until, after a string of failures, their end was announced in the budget of October 2018.

By then, the hospital trusts were paying £2 billion a year to private companies, a figure set to rise, for building and operating new hospitals and renovating old ones. While the deals financed £13 billion of hospital building, the trusts are locked into arrangements to repay £79 billion over the twenty-five to thirty years the arrangements are set to last, which is six times the building cost and far more than if the government had borrowed the money on their behalf. Just four firms will be paid £39 billion.[31] Meanwhile, NHS hospitals are collectively deep in the red and struggling to cope with continuing increases in patient numbers.

Across Britain, expensive PFI contracts have also been used to fund schools, roads, streetlights, prisons, police stations and care homes, burdening central and local government with huge debts to financial capital. The annual charge on the existing 716 private finance deals, with a capital value of about £60 billion, amounted to £10.3 billion in 2016–17, with some £100 billion already paid out and £200 billion due in future payments into the 2040s.[32]

Schools built using the PFI cost 40 per cent more and hospitals 60 per cent more than the public sector alternative. As a consequence, these public services are locked into paying absurdly high costs on PFI contracts at a time of shrinking budgets due to austerity cuts by central government, representing a double squeeze on essential spending. Much of the money has gone to lucrative investment funds based in tax havens.[33] And yet the government planned to continue using PFI contracts until shamed by the Carillion collapse into ending the scheme for future projects.

The folly of the PFI system showed many signs of failure before the collapse of Carillion, a huge construction and outsourcing company, in January 2018. Government decisions on contracts have been driven by price, with only secondary regard for quality. To secure contracts, companies competed to underbid each other, sometimes offering less than the cost of providing the services and failing to provide adequately for cost overruns and delays on construction projects. By bidding low, Carillion won hundreds of contracts to build roads, hospitals and schools and provide services from prison maintenance to NHS cleaning and school meals. The inevitable outcomes were poor services for the public and consistent losses for the company, which ran up massive debt. That did not stop the directors awarding themselves large bonuses and paying out generous dividends to shareholders.

Despite repeated profit warnings, the government went on awarding Carillion large and socially sensitive contracts. Its eventual bankruptcy exposed as a sham the claim commonly made that paying private companies extra was justified because they were bearing the risk. When Carillion went bankrupt, the government was left to find the money to finish building the hospitals and roads, deliver school dinners, and the rest. And Carillion was not alone in bidding too low for contracts. In the eighteen months from January 2016 the government was obliged to renegotiate contracts worth more than £120 million to keep public services running because they were initially outsourced too cheaply.[34]

There was also no evidence to support the claim that privatized health services increased efficiency. NHS reforms introduced more layers of highly paid managers to impose more bureaucracy, supervise an increasingly insecure workforce, and award contracts to private companies more intent on profits and rent-seeking than patient care. A report by the

National Audit Office in 2018 said outsourcing of primary care administration services to Capita, another giant outsourcing company, had put patients at risk and encouraged the company to shut down services to minimize losses.[35] In early 2019, top NHS officials called for the repeal of parts of the Health and Social Care Act 2012 to end automatic tendering for NHS contracts and facilitate the planned integration of health and care services now hindered by the fragmentation of care delivery brought about by privatization.[36]

Meanwhile, the government's allocation of resources to the NHS has not kept pace with rising demand for healthcare, due to an ageing population, an increase in chronic illness and bigger bills for staff, drugs and equipment. And reforms have contributed to an increase in inequality, with bigger cuts to health services in poorer areas than in richer ones. In some areas tight budgets have led to random treatment restrictions including cutbacks in IVF (in vitro fertilization), hip and knee operations, even to the extent of fixing eye cataracts in just one eye rather than both. In many areas, general practitioners (GPs), now nominally 'independent contractors', have been banned from prescribing medicines such as painkillers that can be purchased over the counter, hitting low-income households previously entitled to free prescriptions most severely.[37]

As of 2017, the NHS was short of 40,000 nurses and 6,000 doctors. Four million people were on hospital waiting lists. The British Red Cross warned of an unfolding 'humanitarian crisis' in NHS hospitals due to overcrowding and understaffing.[38] Sir Robert Francis QC, who chaired the public inquiry into the failings of the Mid-Staffordshire NHS foundation trust when staff shortages and exhaustion led to patient mis-treatment and unnecessary deaths, said the NHS was facing 'an existential crisis'. It had ceased to be part of the social commons.

The drip-by-drip privatization of the NHS has reflected a global trend. Although starting from very different struc-tures, other countries have also seen extended privatization of healthcare in the neo-liberal era. Developments in the United States have been particularly regressive. In January 2018, the Trump administration established a Conscience and Religious Freedom Division in the Department of Health and Human Services, which will allow nurses and doctors to refuse to conduct abortions and other procedures that run counter to their religious beliefs. These could include legal-ized assisted suicide, care for transgender transition, and even conventional medical care for LGBT people. The move is clearly discriminatory and represents a narrowing of the healthcare commons.

In 2018 several US states decided, with the approval of the Trump administration, to extend work requirements for receipt of Medicaid that ensures healthcare for low-income households. Many poor people are expected to lose health coverage as a result, including those working irregular hours who may not be able to meet the minimum stipulated hours every month.

But the unfolding tragedy in the UK is worse because the NHS since 1948 has been an embodiment of the social commons. It was designed as a universal service – not a safety net for the poor – that would treat all citizens equal-ly, with everyone entitled to the best possible care based on need rather than ability to pay. It has been universalistic in the true meaning, not just providing a universal service free at the point of delivery but expressing solidarity between commoners as users and commoners as providers. Patients and providers – whether surgeons, doctors, nurses or auxiliaries – can see each other as sharing equally in a collective endeavour. By 2018, that sharing sense of universalism was endangered as providers, increasingly treated as part of the precariat, struggled in a competitive environment. It was a time of crisis, in need of a new social compact.

## Care for the elderly: commercializing common life

In our ageing societies, social care for the elderly has become a highly charged part of the social commons. In England, social care for the elderly is a statutory responsibility of local authorities; it now accounts for about a third of their budget at a time of unprecedented cuts in council spending on services and rising demand for care.

As with other social services, elder care has been steadily privatized, to the detriment of both quality and reliability. Care homes are being run by businesses for profit; three of the biggest commercial chains – HC-One, Four Seasons and Care UK – are owned by private equity companies. If a home is not sufficiently profitable, it can be closed or left in a run-down state for a local authority to take over.

Tens of thousands of elderly and vulnerable people have been left with inadequate care or have been forced to move following a series of closures and bankruptcies in recent years. These have been blamed by the owners on cuts in local council funding for the 60 per cent of care home residents who depend on public support, as well as the impact of the increased 'living wage' on their costs.[39] However, care of the elderly should not be in the hands of private companies more concerned about making money than about the people in their charge.

The privatization and commodification of care was accelerated by the NHS and Community Care Act of 1990, under which local authorities were obliged to become 'purchasers' of care services, while the private commercial and non-profit sectors became 'providers'. The reform ushered in competitive tendering, with contracts tending to be awarded to the lowest bidder. Cost-cutting has lowered the quality of the public service, partly by driving down the wages and working conditions of the front-line service providers.[40] And a widening gap has emerged between a growing 'care worker' precariat and highly paid senior managers. Meanwhile, NGOs, reliant on local authority contracts, have ceased to be advocacy groups or part of the social commons.

Between 2009–10 and 2016–17, 400,000 fewer elderly people received social care as eligibility criteria were tightened to reduce the demand on restricted council budgets.[41] As of 2018, 1.2 million older and disabled people in England were unable to get the care they needed, almost double the number in 2010.[42] Many were stuck in hospital, blocking badly needed bed space and adding to NHS costs, because there was nowhere else for them to go. Care has been commodified, eroding the social commons by devaluing shared community responsibility for caring for its elderly citizens.

## Playgrounds

Children's public playgrounds, free and open to all, are an integral part of the social commons. Their commons status is cemented by their longevity and by the fact that they reflect commoning – shared activity from an early age that brings children of all backgrounds together to play. But playgrounds have proved an easy target for councils and other organizations forced by austerity to wield cuts to the social commons. Hundreds of public playgrounds in England have been closed, while others have been converted into commercial ventures.[43]

A public, free adventure playground in Battersea Park in south London, with equipment painted by the children themselves, has been bulldozed and replaced by a 'swings-and-slides' park for younger children. Directly above them are the zip wires and rope bridges of Go Ape, a private 'tree-top adventure company', that offers climbing sessions for between £21 and £36 per child, well beyond the means of low-income families.[44]

Queen Victoria gave Battersea Park to the nation as a free public space. Renting part of it out, after spending £250,000 of public money on clearance and new equipment, has created a divisive landscape, leaving poorer children literally looking up at their more affluent peers. It epitomizes the plunder of the social commons, and in a small cruel way accentuates social income inequality and erodes social solidarity.

## The mail

Mail services are an often overlooked part of the social commons. Many people, especially the elderly and those on low incomes without access to or ability to use fast broadband services, rely on snail mail.

The Royal Mail was established in 1516 when Henry VIII appointed a 'Master of the Posts' and became a public service a little over a century later. It has been a venerable part of the social commons. But in 2013, mail services in Britain were privatized by the Coalition government, the new owners of the Royal Mail receiving a hefty subsidy in the process.

Instead of having faith in the market, which would have required auctioning the newly created shares for sale to the highest credible bidders, the government set the initial price of shares at 330p a share, well below the market value. Within a day, the price rose to 445p, providing a £750 million windfall to their holders on flotation. Most of this went to large investors such as pension and hedge funds. Among the major beneficiaries were the financial institutions appointed to advise the government on the selling price. Besides handsome payment for their advice, they had been sold large bundles of shares at the price they themselves set. They promptly sold those shares when the price rose, making huge profits. As the shares subsequently rose further, the government had effectively given away over £1 billion of the public's social commons.[45]

In 2015, the British regulator, Ofcom, charged Royal Mail with breach of competition laws in relation to its proposed charges to rival operators for bulk mail delivery services. Ofcom had earlier launched a 'fundamental review' to assess whether existing regulation needed strengthening to prevent abuse of the company's near-monopoly position, including excessive charges for letters and parcels. Another issue is the extension of Royal Mail's obligation to provide a universal service, delivering post to all areas of Britain, which expires in 2021. Some fifty-two delivery offices have been closed since privatization to cut costs, worsening postal services to the public.[46] A public service has been handed over to private commercial interests. Surely, no one should be surprised if a private near-monopoly acts like one.

## Transport services

Public transport services are vital. They enable people to get to jobs, schools, shops, libraries, doctors and social and cultural activities; they, too, are part of the social commons. But the standard of Britain's transport infrastructure has been in serious decline since the onset of the austerity strategy in 2010. Public sector investment is planned to fall from 3.2 per cent of GDP in 2010 to 1.4 per cent in 2020.[47] Funding for local roads was cut by 20 per cent between 2010 and 2016. Infrastructure was hit even harder outside London, which was allocated a bigger share of the total.

The experience of water privatization in Britain has been matched by the record of the privatization of Britain's railways since 1993. Investment has increased, along with the number of services; passenger numbers have more than doubled. But fares have soared despite continuing generous government subsidies, as have profits, much diverted abroad. Train companies paid out nearly all the £868 million operating profits between 2012–13 and 2015–16 as dividends, despite the pressing need for reinvestment to improve service quality.[48] Nor has privatization led to increased efficiency. Operating costs are higher than anywhere else in Europe and, despite more intensive use of the network, unit costs per passenger are the same as they were on privatization.

Much of this is due to the then government's decision to split the former British Rail into separate track, rolling stock and train operations, which were then sold off in 100 pieces between 1995 and 1997. 'The train you catch is owned by a bank, leased to a private company, which has a franchise from the Department of Transport to run it on this track owned by Network Rail, all regulated by another office, and all paid for by taxpayers or passengers,' one commentator explained to the *Financial Times*.[49] Each part of the system prioritizes its own profits, to the detriment of the network as a whole.

Meanwhile, as with water privatization, the experience of rail privatization has exposed as nonsense the claim that private operators deserve a return for taking on business risk. Their risk is minimal as the government has opted to bail out the operators or release them from their contracts without significant penalty rather than admit that privatization has failed. When the East Coast line was renationalized in 2009, the subsequent five years saw increased ticket sales, record levels of customer satisfaction and a return of about £1 billion to the Exchequer. Yet the government still chose to re-privatize that line, only to renationalize it yet again in 2018 when operators Virgin and Stagecoach could no longer meet the terms of the contract. Predictably, they were allowed to walk away from the contract rather than pay the government what they owed.

Ironically, section 25 of the Railway Act of 1993 effectively states that the only government barred from owning Britain's railways is Britain's. This is self-induced colonization. Today, two-thirds of Britain's rail operators are foreign companies, including state-owned railways from Germany, the Netherlands and France. Yet the companies require even more subsidy than the nationalized industry ever did. In 1993, before privatization, British Rail was paid £1.3 billion in subsidies.[50] By 2016–17, the government was subsidizing private operators to the tune of over £6.8 billion a year.

Although only 2 per cent of trips in England are made by rail, over half of those trips involve journeys to work and a reliable affordable service is essential. In north-west England poor services by Northern Rail after service reductions in 2018 reportedly cost some their jobs for persistent lateness and led others to quit. Passengers missed medical appointments and flights, weddings, funerals and social events; disabled people were allegedly left stranded 'like animals' at stations. These are the personal, economic and social costs of losing a vital part of the social commons.

Rail privatization has also affected the many small businesses and start-ups that have thrived under the 4,455 railway arches built over generations. In 2018, state-owned Network Rail, which took back responsibility for railway infrastructure in the early 2000s, sold 5,200 properties, mostly comprising arches, to two investors: Telereal Trillium, a British property group, and Blackstone Property Partners, an American private equity company.[51] Those small businesses now fear being forced out by unaffordable rents.

Bus services, which are used by many more people than

trains, have performed an important social function since their introduction early in the twentieth century. In most parts of Britain, but especially in rural areas, buses are the only form of public transport available and unprofitable routes have often been subsidized to ensure essential services. A quarter of British households have no car, including half of low-income households. Young people and the elderly are especially dependent on bus services.

Deregulation under the Thatcher government generated a chaotic multitude of competing operators seeking the most profitable routes. In London, order was eventually restored when Transport for London introduced a franchising system that contracts out specific routes to a single operator. But in most other places the bus system is a mess, with no overall coordination, no tie-in with other transport services and little accountability. Operators have withdrawn unprofitable routes and passenger numbers have fallen.

However, in the austerity era, the loss of vital bus services has become a rout. Between 2010 and 2017, more than 3,000 bus services and routes, most in rural areas, were reduced or withdrawn altogether in England and Wales, due to funding cuts by government, and more were earmarked for closure in 2018.[52] Funding for buses was cut by a third in the same period, the biggest reductions coming in areas where the need to reach low-income groups was greatest. Eleven local councils are now spending nothing at all on bus support, including Stockton-on-Tees, Stoke-on-Trent, Blackpool, Southend and Luton.

Besides the environmental cost of the increased use of cars and taxis, eroding the social commons by such cuts leads to more inequality. The young, the elderly, and those on low incomes and in the precariat, are the most hurt by higher fares and poorer services. There are ripple effects on many other aspects of living, making the personal losses far greater than the loss of the bus service alone. They include growing isolation among older people in rural areas who rely on buses to access healthcare, social activities, community events and shops, as well as visiting friends and family (or having them visit). Free bus passes are not much use if there is no bus service. And, paradoxically, free off-peak bus travel for pensioners has prompted cuts in services used predominantly by the elderly because operators claim they are not adequately compensated.

More people commute to work by bus than by any other means of transport, so worsening services make travel to work more difficult and stressful and may even make getting to work impossible. Meanwhile, cuts make it harder for benefit claimants to search for jobs or attend employment offices for obligatory appointments. If they are just five minutes late, they can be sanctioned and lose a month's benefits, including housing benefit, which can lead to more debt, rent arrears and eviction. Cutting the bus service is just part of a chain of deprivation.

Cuts to rural bus services are culturally impoverishing as well. Many rural buses now cease running at 6 p.m., making it impossible for people reliant on buses to go to cinemas, theatres, choirs, children's music centres, bingo, sports facilities and other recreations.[53] Even national parks are increasingly inaccessible via public transport, as are hundreds of national landmarks and thousands of miles of coastline. This too has class implications, since those cut off from such places are often the precariat and proletariat. It is scarcely surprising that organizations such as the National Trust are run by and largely for middle-income and wealthy interests.

Some see hope in the Bus Services Act 2017, which gives local authorities more powers over bus services in their areas through partnerships with operators or London-style franchising. But if we continue down the path of austerity, bus services may be beyond rescue as part of the social commons.

## Labour market services: from help to coercion

Labour exchanges to help unemployed workers find jobs and employers to fill vacancies have existed since 'time immemorial': the first in Britain were set up in 1911. They lowered the cost of searching for a job and the cost of unemployment. But the ethos and model of labour market services as part of the social commons have long since been shredded. Some services have been privatized, through temp agencies and commercial training providers. The remainder have been converted into directive, selective instruments geared to the perceived needs of employers and the state, rather than those of the workers. The old labour or employment exchanges have been turned into 'Jobcentres', intended to coerce the unemployed into jobs, however unsuitable, on pain of losing social benefits. This is a clear rejection of the right to work as enshrined in the Charter of the Forest.

The stated intentions behind Universal Credit (UC), which is neither universal nor a form of credit, were to teach welfare 'claimants' financial 'management' or 'discipline' and to make the experience of being on UC as close as possible to being in a job. Claimants had to wait six weeks from the date of a claim before receiving UC, and benefits were withdrawn if they failed to behave in ways stipulated by the Jobcentre 'advisers'. When evidence accumulated that the six-week wait (in practice often longer) was causing desperate claimants real hardship, the required waiting period was cut to five weeks. How many people in jobs have to wait more than a month before being paid, and are not paid at all for the first month of work? The character of the service has been steadily altered to the point where it is not part of the social commons at all. It is about reforming people presumed – without evidence – to lack financial management skills and work discipline.

Meanwhile, the actions of Jobcentre 'advisers' have been more arbitrary and punitive than those of the worst kind of employer. Requiring claimants to report for interviews at any time of the day, at short notice, when they might be living a long way away, under threat of having benefits withdrawn, is eroding what remains of a public social service which, it should be recalled, is meant to supply something that the 'client' wants and needs.

Employment and welfare services used to be integral parts of the public domain. It is not much of an exaggeration to state that with privatization of a public service, unemployed, disabled or otherwise disadvantaged people are being treated as commodities. This is not unique to Britain. Denmark, Germany, the Netherlands, Sweden, Australia and the USA are all contracting out these services to private providers. Their public ethos is being eroded.

In Britain, as of 2018, the main privatized employment programmes were the Work Programme, aimed at pushing the unemployed into jobs, and the Work Capability Assessment, which is supposed to determine whether a disabled person is fit for employment. In principle, Work Programme contracts, estimated to total between £3 billion and £5 billion up to 2017, are funded by the consequent benefit savings of putting more people into jobs more quickly. The private commercial providers are paid according to the number of people they place in jobs. But these are services people are obliged to use in order to receive a benefit. The private companies are making money from a captive market created by the state.

Even before the Coalition government introduced the present Work Programme, the deficiencies of private provision were clear from the experience of other countries. Payment systems give private providers incentives to focus resources on the easiest-to-place people ('creaming'), ignore the hardest-to-place ('parking') and game the system by claiming credit for jobs found by unemployed people themselves, or by fabricating evidence of sustained employment. Even according to official figures, the Work Programme is not working. The evidence suggests that an unemployed person is no more likely to find a job through the programme than by searching themselves and no more likely to obtain one matching their qualifications. The service is earning its keep, from the government's viewpoint, not by putting people into jobs but by withdrawing benefits from more people for alleged breaches of a multiplicity of petty rules. Similarly, the privatized work assessments applied to disabled people, which determine what if any disability payments they should receive, have judged many people 'fit for work' when by any reasonable standard they are not. The consequences have been penury, premature deaths and suicides.

In less than two years over £108 million was spent by the Department for Work and Pensions on administrative reviews and appeals by people with disabilities who were ruled to be 'fit for work'.[54] And the Ministry of Justice, which was obliged to spend £103 million in 2016–17 on social security and child support tribunals, was facing rising costs as a result of decisions by the private contractors to deny benefits.

For over a century, the vocational training efforts of firms, public sector employers, professions and crafts were complemented by public training services. They became part of the twentieth-century social commons, epitomized by extension colleges and 'polytechnics' that were converted into 'universities' under Thatcher, to coincide with the corrosion of the enlightenment values of old universities. However, in 2011, the Coalition government sold off Learndirect, its adult training and apprenticeship service, to a private equity arm of Lloyds Bank. Learndirect continued to rely almost entirely on government contracts, receiving £158 million in the year to July 2017 alone, and £631 million since 2011. Yet, from having no debt initially, by mid-2015, while it had run down its cash holdings by 80 per cent, it had built up debts of £90 million, over ten times its operating cash flow and more than seven times its gross earnings. And despite declining profits over the previous three years, it paid out £20 million in dividends to its holding company.[55]

A report by the regulatory body Ofsted in 2017, which Learndirect tried to suppress, revealed that many of the 73,000 people on its training courses were not receiving any training or only rudimentary, inadequate training. Over a four-year period, 84 per cent of the cash generated by the business went to managers and financiers, and the parent company had spent £500,000 sponsoring an unsuccessful Formula One team backed by its private equity owners. The evidence makes a mockery of claims that the privatization would improve efficiency.

When confronted with the accumulation of evidence, the Department for Education said it would withdraw funding from Learndirect once its existing contracts expired in 2018. But it had no plans to end contracts with Learndirect Apprenticeships, owned by the same private equity company, which is offering apprenticeships under a new scheme launched by the government in May 2017. Meanwhile, the real losers were the commoners, who were induced to make use of the so-called training on offer.

Labour market services are no longer predominantly services intended to help citizens. Their intention is to change citizens' behaviour, backed by threats and punishments. A 'service' reflects and responds to what those using it want. If the service is a commons, what is provided is determined mainly by those making use of it. But today the government and companies determine what is provided and what is not. There are no stewards retaining the ethos of the commons and there are no gatekeepers working on behalf of the commoners obliged to use the services. Even if the motives of commercial front-line providers were benevolent, they are part of the paternalistic state which denies commoners any say in the services they may be obliged to use.

## The guilds as commons

One of the great symbols of the social commons has been the occupational guilds, which stretch back to ancient times. They existed in ancient China and Rome, and reached their maturity in fourteenth-century Florence, when twenty-one occupational guilds shaped the ethical and working life of the city and provided its governing council. Although there and elsewhere they were always prone to being bastions of privilege for their members, they epitomized the social commons in their unparalleled sense of community and social solidarity.

Throughout history they have protected the ethics of empathy, civic pride, craftsmanship and professional conduct, and nurtured social memory. For this reason, in times of social and economic transformation, the state has sought to crush them. In Britain, they were suppressed in the 1530s and 1540s, and in France they were banned after the Revolution in 1791. They were recognized for what they were, groups of like-minded commoners standing against the state and against market capitalism. Ever since, they have struggled to embody the social commons and uphold occupational citizenship.[56]

In myriad ways, the guilds have always stood against 'the market' – against commodification, standardization and commercial opportunism. They provided and reinforced community values and extolled 'character' above efficiency at all costs. In emphasizing civic friendship, they have always cultivated a wider sense of justice. Robust occupational communities are a barrier to opportunistic market forces because they limit competition between their members.

In the 1980s the neo-liberals set out to destroy the guilds, which they saw as restricting competition. And they largely succeeded, to the detriment of society. Milton Friedman wrote his first book on the medical guild system in the United States, advocating that it should be dismantled. Once neo-liberal ideology achieved ascendancy as the new orthodoxy, there was a trend away from self-regulation by guilds of their professions or crafts towards state regulation via occupational licensing. About 1,100 occupations in the USA are subject in at least one state to licensing by external boards, many dominated by the insurance industry and financial institutions. One consequence, in the USA, the UK and many other countries, has been the destruction of occupational commons. In Britain, this was advanced most by two Acts passed in 2007 relating to the legal and medical professions that took control away from the respective occupational communities and handed them to boards oriented to 'consumers' rather than to those inside the professions. The reforms thereby strengthened state control and debased the power of social memory.

The neo-liberal shift to licensing has been linked to the subsequent rise in wage differentials within occupations. While licensing does not result in wage gains for so-called low-skilled workers, it substantially boosts the earnings of higher-income earners. Yet the figures understate the loss of income for lower-earning workers, since the guilds also provided a complex network of social protection that has now been lost.

## 'Corporate commons'

Some of the early corporations of industrial capitalism in the nineteenth century provided their proletariat workforce with 'factory gardens', the pioneering example of which was

Robert Owen's 'pleasant manufactory' at his New Lanark textile mills in Scotland. His ideas inspired initiatives by several great paternalistic companies to improve workers' living and working conditions, which reached their apex at the end of the nineteenth century with Bournville, Cadbury's model village.[57] These initiatives were designed to supplement the earnings of their workers and induce them to be stable, hard-working employees. Workers in those firms thus had non-wage benefits that the majority did not have; even infant mortality amongst the workers' families declined due to the healthier environment.

This type of corporate benefit has become a major source of inequality again in the early twenty-first century, accentuating differences in social income between the salariat and the precariat. For instance, Google's new London campus at King's Cross will have a 300-metre-long rooftop garden, with a 'trim-track' running route. It is a 'landscraper'. Nomura has riverside offices in London with a large rooftop garden and vegetable plots. These are sources of social income for a privileged salariat, and a denial of the social commons for others.

## The allotment: a metaphor for the commons

The time-honoured institution of the allotment – or community garden, as it is known in the USA, or 'victory garden' as it was called in the UK during the Second World War – is a metaphor for the commons. It has existed for many generations in some form or another and in many countries and cultures. In Germany, where they are known as *Schrebergarten*, there are 1.4 million allotments, with 833 complexes in Berlin alone. In Italy, they burgeoned in the Second World War – hence their name, *orti di guerra*. They have also proliferated in Denmark, the Netherlands, Norway (where people can wait up to twenty years for one) and Sweden. They fulfil several socio-economic roles and images, being both sources of family food, and thus implied income, and sites of cultural activity.

Allotments are publicly owned plots rented to families to grow vegetables and fruit, mainly for consumption by themselves, family and friends. (Some sites also permit keeping hens, bees and rabbits.) They symbolize the historical continuity of the commons. In the UK, allotments have had a chequered history. At the time of the Speenhamland system at the end of the eighteenth century, Thomas Malthus and Edmund Burke opposed them, on the grounds that they would reduce labour supply to employers and slow capital accumulation. They survived and, during the nineteenth century, public and political sentiment changed in their favour. Three parliamentary Acts between 1887 and 1908 empowered local authorities to acquire land to turn into municipal allotments and, in rural areas, county farms for leasing cheaply to small tenant farmers.

In the twentieth century, attitudes fluctuated, as did the number of allotments. But in our era of rentier capitalism, they have been under relentless attack as councils have sold off allotment sites for private development. There are some 250,000 allotments in Britain today, against 1.3 million just after the Second World War, and the number is still shrinking despite nearly 100,000 people on waiting lists for one. The Olympic Park at Stratford, taken for London's Olympics in 2012, was built over thousands of allotments granted to residents of East London after the war. The County

Smallholdings Estate (the area allotted to county farms) has also been depleted, its partial sale encouraged by the Conservative government's rural white paper (policy document) of 1995. By 2015, the Estate had been reduced by a third, as local councils implemented cuts in response to dwindling funds from central government.

For those who manage to obtain one, an allotment is part of their social income. It also provides a source of informal social protection, as with any small garden. In the aftermath of the break-up of the Soviet Union in the early 1990s, Russia and Ukraine, the two largest countries of the USSR, were plunged into a terrifying period of hyper-stagflation, with plunging national income and hyperinflation. In Russia, life expectancy also plunged: male life expectancy fell from sixty-four to fifty-eight years. In Ukraine, the economically poorer country, it only fell a little, from a similar starting point. What distinguished Ukraine was that all urban residents had been given small plots on which to grow vegetables, principally potatoes. Those plots saved many lives, even if the work done on them was not recognized as productive activity.

In all countries, the role of allotments has combined both production and gentle, civilizing, leisurely work or working leisure. To some extent, in the twentieth century, allotments were monopolized by middle-class families, intent on weekend escapes from the urban bustle. Nowhere was this more so than in Germany and, in the form of dachas, in Russia and Ukraine. More recently, they have been dominated by pensioners. But their progressive socio-economic and cultural role should not be overlooked.

Allotments offer a place for retreat, a place to dissipate

stress, giving a sense of security and a link back with many generations of common folk. They convey a sense of citizenship, a welcome combination of cultural, social and economic rights, because of the connection to local land and the right to produce for one's family, friends and community. They also help to reproduce a sense of community standing against commercialization. No more than 49 per cent of produce can be sold but informal exchange and barter have never gone amiss. There is a pride and status in the reproductive work that gardening conveys.

Allotments have also had a political role, enabling families and friends to discuss political movements, facilitating reflective talk, undisturbed by commercial pressures or bosses' dictats. In many countries, they have been an outside equivalent of the bistro – Honoré de Balzac's parliament of the people – where conviviality and animated debates on politics flourished.

For the precariat, allotments are a harbinger of a struggle for the revival of the commons. They offer a vision of desirable elements of a good life, bestowing not just nutritional benefits but an assertion of the value of reproductive work over the dictates of labour. Work on allotments, for whatever reason, is real work – re-creating a little space at least as valuable and productive as shelf-stacking in a supermarket.

The allotment movement in Britain began in earnest with industrialization and urbanization, though allotments existed in rural areas and around small towns in the eighteenth century. Popular demand surged early in the twentieth century, leading to the Small Holdings and Allotments Act of 1908, parts of which are still in force. It placed a duty on local authorities to provide allotments according to demand. But demand has always outstripped the supply of land, partly because public ownership was preserved to keep down the price, to respect the idea that allotments are part of the commons.

In Britain as elsewhere, since their early days, responsibility for handing out allotments has been delegated to local councils. Since 1908, the amount of land made available has fluctuated. By 1913, there were 600,000 allotments in England and Wales. In the First World War, a lot more land was requisitioned for allotments to increase the food supply for a beleaguered nation. By 1918, there were 1,500,000. Although much of the land was returned to its owners, the spike in numbers had shown that land for common use could be mobilized quickly, could be put to productive use by working people, and was an appropriate response to national crises.

In the early 1920s the number of allotments shrank, before troubled economic times led to a new revival. In 1925 local authorities were banned from selling or converting allotment land without ministerial consent. In 1926, the Quakers launched a scheme called 'Allotment Gardens for the Unemployed' in south Wales, treating them as a source of food and of work. The success of the scheme led to a renewed burgeoning of allotments all over Britain, supported by a government keen to deflect social unrest. (Not for nothing did Lenin sniff that allotments reduce the proletariat's revolutionary fervour after being taken to one in Sweden en route to lead the Bolshevik Revolution in 1917.) They boomed again during the Second World War, before shrinking after the war due to a diminishing supply of land.

Today, the social institution of allotments is under attack

more than ever. Councils all over Britain are considering selling allotment land for commercial development, using well-worn rationalizations about growth and job-creation. And government, looking kindly on property developers who offer donations to party coffers and possible future board memberships to ministers facilitating access, has eyed allotment areas that could be made 'productive' and bring jobs. Take the Farm Terrace allotment area near Watford, west of London, set up in 1896 on a piece of land known for its fertile soil: in 2013 it consisted of sixty working sites overlooked by Watford General Hospital.[58] That year, Watford Borough Council, in partnership with a property development company, drew up plans to sell the allotment site to the developer for a 'health campus' and a 'business incubator and retail units', including a hotel, restaurant and cafés. In very quick time, this was approved by the government's 'Communities' Minister, a prominent advocate of privatization. The allotment holders were offered alternative plots two miles away on less fertile soil. But a time-honoured economic right was being trampled on. One allotment holder who had worked on her plot for five years put it well:

> Emotionally, it's been very hard. The thing is, how could you recreate somewhere like this? And I'm worried about the detrimental effect that getting rid of these plots will have on people's health. For a lot of us, this is physical work. But there is also the emotional release you get.

Similar encroachments have occurred across the country. The National Allotment Society reported in early 2013 that it was receiving news of fresh threats to allotments every day, while a survey had found that three-quarters of allotment holders were most worried about the sale of their plots. When allotments are sold by government for 'development', private riches are increased at the cost of lower living standards and quality of life for many commoners, a decline that is not recorded or recognized. Selling allotments may increase measured 'economic growth', but it does so to the detriment of 'public wealth'.

Though allotments that lack legal protection are threatened by developers, there are some encouraging signs: councils in Liverpool and Chorley have created new allotments, as have housing developers in Budleigh Salterton, Devon. The National Allotment Society has helped to create sixty new sites in south-west England, leased by collectives of local people. This do-it-yourself approach has been adopted in Ashburton, Devon, where a group of residents created their own hilltop allotment.

Elsewhere, in 2001, OrganicLea, a group of local food enthusiasts, acquired the right to farm on derelict allotment land in east London, at Chingford in the Lea Valley. Working with a supportive local council, they have expanded to a 12-acre site that now functions as a community market garden and have turned themselves into a workers' cooperative, employing fifteen members. By 2017, OrganicLea was producing eight tonnes of fruit and vegetables a year, feeding 330 households through a 'veg box' scheme, as well as selling to market stalls across London.

\*

As the OrganicLea initiative suggests, allotments and local cooperative farming have a close relationship to one of the most loved aspects of the social commons, the local food market. They have been a feature of every viable community throughout history. But today they are locked in a struggle for survival with supermarkets and online delivery systems. It is not just sentiment that leads many of us to hope they survive. They are an expression of community and social memory that allows the small-scale producer to show humble craftsmanship. They should be preserved and revived.

In addition, we should respect the principles of the People's Food Policy, launched in June 2017 by the Food Sovereignty Movement, a coalition of over 100 food, farming and human rights organizations. These aim to ensure food security for all, while protecting the environment and farm livelihoods, for current and future generations.[59] The six principles are: food production geared to feeding people, not to selling commodities in the global market; decent rewards and respect for food producers; local food provision wherever possible; democratic control over the food system; building knowledge and skills that can be passed on to future generations; and working with nature to protect natural resources and reduce environmental impact.

The following articles for a Charter of the Commons cover identified priorities for a revival of the social commons:

> Article 20: The right to a home must be restored. The 'right to buy' and the compulsory sale of social housing must be scrapped, and more social housing built.
> Local authorities should have the power to requisition unoccupied housing. The 'bedroom tax' should be abolished.

Article 21: Local communities must have more say in the planning and design of local housing, including community ownership.

Article 22: Student accommodation must be affordable for all and comply with normal rules for social housing, including safety, liveable space and access for those with disabilities.

Article 23: We must combat the homelessness epidemic. Conventional hostels and shelters should be replaced by 'housing commons', places where people are assured of shelter and food and can recover a sense of basic security.

Article 24: Cuts in spending on public services and amenities must be reversed. Privatized and outsourced services should be brought back into common ownership or strictly regulated in the interests of users, the commoners.

Article 25: People with physical or mental disabilities should have equal access to public spaces and facilities, including POPS, and equal rights of use. All public spaces and facilities must be made accessible for those with disabilities.

Article 26: The number of allotments should be preserved and expanded. Sites must be protected from privatization or conversion to other uses.

Article 27: Local markets selling fresh and local produce should be encouraged and protected.

Article 28: Policies must ensure food security for all, as part of the right to subsistence. Hunger has no place in an affluent society.

Article 29: The commons traditions of the guilds must be regenerated by reviving occupational communities and encouraging accreditation-based practices in place of licensing.

## Concluding reflections

The plunder of the social commons has hit the precariat much harder than the better-off, worsening their quality of life and raising their cost of living. We cannot sensibly measure changing inequality without taking this into account. At every point, it is lower-income groups that have been made worse off by cuts in public services and by their commercialization and privatization – whether affordable social housing, student accommodation, health and care services, fire services, playgrounds or labour market services. It is the precariat in the professions and crafts that lose most when occupational communities are weakened, partly because internal channels of upward mobility are broken. It is low-income groups who suffer most when social care is made harder to obtain and of lower quality. All of these developments increase social income inequality.

The National Audit Office reported in 2018 that government funding for local authorities in England had been slashed by half between 2010–11 and 2016–17.[60] To meet rising demand for social care, which is a statutory responsibility, local authorities had cut spending on other services by a third. Despite this, the NAO predicted that on current rates of spending on social care, up to fifteen English councils (10 per cent) would have exhausted their reserves by 2020 and would be technically bankrupt. In early 2018 Northamptonshire County Council became the first council in two decades to go bust. The government was obliged to send commissioners to run the council until the local elections, scheduled for 2020, and the council was forced to make cuts of over £70 million in spending on basic social services. Other councils were teetering on the edge. 'Even if councils stopped filling in potholes, maintaining parks, closed all children's centres, libraries, museums, leisure centres and turned off every street light, that will not have saved enough money to plug the financial black hole they face by 2020,' the chair of the Local Government Association warned in 2015.[61] And the most deprived fifth of English local authorities, especially towns and cities in northern England, have been hit hardest.[62]

Bit by bit, the 'banality of evil' that has underpinned the austerity agenda has done increasing harm and many more vulnerable people have been rendered ill, impoverished or suicidal. None of this was intended by the politicians or their civil servants, but the economic course chosen by the government was bound to have those effects. Between 2010 and 2018, in response to budget cuts, the Merseyside Fire and Rescue Service closed five fire stations, while cutting the number of firefighters from about 1,000 to 620. Analysing the eighty-three deaths in accidental house fires in the Merseyside area from 2007 to 2017, the service found that a majority of the victims were living alone and in need of care, which had also been cut; many had been reduced by poverty to using candles, an obvious fire risk.[63] The connection between benefit cuts, lack of care, poverty, candle use, fires, inadequate fire services and the rising number of deaths due to house fires was undeniable. Austerity is an unequal health hazard.

Privatizing the social commons has been a form of historical vandalism. Successive governments – the Conservatives and Liberal Democrats from 2010 to 2015, the Conservatives from 2015 onwards – knowingly embarked on a macroeconomic strategy that would inevitably destroy the social commons. It was a deliberate choice made from an array of choices and cannot be excused by claims that 'there was no alternative'. It was a politically expedient action for which all who supported it must bear responsibility.

Among the consequences is a thinning of Britain's historical legacy. Take the great city of Sheffield. Faced with a massive budget deficit due to funding cuts from central government, and the prospect of much more of the same to come, in 2017 the city council was obliged to sell its Grade II-listed central library to a Chinese consortium with permission to convert it into a posh five-star hotel. In the end, the sale fell through, but only because questions emerged about the buyer's credibility.

Meanwhile in London, the local council was allowing part of Ealing's Grade II-listed town hall to be redeveloped as a hotel, and the London Borough of Haringey was selling the former Hornsey town hall to the Far Eastern Consortium International so that they could convert it into a hotel and apartment complex. It was as if government was intent on destroying the social memory.

A report issued in June 2018 estimated that over 4,000 public buildings and spaces were being sold off by local authorities in England each year, mainly to private property developers.[64] This trend was accelerated by a 2016 government decision to allow local authorities to use proceeds from the sale of public buildings as current revenue, an implicit denial of the essence of the commons which is to preserve the capital value of the commons for the benefit of future generations as well. Since the Treasury was depriving local authorities of revenue in the first place, the decision by the Chancellor of the Exchequer was nothing less than the destruction of the social commons. The enforced sales in effect were paying for tax cuts for the well-off and companies.

In a remarkable demonstration of chutzpah, a government paper in August 2018 announced measures to encourage and help charities and voluntary organizations to play a bigger role in the provision of public services. A foreword to the report signed by the Culture Secretary and the Civil Society Minister noted that 'new providers are taking responsibility' for local services, adding, 'All this is happening because of the resourcefulness of the British people'. By comparison with the budget cuts it had imposed, the government was promising to spend a tiny sum on inducing non-profit groups to fill the void created over the previous eight years by its cuts. It was an innovative way of saying the cull in public social services would continue.

CHAPTER 5

# The Civil Commons

> For a trivial offence, a free man shall be fined only in
> proportion to the degree of his offence, and for a serious
> offence correspondingly, but not so heavily as to deprive
> him of his livelihood . . . None of these fines shall be
> imposed except by the assessment on oath of reputable
> men of the neighbourhood.
> — Magna Carta, Clause 20

The right to justice is a precious form of commons: it is universal and based on due process and equality before the law. The activity of commoning is also embedded in the practice of common law, with its respect for precedent, which builds on what many generations have come to regard as just behaviour.

The civil commons were enshrined in the Magna Carta. Clause 20 above established the principle of proportionality in the punishment for a crime, with the vital caveat that, whatever the punishment, it should not deprive the person of their livelihood, their source of subsistence. Clause 38 required witnesses, Clause 39 stated that an accused person should be judged by his equals, and Clause 40 upheld the right to justice for all:

38. In future no official shall place a man on trial upon his own unsupported statement, without producing credible witnesses to the truth of it.

39. No free man shall be seized or imprisoned, or stripped of his rights or possessions, or outlawed or exiled, or deprived of his standing in any other way, nor will we proceed with force against him, or send others to do so, except by the lawful judgement of his equals or by the law of the land.

40. To no one will we sell, to no one deny or delay right or justice.

Every modern government has paid lip service to these commitments. The Charter of the Forest added a crucial dimension in stressing the importance of *local* common law, administered by verderers and other such, which later evolved into local magistrates' courts. Local people could understand local contexts and traditions set in the commons.

E. P. Thompson, in his justly famous 1968 book *The Making of the English Working Class*, saw the rule of law as being part of the commons. Common law, and common rights and accepted behaviour derived from custom, limited exploitation and oppression. Access to a civil commons was the ultimate 'poor's overcoat'.

In the seventeenth and eighteenth centuries many of these common laws came to be perceived by the rich and the bourgeoisie as impediments to commercial expansion, since they enabled many commoners – the emerging proletariat – to survive independently rather than labouring for them. If commoners retained access to the natural commons, they were deemed to be 'idling'. So ruling elites sought to shrink the commons and whittle away common rights, to induce the poor to labour, under fear of punishment.[1]

This was to be echoed in the mid-twentieth century, when governments wedded to the gospel of 'full employment' strove to have as many commoners as possible in jobs, paving the way for coercive policies such as 'workfare' that involved more sacrifice of the civil commons. But erosion of the civil commons and common rights has greatly intensified in the austerity era.

## Tottenham rough justice vs. white-collar leniency

There are moments in history that expose the fragility of the civil commons and its values of customary justice, due process, proportionality and universalism. The Peterloo Massacre in Manchester in 1819, the Tolpuddle Martyrs of 1834, the suppression of the Chartists in the 1830s, and the vicious class-based actions taken against the General Strike in 1926 all show governments deliberately ignoring the basic precepts of universal justice. To these can be added the Tottenham riots.

One warm summer's evening, in August 2011, police shot dead an unarmed black man during an attempted arrest. Spontaneous riots and acts of arson followed, initially in Tottenham, north London, and subsequently elsewhere across England. Watching fires light up the night sky, politicians and TV viewers were shocked and perplexed.

In the immediate aftermath, the middle classes joined with the elite in alarmed retribution. A total of 1,800 years of prison sentences were handed out to 1,292 people by fast-track courts set up in record time. If justice delayed is justice denied, then so too is justice rushed. One youth, with no previous criminal record, was jailed for fourteen months for taking an ice cream. Another, also without form, was jailed for four months for taking fizzy water worth £3.50 from a broken shop window that he had not broken. So much for the principle of proportionality.

While the teenagers were kicking their heels in prison, the Independent Police Complaints Commission's investigation into Mark Duggan's killing, which sparked the riots, stretched on for over three years, before predictably clearing the police officer who fired the fatal shot. Indecent haste and summary justice for some; indecent delay for others. These double standards offend the ethos of the civil commons. While lower-income groups are increasingly at risk of being criminalized and impoverished by the loss of common rights, harmful behaviour by corporations and privileged individuals often goes virtually unpunished.

Sir Philip Green, former owner of BHS, lined his own pocket with hundreds of millions of pounds from the firm's pension fund. When the company collapsed in 2016, a year after he sold it to a known bankrupt for £1, employees found themselves not only jobless but facing penury in old age. He was not prosecuted, after grudgingly agreeing to pay back most of the money. He was not barred from serving as a company director and did not even lose his knighthood.

The leniency shown to Green was typical of that shown to other white-collar acts of immorality. Nobody was prosecuted after Thames Water poured millions of tons of untreated sewage into the Thames, endangering people and nature. Surely that was a crime and somebody must have been responsible. It was hardly comparable to stealing a bottle of water.

Some defend the leniency meted out to corporate crime on the grounds that it is usually the result of collective action rather than individual wrongdoing.[2] This is to absolve senior executives from the responsibilities for which they are richly paid. It is not enough to fine the corporation. The individuals who shared the decision should be punished in proportion to the magnitude of the offence – the principle set out in the Magna Carta.

## The arms of the law

Many more actions today are deemed to be criminal than they were thirty years ago. This is an international trend but has been especially marked in Britain since the 1990s. The Criminal Justice and Public Order Act 1994, introduced by John Major's Conservative government, circumscribed a number of existing commoners' rights and increased penalties for certain 'anti-social behaviours'. It made some offences of trespass, squatting and unauthorized camping into crimes and banned 'aggravated trespass' intended to disrupt 'lawful activity'. These changes have had a chilling effect on many forms of protest, including action to defend the commons against fracking or tree-felling. Another section of the Act removed the obligation on local authorities to provide sites for gypsy and traveller use.

New Labour continued the criminalization trend, adding one new crime to the statute books for every day it was in office. These included such heinous offences as selling a game bird killed on a Sunday. Under ASBOs (Anti-Social Behaviour Orders), introduced by the 1998 Crime and Disorder Act, children as young as ten could be banned from playing noisy games or congregating in groups. Someone failing to comply with an ASBO could end up in prison. In this 'zero tolerance' approach, all acts deemed to have a harmful effect are regarded as individual choices and therefore culpable. Youngsters are punished for hanging around the streets when they have nowhere else to go. More than 600 youth centres and clubs where young people could meet, and mix socially with those from different backgrounds, have closed since 2010.[3]

The Coalition government further ratcheted up the criminalization of disliked behaviour with the Anti-Social Behaviour, Criminal and Policing Act in 2014. This replaced ASBOs with Criminal Behaviour Orders (nicknamed 'Crimbos'), directed at 'serious and persistent' anti-social behaviour, and Community Protection Notices aimed at minor, even petty offences that annoy the neighbours, such as littering, rubbish in gardens and noisy parties. There is no due process; objection by a neighbour is enough for a notice to be issued. And as with ASBOs, disobeying a notice is a crime.

In practice, these measures have been largely directed at poor people living in crowded communities and have been less about reducing crime than about branding people as social pariahs, echoing the historical branding of commoners as idlers and subversives to justify enclosure of common land. What were once misdemeanours can now give someone a criminal record, blighting their life chances for good.

Each step taken by governments – involving all three main political parties – has chipped away at personal freedom and common justice to give precedence to public order. Youths on the street, eccentrics, racial minorities and the homeless are not just seen as undesirable but presumed to be actual or potential criminals. By contrast, these same governments were making it easier for rich foreign oligarchs with very dubious records to enter the country and even join a fast track to citizenship.

In 2018, the Home Office said it was trialling a scheme permitted by the 2014 Act whereby the family of a gang member could be evicted from their council home.[4] This is contrary to common law that states that only the guilty should be punished; it is a form of collective punishment. It is also regressive and discriminatory. It applies only to those living in rented public housing and to families of alleged gang members. Young men from black and other ethnic minority communities are much more likely than whites in similar circumstances to be classified as gang members.[5]

Austerity has put access to justice increasingly out of reach of commoners. Between 2010 and 2018, spending by the Ministry of Justice was cut in real (inflation-adjusted) terms by 40 per cent. Costs for defendants and delays in the criminal justice system have risen remorselessly. In this respect, among many others, Britain has been following trends in the USA, where 95 per cent of defendants enter a plea bargain or plead guilty to a lesser offence rather than risk the expense of going to trial. In the UK, before legislation in 2012, defendants who went to trial and were acquitted had their legal costs reimbursed. Now they can reclaim only a fraction of those costs, which can run into tens of thousands of pounds. Meanwhile, legal aid has been made much harder to obtain, not only through tighter conditions for entitlement but also through cuts in fees paid to solicitors and barristers that has led to a shortage of criminal lawyers willing to take legal aid cases.

Access to legal aid is a civil right. It is meant to ensure that all have the means to defend themselves and have legally qualified representatives to do so. Making the justice system more expensive and harder to access denies commoners their right to an adequate defence against wrongful accusations.

In another attack on justice for all, in 2015 the government introduced mandatory criminal court charges to help finance the court system in England and Wales. People found guilty after a hearing or trial had to pay up to £1,200, whereas if they pleaded guilty the charge was only about £150. Condemning the charges, the parliamentary Justice Select Committee said they provided perverse incentives to plead guilty and were grossly disproportionate for minor offences. More than 100 magistrates resigned in protest and the Lord Chief Justice himself argued, 'The scale of court fees, together with the cost of legal assistance, is putting access to justice out of reach of most, imperilling a core principle of Magna Carta.'[6]

Magistrates were not allowed to use discretion in applying the charge or to vary it according to ability to pay. To compound the inequity, those who could not pay were sent to prison. After just a few months, the government was forced to drop the scheme. But the direction of policy remains the same: a reduction in access to justice and to the civil commons for those most in need, in order to lower the fiscal costs of the judicial system.

The assault on basic principles of justice is not unique to Britain. In the USA, many jurisdictions rely on court fees to help finance the criminal justice system and people who cannot afford to pay can face prison. The prevalent practice of 'money bail' – granting pre-trial bail only on payment – means half a million people are in jail on any one day because they cannot afford bail. As a consequence, they may lose their job, their home and fall into deeper destitution. Some plead guilty, even though they are innocent, just to avoid incarceration.[7]

In Canada, in 2013, the Conservative government made mandatory a so-called 'victim surcharge' that requires a convicted person to pay a certain amount in addition to their sentence.[8] The surcharge is 30 per cent of any fine, or Canadian $100 for each summary conviction and Canadian $200 for each indictable offence. Homeless or marginalized people who commit petty crimes in their struggle to survive have ended up owing more than their total anticipated annual income. In some provinces the amount owing can be deducted from already meagre welfare payments. In others the debt is discharged if the person signs up for a 'compensatory work programme' – effectively an additional punishment.

The civil justice system in Britain has fared no better than the system for criminal justice. Legal aid has been scrapped altogether for many areas of civil, family and migration law, deterring people from seeking redress when their rights are breached and forcing those obliged to go to court to represent themselves or go without anyone to speak for them.[9]

Courts are overloaded. And as well as making access to legal services more difficult financially, budget cuts have made physical access more difficult. Between 2010 and 2018, more than 250 courts, including half of all the magistrates' courts in England and Wales, were shut and most sold off to raise money. 'Anyone who thinks we currently have a network of courts which enables proper access to justice is deluding themselves,' the outgoing President of the Family Division said in July 2018, suggesting that people should be asked if they want to 'Skype the judge' instead![10]

A commercial market in judicial services has emerged in the UK, weakening any notion of universal justice, with companies answerable to their shareholders rather than to the public, the commoners. This ongoing privatization of legal services reduces public accountability. Services delivered by public bodies are subject to 'freedom-of-information' scrutiny. Politicians, the media and the public can request information on performance and outcomes. But private entities are under no such obligation and can cite 'commercial confidentiality' in refusing to disclose information relating to their contracts and performance.

Since 2015 the erosion of public accountability has been compounded by the privatization of local council auditing and by the abolition of the independent Audit Commission as part of the austerity drive. Private auditors have a mixed record in protecting the commercial interests of their private clients. They have no statutory obligation to serve the civil commons, or any incentive to do so. Meanwhile, the Audit Commission was replaced by a cheaper National Audit Office. The Commission had been responsible for scrutinizing contracts made between public bodies and privatized contractors to make sure they did not harm the public interest. Its abolition confirmed the ideological bias in favour of commercial firms, allowing wealthy owners and managers to escape public surveillance at a time when the government was tightening scrutiny of poorer citizens to ensure they did not gain undue meagre benefits.

A glaring example of the failings of privatization and the lack of public oversight came in early 2018 with the bankruptcy of Carillion. Its private auditors allowed the firm to declare profits, later shown to be non-existent, to justify continued dividends for its shareholders and bonuses for its top executives. The firm's well-paid private auditors were culpable, but the absence of a properly funded national auditor operating in the public interest, which could have revealed the management's 'recklessness, hubris and greed' early on, had allowed that to happen.[11]

As with other commons, judicial services need a gatekeeper to safeguard the common interest, coming between the government (acting as the steward) and commercial interests. The government's immediate saving from abolishing the Audit Commission was far outweighed by the costs of the Carillion collapse. Those costs included the payment of state benefits to the thousands of people who had lost their jobs, a record Pension Protection Fund liability, and the need to maintain the public services that Carillion had been contracted to provide. Carillion is unlikely to be the last failure of its kind.[12]

Even prosecution services are being privatized as a consequence of austerity. Between 2010 and 2018, the Crown

Prosecution Service lost a quarter of its budget and a third of its staff. Declining funds for public judicial procedures have prompted lawyers to move into private firms and commercial interests to undertake formerly public functions. The number of private prosecutions has been rising in cases that would previously have been taken (or refused) by the public prosecution service.

At least one private firm, Edmonds Marshall McMahon, now employs prosecution lawyers who used to work in the public sector to undertake private prosecutions. Instead of bringing justice to commoners, lawyers in private practice will tend to prosecute on behalf of rich clients and companies who will pay them the most. Some altruistic lawyers may take on pro bono cases or commit to doing a few cases for worthy causes. But the logic of the market will prevail. One reported motive for establishing Edmonds Marshall McMahon was the substantial reduction in the number and strength of specialist crime teams dealing with fraud. These handle white-collar crime, involving corporations, executives, financiers and their kind. As journalist Nick Cohen noted, 'Fraud has become a virtually risk-free crime.'[13] He should have added, 'unless it is petty and committed by someone on welfare'. While the government was cutting funds and staff for investigating white-collar crime, it was increasing resources to monitor and sanction the precariat and the socially marginalized. 'We are well on the way to a society that will be able to boast it offers the best justice that money can buy,' Cohen rightly concluded.

Criminal forensic research, too, has been privatized. The Coalition government abolished the public Forensic Science

Service in 2012. Police forces promptly contracted out forensic investigations to a bevy of private firms, which then cut costs to increase profits. The private firms, predictably, failed to meet required quality standards which, according to the Forensic Science Regulator, may have led to miscarriages of justice, including the conviction of innocent people and the guilty walking free.[14] The government did not even give the regulator statutory powers to bar sub-standard firms. Commercial interests had to come first. The public gatekeeper was left in the wilderness.

In response to the regulator's criticisms of shoddy research by private forensic laboratories, a Home Office spokesperson said: 'It is for chief constables and police and crime commissioners to decide how best to deploy resources to effectively manage crime and local priorities, including forensic services. However, we are clear that cost savings must not come at the expense of a reduction in quality standards.' This disingenuous comment was made six years after the public forensic service had been abolished, during which time nothing had been done to convert that 'must' into a meaningful safeguard. Instead, the government slashed funds for police forces countrywide, obliging them to cut costs where they could. A mixture of privatization and official neglect has eroded yet another part of the commons, jeopardizing the right to justice.

The independence of the judiciary from government has also been compromised. In 2018, without any due process, the Justice Secretary forced the chair of the Parole Board to resign over the board's decision to release a serial sex offender. It was a clear breach of the principle of judicial independence enshrined in the Act of Settlement of 1701, intended to ensure the impartiality of judges and prevent politicians from subverting the law. As David Neuberger, past president of the Supreme Court, has written, one of the most important functions of the judiciary is to protect citizens – commoners – from unreasonable or unlawful decisions of the executive.[15]

The government, once more citing austerity savings, has allowed the cost of legal training to rise sharply, which indirectly erodes the civil commons. Morale has collapsed among young barristers, who are struggling with high debt run up in training and reduced fees for legal aid cases. More than a third of criminal barristers were actively considering leaving the profession as of 2018, and there was a growing shortage of defence solicitors.[16] Justice has increasingly become a preserve of the rich, mocking the Magna Carta precept that justice must neither be sold nor denied.

## Privatized policing

Not even the police force has been safe from austerity. In 2014 New Scotland Yard, the famous old headquarters of the London Metropolitan Police, was sold to an Abu Dhabi investment fund to build luxury apartments. More seriously, over 600 police stations have been closed and in a growing number of towns and cities – Bath and Peterborough are just two examples – there are no police stations at all. This obviously handicaps the ability of the police to respond quickly to emergencies, makes it difficult for people to report crime, and severs the local ties between police and the communities they serve that are vital in preventing crime.

The number of local bobbies on the beat in England and Wales has been cut by more than a third since 2010 and some forces have lost more than two-thirds of their neighbourhood officers. The government claims that the reduction in police numbers has had nothing to do with the recorded increase in homicides, violent crime and robberies, and the recorded drop in charges and arrests. Ministers must think there is no need for a police force at all.

Since 2010 police pay has fallen by nearly a fifth in real terms, many police officers are struggling to make ends meet and a rising number have taken on a second job, including taxi driving, plumbing, photography and gardening.[17] And besides the cuts to public police forces, policing itself is being privatized. A scheme called Met Patrol Plus enables London boroughs to buy extra police services by paying officers' salaries. Initially the scheme operated to protect business property in 'business improvement districts', where local businesses pay a special levy to local councils for additional services or improvements. However, by late 2016 it was being used in twenty-four of London's thirty-two boroughs for a variety of policing tasks. For each officer the boroughs pay for, they get another free!

Our policing system is being divided into two tiers: richer boroughs, or their private development partners, can buy better policing, displacing crime to poorer and less well-policed neighbourhoods. In theory, private residents and community groups can also buy extra policing of their residential areas in the same way, dubbed 'rent-a-cop'. If richer people and areas can purchase more or better policing, they will have less incentive to join with others in pressing the state to provide better policing for all. The commonality of the civil commons, in which we all have or should have equal rights to security and justice, is weakened.

Legal powers granted in 2002 to private security guards and 'neighbourhood wardens' have also legitimized private law enforcement. They can stop cyclists on footpaths, make under-eighteens surrender alcohol, ask any person they regard as an 'offender' to give their name and address, and issue a 'fixed penalty notice' (a fine by ticket) for spraying graffiti or being disorderly.[18] Law enforcement is being outsourced with no guarantees of due process against arbitrary or malicious decisions. And again, companies and richer areas can buy private security that poorer areas cannot. Privatized policing is another form of inequality.

## Probationary services

In 2014, another essential judicial service was partially privatized when 70 per cent of probation work in England and Wales was outsourced to twenty-one 'Community Rehabilitation Companies' (CRCs). The public National Probation Service was left to handle only 'high-risk' cases such as those convicted of violence or sexual assault.

As with other commons, privatization has attracted foreign capital. One CRC is Working Links, a global corporation now owned by a Germany-based investment company that also provides a wide range of 'welfare-to-work' services for the British government. When it took on the probation contract, it had already faced criticism for its handling of contracts under the government's Work Programme, including allegations that staff were falsifying claims to have placed unemployed people in jobs.[19] Then in 2017 the company was slated by the probation inspectorate for cutting staff by 40 per cent, resulting in unacceptable workloads for the remainder. Lack of time for proper supervision and counselling denied ex-offenders a decent chance of rehabilitation and increased the risk of reoffending.

Staff were sometimes obliged to interview ex-offenders in public libraries, in public, surrounded by people wanting to read books or browse in silence.[20] The company was using the commons in its pursuit of profits. And for ex-offenders, discussing personal details in public is embarrassing and stigmatizing. Their needs were being ignored, another source of inequality since most will have come from lower-income families and communities.

In February 2018 the HM Inspectorate of Probation issued a damning assessment of privatized probationary services overall, concluding that the twenty-one CRCs were 'stretched beyond their capacity' and were failing to fulfil their contractual agreement to meet and supervise ex-offenders.[21] Some probation staff were handling more than 200 cases each, against a recommended maximum of sixty. An earlier report said privatization was putting the public at risk because the CRCs were failing to properly assess the risk of harm; they were supervising thousands of ex-offenders with phone calls every six weeks instead of more frequent face-to-face meetings required by the courts as a condition of probation.[22] Re-offending, including crimes of violence, has increased since 2014, as have returns to prison for breach of probation terms.

The probation inspectorate said the performance of

CRCs was worse than the National Probation Service on every measure it looked at. Yet the Ministry of Justice initially reacted by saying that even though the privatized system needed improvement, it would be continued. In July 2018 the government said it would cancel the existing CRC contracts in 2020, two years earlier than agreed, and put new contracts out to tender. Less than a year later, it announced that probation services would be returned to the public sector from 2021.

Meanwhile, it has bailed out the private companies to the tune of over £500 million, topping up contracts that were awarded at too low a price and waiving penalties owed by the CRCs for failing to meet their contractual targets. This is yet another example of double standards and unequal treatment. If low-income benefit claimants fail to comply with a contract imposed by a Jobcentre, they are sanctioned and lose benefit. If a for-profit CRC fails to deliver on a contract it voluntarily entered into, it is given more money and penalties are forgiven.

Privatized supervision of community service orders has also been a failure. First tried in Germany in the 1950s, community service orders were introduced on a pilot basis in Britain in 1973, and eventually nationally, as an alternative to custodial sentences. Community service was conceived as a mild and proportionate punishment that encouraged rehabilitation. In the quarter of a century after its introduction, community service orders were adopted in much of Europe, and in Australasia, the USA and parts of Asia.

Studies show that, by comparison with prison sentences, they reduced the probability of re-offending. However, in 2003 the government stipulated that every community service order had to contain a mandatory punitive element, rebranding community service as 'community payback', in effect, community punishment and a way to extract unpaid labour. Tasks include street clean-ups, rubbish removal, gardening, repair projects and removing graffiti. These orders are designed to be stigmatizing. 'Today's offenders,' said one saddened pioneer of community service, 'wear fluorescent tabards over their clothes to indicate they are offenders, easily recognizable by members of the public'.[23] Offenders given community service orders are now allocated tasks and supervised by private for-profit CRCs. In 2016, HM Inspectorate of Probation said the unpaid labour was just another punishment, ignoring the rehabilitation potential. 'Much of [the delivery of unpaid work] was simply not good enough, lacking in focus on the basic requirement to deliver and enforce the sentence of the court,' it said.[24]

One CRC heavily involved in community payback is Serco, a British multinational specializing in government services. Its first contract was to handle the London community payback scheme in 2012, a trial run for the later privatization decision. The contract was terminated early after allegations that participants were not properly supervised. Yet Serco was given a new contract and in 2018 was still operating the London scheme.

In 2013, it was revealed that Serco and rival G4S, another private security company, had been overcharging the government for electronic tagging of offenders for almost a decade, claiming payment for tagging offenders who were dead or still in prison. They were subsequently stripped of the contracts and agreed to pay back a total of £180 million.

Although the Serious Fraud Squad opened an investigation, by early 2019 it had still not been concluded. Meanwhile, G4S was given another electronic tagging contract and both it and Serco have been allowed to bid for and receive lucrative contracts for other justice services including prisons, where they have demonstrated the same mixture of incompetence and worse.

## Private prisons

Prisons are another area of the civil commons where justice services have been outsourced to private profit-making companies. Privatization, which began in 1992, has accompanied rising prison numbers – the number of actions deemed imprisonable has grown and more offenders are being sent to prison and for longer.

Private prison services in Britain are dominated by three multinational firms: Britain's G4S and Serco, and France's Sodexo. Initially, the government claimed that more prisons were needed because of overcrowding due to tougher sentencing; handing responsibility for building and operating prisons to private firms would be more cost-effective, improve conditions and reduce the call on the public purse. By 2018, 15 per cent of Britain's 86,000 prisoners were in private commercial prisons and the operating companies were receiving £4 billion a year from the government, that is, from the public as taxpayers.[25] Many of their prisons had been built under PFI contracts.

However, plans by the Ministry of Justice to extend privatization to cover at least 25 per cent of all prisoners have faltered. Conditions in private prisons have worsened, due to cost-cutting and staff shortages that have also affected public prisons, and any cost advantage has been eroded. Riots have broken out in private prisons, due to overcrowding, degrading conditions and a lack of experienced prison officers. Two contracted prisons have been returned to the public sector, and in 2018 the Ministry of Justice was forced to take temporary control of the Birmingham prison from G4S after an inspection found prisoners were using drink, drugs and violence with impunity and filthy communal areas were littered with cockroaches, blood and vomit.[26]

There have also been repeated criticisms of conditions at immigration removal centres run by private companies, which operate seven of the nine centres in the UK. Mitie, which runs the largest immigration detention centre in Europe at Harmondsworth close to Heathrow airport, was blasted by the prison inspectorate in 2016 for 'dirty', 'rundown' and 'insanitary' facilities.[27] In 2013 Serco was accused of covering up numerous cases of sexual abuse at the Yarl's Wood Immigration Removal Centre for women that it runs in Bedford,[28] and a report on the centre by the National Audit Office in 2016 slated the company for staff cuts and inadequate training.[29]

In 2017, an undercover BBC *Panorama* film showed employees of G4S assaulting detainees at Brook House immigration removal centre near Gatwick airport, forcing the resignation of its manager, but there was no penalty for the firm itself. Shortly after G4S's abusive behaviour had been shown on television, the government gave the firm a new contract to continue running the detention centre, even though the Home Office itself found there had been collusion to conceal the abuses.[30]

Meanwhile, Serco, G4S and GEO, an American company, have all been using detainees as cheap labour to cook and clean, enabling them to cut payroll bills and boost profits.[31] To cut costs at Yarl's Wood as required by its contract, Serco has replaced employees with 'self-service kiosks' for inmates to order food, send their own faxes and book their own visitors, which has led to a shortage of needed operational staff.[32] Reducing the quality of service is an inevitable response to cut-price contracts, particularly since immigration and asylum services serve the most vulnerable and least popular of 'customers', and those least likely to be noticed.[33]

G4S, infamous for failing to honour its contract to provide security guards during the London Olympics, was forced to sell its children's services arm after another undercover film by BBC *Panorama* in 2015 prompted a police investigation into assault and abuse by staff in its Medway secure youth training centre in Kent. G4S had already lost its contract to run Rainsbrook Secure Training Centre near Rugby after a government inspection disclosed that children had been subject to degrading treatment and racist comments.[34]

Privatizing prisons and detention centres provides perverse incentives for companies to support more and longer imprisonment, and to cut costs and worsen overcrowding and conditions to the greatest extent possible. Given their track record, why should they be presumed to act as a social service? Most of those in the prison system, probably including most of the staff, come from lower-income groups. Those gaining from privatization have been relatively affluent shareholders.

## Punishing the vulnerable

The most pervasive erosion of our civil commons has been in social protection policy. The network of social policies supposedly intended to ensure the 'right to subsistence' for all has drifted steadily towards denying commoners any such right.

In the neo-liberal era that began in the 1980s, the UK, along with other countries, went down the road of converting social protection policy to a mainly means-tested system. This had the superficially appealing rationale that public social spending should be limited to assisting those most in need, the key words used being 'targeting' and 'the poor'. Means-testing erodes the civil commons by dividing people into categories given different treatment. The 'deserving poor' are contrasted with the 'undeserving poor', perceived to be poor because of some character defect, such as 'laziness', 'skiving' or 'dependency'. And these two 'poor' groups are differentiated from the 'non-poor'. The impression is then easily given that 'we', the non-poor, are having to pay for 'them', many of whom are probably undeserving, which is convenient because then we can say we should not be paying tax for 'them'. This utilitarian perspective stands in contrast with a commons, which is about sharing and universalism in the widest sense of partnership, commonality and equal basic rights.

Means-testing also tends to split the various risks of living into their components – the risk of illness, the risk of an accident, the risk of unemployment, the risk of disability and so on – so that a morass of means-tested schemes emerges, each with rules of entitlement for identifying the 'deserving'.

With such rules come penalties designed to exclude the 'undeserving'. And the authorities then try to cut the high cost of administering the rules by dispensing with lengthy determination procedures. The first casualty is due process.

The shift in Britain started symbolically with Thatcher's renaming of unemployment benefit as Jobseeker's Allowance. Instead of regarding unemployment as ill-luck due to economic policies and structural change, for which someone should be compensated, joblessness became a matter of personal responsibility for which the government was kindly giving temporary help if the unemployed person deserved it. Once that road is taken, a castle of arbitrary rules must be devised to determine entitlement.[35]

In 2015, the main means-tested schemes were Pension Credit, Housing Benefit, Employment and Support Allowance (ESA) for those with disabilities, Jobseeker's Allowance (JSA), Child Tax Credit, Income Support, and Working Tax Credit. However, in 2010, the government decided to convert the last six into a single integrated means-tested benefit called, misleadingly, Universal Credit. It is anything but universal, which means applying to everybody. The plan was to roll out the new benefit across the country, phasing out the old system by 2015, but the scheme has been dogged by delays, mishaps and errors in the computerized system that has already cost £1.3 billon to set up.

The average cost of administering a claim for Universal Credit in 2018 was a staggering £699, against a target of £173.[36] By late 2018 fewer than 1 million people were covered, out of the 8 million the government estimates will be drawing something from the scheme when fully operational. And, after prolonged denial, the government finally admitted that a large proportion of those drawing the old benefits would lose financially after transferring to Universal Credit.

The government was also doing nothing to correct for another failing of all means-tested schemes – low take-up. Every study in every country where means-testing operates has shown that only a proportion of those entitled to benefits actually receive them. This does not mean people who do not claim do not need the benefits. Many will be ashamed, fear stigmatization, or will not know how to apply or how to navigate the rules. Official estimates of non-take-up, which may be underestimates, show that about 40 per cent of households entitled to Pension Credit were not receiving it, 20 per cent of those entitled to Housing Benefit were not receiving it, 44 per cent of those entitled to JSA did not receive it (a share that was rising) and half a million families with a disabled member entitled to ESA were not receiving it. These figures are indicative of a system in bad shape.

The worst failings have related to benefits for the disabled (ESA) which are paid to people unable to work, and the non-means-tested Personal Independence Payment (PIP), intended to meet the extra costs of disability, that has replaced the Disability Living Allowance (DLA). To claim ESA, in addition to the means test, disabled people must undergo repeated 'work capability assessments' to check they are unable to take a job. If they are deemed to be capable of employment, they lose the ESA and must go on to JSA or Income Support. Similarly, those claiming PIP, which is paid at different levels depending on the degree of disability, face repeated assessments to check they are still entitled.

Responsibility for making these assessments – the purpose of which is to reduce the cost to the Exchequer of disability payments – has been handed over to private companies. The result has been denial of benefits, or reduced benefits, for many thousands of vulnerable people in need.

These privatized assessments lack respect for all principles of justice enshrined in the Magna Carta and the Charter of the Forest. Privatizing the procedures has given quasi-judicial powers to employees in private firms. They can decide whether to grant benefits, delay entitlement, deny entitlement altogether, or impose sanctions by withdrawing benefits. Disabled people are often not given their assessment report, so cannot correct errors ahead of decisions being made. There is no due process. But the company bosses, their shareholders and the DWP have shown they do not care. The privatized 'assessor' has an incentive to delay payment or to sanction the claimant, since that saves money for the real customer, the DWP, makes more profit for the firm, and makes it more likely that the firm will obtain new government contracts. For good measure, the government can escape direct responsibility for 'errors'.

A DWP audit found that one in every three PIP assessment reports completed by the private firm Capita between April and December 2016 contained errors or omitted relevant information, rendering decisions made on them suspect.[37] Reassessments in the year to October 2017 of those previously receiving Disability Living Allowance led to 47 per cent receiving less or nothing at all under the PIP that replaced it. Meanwhile, the firms dealing with the assessments, Capita and IAS (Atos), were paid 30 per cent more.[38]

Some of the more outrageous mistakes made in assessments for ESA and PIP by Capita and IAS, cited in evidence to the parliamentary Work and Pensions Select Committee, included: 'Apparently I walk my dog daily, which was baffling because I can barely walk and I do not have a dog'; 'She wrote I arose from the chair without any difficulty. I was in bed the whole time (she let herself in) and I only have the one chair in the room and she was sitting in it'; 'She said that I had no difficulty reading with my glasses yet I do not wear glasses to read.'[39]

Characteristic of the haughty attitude of the privatized assessment 'service' is the case of a forty-year-old woman suffering from bipolar disorder and severe anxiety, who received a letter from Capita informing her she was being sanctioned and had lost her benefits because she had not met her assessor at her home at the arranged time. Distraught, she eventually obtained help to write to a national newspaper, which investigated. It turned out that Capita had sent someone to her home at a different time from the time notified to her. The woman lost nearly £700 before the situation was rectified, leaving her unable to buy groceries and causing her acute anxiety. Capita paid no penalty.[40]

By 2018, the DWP and Ministry of Justice were spending over £200 million annually to deal with 'mandatory reconsiderations' and appeals against ESA and PIP decisions. It is a scathing indictment of the system that an astonishing two-thirds of PIP and ESA claimants had the decision changed at 'mandatory reconsideration' stage or won their appeals at the tribunal.[41] Yet no penalty was imposed on the firms making so many erroneous judgements. All the costs of any error in the original decision are borne by the commoner, none by the firm or its employees.

Cases take about six months to be heard by the ESA tribunal, during which time claimants may have no income. They cannot apply for Jobseeker's Allowance or make a fresh claim for ESA while contesting the original decision. So, even if they end up winning their appeal and receive back-paid benefits, they will have lost a lot of income and, in many cases, run up a lot of debt to meet basic needs. Often borrowed at high rates of interest, the debts then have to be paid off.

During PIP appeals too, disabled people must get by with no benefit or a reduced one while waiting for the outcome. And in both ESA and PIP appeals they must pay any direct costs because, in England and Wales, legal aid has been withdrawn. If they then win their case, they have no assurance the benefit will be backdated to the point when it was unfairly denied.

The hardship and stress endured by people fighting to overturn an unjust decision unsurprisingly has a devastating impact on their health. For many, it has become a revolving door of seemingly endless assessments, lost or denied benefits due to wrong assessments, appeals, reinstatement, and more routine assessments three or four months later. For some, it has been a death sentence.[42] One woman, forced by severe back pain to give up her retailing job, was consistently judged fit for work in assessments over five years, appealed successfully several times but went into severe debt during the months the appeals took. The fifty-seven-year-old eventually died of a massive heart attack her relatives claim was brought on by stress. She was found dead at the foot of her stairs, surrounded by letters informing her that the gas, electricity, water, telephone and television were all in danger of being cut off.

For the DWP, the cost of undertaking a 'reconsideration' of a denial of ESA or PIP is minimal – £38 as of 2018.[43] The savings from denying a claimant disability benefits can be a hundred times as much as the cost of a reconsideration, so even losing most reconsiderations means the DWP and the companies still make a profit. And as most claimants who lose at the mandatory reconsideration stage do not go on to appeal to the tribunal, for whatever reason, a wrong decision to deny benefits will yield the DWP substantial savings. If a disabled person does appeal, this costs the DWP a mere £140, which is much less than the cost of paying the benefit in the interval.

According to the Senior President of Tribunals, exasperated by the number of 'hopeless' cases brought to court for which the DWP had no credible defence, most appeals are 'no-brainers', putting people who have been wrongly assessed for benefits through unnecessary stress and wasting judges' time. Speaking in late 2017, Sir Ernest Ryder said the quality of evidence provided by the Department was so poor it would be 'wholly inadmissible' in any other court. He and his fellow judges were considering sending back cases where there was 'no justiciable defence to the appeal' or even charging the DWP for the cases it loses.[44] That would be a modest improvement but seems unlikely to happen.

In 2018, the parliamentary Public Accounts Committee (PAC) reported that, due to an error, the DWP had underpaid about 70,000 disabled claimants for six years and had even denied them dentistry and prescription costs. The DWP apparently became aware of the error after three years but did nothing to remedy it. When exposed, the Department admitted it had deprived people of their benefit entitlement, but said it would only make back payments from 2014, the year it had identified the error. The PAC castigated the DWP for 'a culture of indifference'. The error and deliberate cover-up caused undeniable suffering to many thousands of disabled people, and yet the DWP was allowed to get away with wrongdoing. The hypocrisy was disgraceful.

The extraordinary complexity of the welfare system seems designed to make it as hard as possible for ordinary people to understand and use. While the network of Citizens Advice exists to advise claimants, it has been overstretched by the tide of demands made on its service, compounded by enforced budget cuts. Consider the pain in the following email received from one frustrated disability claimant (reproduced without grammatical correction):

> At Kilburn Unemployed Workers Group we early on realised that applying and appealing is expensive and wears people down, so we set up photocopying of forms (loads of awkward sized pages), phone credit given out, paying for Drs' Letters, Taxi-cabs upfront, Recorded Deliveries, refreshments for caseworkers and claimants when discussing cases so a more sociable experience, organising our own Hardship Fund to help with Gas/Leccy etc receipts, and having Quex Road Methodist Church provide a Hardship Fund for less recordable needs, and now having Referral Status to Neasden Sufra Foodbank. I personally have used all of KUWG's above facilities, or I would have had no money or spirit to win my PIP money after 2½ YEARS.

Another claimant emailed to say how much he had appreciated a factsheet produced by the Newcastle Welfare Rights Service in pursuing a year-long appeal. Reading the guide showed just how complex the DWP had made the process. Many vulnerable people would be put off even trying to correct a perceived injustice. One can only conclude that this was the intention.

In late 2018, under pressure from a Freedom of Information request, the DWP was forced to reveal its own statistics showing that every day about 100 people were dying while on one or other of the benefits for the disabled. Shockingly, about ten people died every day who had been deemed fit enough to move into jobs.[45] And the death toll can be expected to rise with the roll-out of Universal Credit, which gives disabled people even lower benefits than the system it is replacing.

In 2017, the UK Independent Mechanism that monitors British compliance with the UN Convention on the Rights of Persons with Disabilities concluded that social security reforms made by successive governments since 2010 'have had a particularly disproportionate, cumulative impact on disabled people . . . and have resulted in regression of disabled people's rights to live independently and to an adequate standard of living'.[46] Their situation has worsened since then.

Beyond the treatment of the disabled, Universal Credit is a giant step in the erosion of subsistence rights. It is the endgame of neo-liberal social policy. Billed as reducing complexity by integrating six different state benefits in a single payment, it is moralistic and directive in design. Claimants, mostly vulnerable almost by definition, are obliged to sign a 'claimant commitment' to attend regular interviews, to inform bureaucrats on what they are doing, and to satisfy 'case workers' that they are spending their time appropriately. The system's architect, Iain Duncan Smith, is a committed Catholic and was a military officer. A sense of military discipline, moralistic certainty and duty permeates the scheme, which invades people's privacy, polices their behaviour and restricts their freedom. It epitomizes a class-based presumption that the poor do not need – or cannot be trusted with – freedom; instead they must be reformed and feel grateful for charity, if they demonstrate the required behavioural change. If not, they must be punished for their sins.

An idea behind the design, according to the DWP, is that claimants would be encouraged to learn financial discipline, so as to 'manage' their finances. This bizarre reason was one of the justifications for delaying entitlement to Universal Credit for six weeks once a person became qualified to receive it. Denying impoverished people money was supposed to help them to manage money. Although after widespread protest the official waiting time was later reduced to five weeks, in practice the delay in receiving benefits has often been much longer.[47]

In 2017 a quarter of all new entitled claimants were not paid in full on time (after their six-week wait), with payment delayed on average by an additional four weeks.[48] About 40 per cent of late-paid claimants had to wait eleven weeks or more. The hardship and insecurity were obvious. The use of food banks has surged in areas where Universal Credit has been rolled out and people have gone deeper into debt, fallen behind with the rent, and suffered mental and physical ill-health due to stress and anxiety.[49]

In response to mounting public criticism, the DWP claimed that there was no extra hardship due to the delay because it was providing emergency loans in the form of 'advance payments' in cases of proven need. But obtaining such loans is onerous and they are recovered through subsequent deductions from benefit of up to 40 per cent each month.[50] While writing this chapter, I received the following email from a woman with a child who had been obliged to obtain an 'advance payment':

> They are taking £92 a month off. I am also now a month behind on my rent. I have had debt collectors knocking at my door as I have now fallen behind with payments. It's depressing and worrying.

Another claimant received the following 'advance payment' notice, reproduced verbatim:[51]

> We deduct money from your payment to repay rent arrears, overpayments, and to pay third parties on your behalf such as your landlord or utility companies.
>
> For a list of deductions, please refer to your journal.
>
> **The total we take off for deductions is £528.85.**

She was sure she was not liable for the payments. In panic, she spent considerable time on the phone to the DWP and online. She had the fortitude to persist. Many in her circumstances would not. It turned out to be a 'mistake'. There is no compensation when such 'mistakes' happen. Nobody is punished for making them. This is unjust and regressive.

The DWP claimed Universal Credit would focus benefits on those 'who need it most'. This is untrue. For instance, it abolished the Enhanced Disability Premium (EDP) and the Severe Disability Premium (SDP), paid to the most severely disabled living without carers, worth up to about £400 a month. As a result, 230,000 disabled people were set to lose collectively £2 billion over several years.[52]

In June 2018 the High Court ruled in a case brought by two disabled men that reducing their income in moving them onto Universal Credit constituted unlawful discrimination. One of the plaintiffs was a terminally ill fifty-two-year-old man who had moved from an area where the old benefits system was still operating to a part of London where Universal Credit had been introduced. He had moved solely to obtain the cancer treatment he needed, for which he was punished by having his benefit cut. After the High Court ruled in his favour, the government said it would appeal. The Court refused to allow it.

The whole welfare system has lurched towards widespread use of sanctions. They are imposed if claimants breach rules set by Jobcentres, such as turning up late for appointments or not applying for enough jobs, in the case officer's opinion. Claimants can have their benefits stopped for a minimum of four weeks, which comes to about £300, and for a maximum of three years. This grossly disproportionate punishment trashes the ethos of Clause 20 of the Magna Carta. It also fails any sensible understanding of due process, as enshrined in Clause 39. There is no trial, no legal representation, no opportunity to contest the judgement before it is reached, or before the punishment takes effect.

Nor do the behavioural rules imposed on claimants achieve what the government claims is the objective. The DWP justified mandatory thirty-five-hour-a-week job searches and sanctions on claimants on two grounds, that they would 'weed out' false claimants and that they would encourage and 'incentivize' claimants to take jobs. The evidence on the first is overwhelming: the exclusion of entitled claimants vastly exceeds the unintended inclusion of people not in financial need. The evidence on the second claim is equally clear: the threat and imposition of sanctions do not lead to more employment. A five-year study by researchers from six universities concluded that the threat of sanctions induced a 'culture of counterproductive compliance and futile behaviour', while sanctions not only increased impoverishment but led to more survival crime and loss of capacity to work.[53]

To satisfy the requirement of applying for jobs to keep benefits, some people interviewed in the study said they applied for any job going, irrespective of whether it suited them or they had any chance of getting it. Others responded to the hassle and compulsion by dropping out of the system altogether. One said he had turned to drug-dealing after being sanctioned. Another said the stress of trying to comply with the conditions had made his anxiety and depression so much worse that even his 'work coach' had agreed he was in no state to take a job.

In response to the study, a DWP spokesperson said: 'We tailor requirements to individual cases and sanctions are only used in a very small percentage of cases when people fail to meet their agreed requirements set out in their claimant commitment.'[54] This is misleading in three ways. First, the 'commitment' is forced on claimants, under duress: if they want benefits, they must sign one. A contract signed under duress should be null and void, and surely would be in any self-respecting court of law. Second, there is no due process behind decisions to sanction, which can be for trivial breaches such as being a few minutes late for appointments. The decisions are made by low-level bureaucrats who, despite official denials, are under administrative and political pressure to meet benefit reduction targets. Third, publicly available statistics contradict the assertion that only 'a very small percentage' of people are sanctioned. In 2013 alone, more than 1 million people were sanctioned. Between 2010 and 2015 a quarter of all unemployed who had managed to obtain Jobseeker's Allowance were sanctioned, and in 2015 the total of benefits withdrawn came to £132 million.[55]

In October 2017 the DWP grudgingly admitted that sanctions were causing harm to many and had led to at least one death – of a diabetic man who had been sanctioned for missing two appointments and died because he had no money for the electricity to preserve insulin in his fridge. The Department promised parliament it would experiment with what it called a 'softer' sanctions approach by first issuing written warnings. Yet in February 2018 it said it would not be doing any such trial, citing 'competing priorities in the parliamentary timetable'. This feeble excuse revealed the disdain for the civil rights of the poor. The extra-legal sanctions system was to continue.

There are other regressive features of the erosion of the civil commons by Universal Credit. Built into it is a sly reduction in entitlements for the precariat – the nominally self-employed, agency workers and zero-hour contract employees who have irregular hours and income. They may receive hundreds of pounds a year less in benefit than someone in a full-time job on the same annual income. This is because entitlement to Universal Credit is subject to a 'minimum income floor'. If a person is self-employed for a year or more it is presumed that they are earning the equivalent of the (hourly) national minimum wage for at least thirty-five hours a week. If they earn less than this, Universal Credit will not make up the difference. But if they earn more their benefit is reduced. The DWP, which introduced the minimum income floor ostensibly to weed out claims based on bogus or non-viable businesses, says the rule 'encourages' people to find more opportunities to earn money, ignoring the fact that for many those opportunities do not exist, which is why they are claiming benefit in the first place.

Any rule based on a presumption is intrinsically unjust because it ignores the facts of the individual case. The Office for Budget Responsibility estimates that 400,000 claimants will lose from the minimum income floor, which the government says will 'save' £1.5 billion a year by 2022.[56] A subsequent investigation by the House of Commons Work and Pensions Committee said that the arbitrary rule risked 'crushing the self-employed'.[57] The DWP showed no sign of giving way.

Another erosion of the civil commons is the policy introduced in 2017 of denying entitlement to child tax credit and the child element of Universal Credit for all children born after 6 April 2017 if they were not a first or second child. This amounts to a paternalistic form of eugenics. The minister responsible said the aim was to 'incentivize behavioural change', implying that low-income women who had a third child were behaving irresponsibly and should be penalized. But the person penalized most is the child, who is scarcely responsible. The policy has apparently already led to abortions of wanted babies.[58] In the first year, 70,620 households did not obtain benefits for third or fourth children, 38 per cent of which were lone-parent families. Another 190 households were exempted because the mothers were able to prove they had been raped, under the disgraceful 'rape clause'.[59]

In late 2018, the DWP announced that Citizens Advice, long held in high esteem as a charity representing the citizens against the state, had signed a government contract for £51 million to help in the delivery of Universal Credit. They thereby forfeited their right to be regarded as a gatekeeper of common rights. Shortly afterwards it was revealed that other charities had signed contracts to assist the DWP that now include a commitment not to criticize the Department or the minister. They had surely sold themselves and should be denied tax advantages gained by being a registered charity.

Universal Credit has savagely eroded the civil commons and the citizenry's right to subsistence. It has already brought hardship and distress to commoners across the land and has worsened social income inequality. So awful was the prospect of further roll-out that in late 2018 several elder statesmen, including two former prime ministers, John Major and Gordon Brown, made public statements warning of social devastation and political unrest. In early 2019 a panicked Secretary of State announced a pause to the roll-out that is already six years behind schedule.

## Spare bedrooms: how they are lost

What is a spare bedroom? In some households, it is easy to identify; in others, it is a hazy idea, since a room may be used by one or other partner when ill or just for a change. The wealthy may have many spare bedrooms. The poor have been targeted to have none, under a policy championed by David Cameron as Prime Minister. It is a cruel form of class-based inequality in modern Britain, introduced by a government with members who have lots of spare rooms.

The 'bedroom tax' introduced by the 2012 Welfare Reform Act reduces housing benefit paid to any working-age tenant living in social housing with more bedrooms than an officially calculated allowance. One spare bedroom reduces housing benefit by 14 per cent; two spare bedrooms incur a loss of 25 per cent. A married couple is allowed only one bedroom. Beyond that, complex rules specify who qualifies to have separate bedrooms.[60] It is left to judges to determine what constitutes a bedroom. The policy is both discriminatory and regressive, applying only to people in social housing on incomes low enough to qualify for housing benefit.

From the start, the policy has been controversial. It has had a disproportionately adverse effect on people with disabilities, who are estimated to make up two-thirds of those affected. Less than 10 per cent have been able to avoid the 'tax' by moving to smaller accommodation; for most, the loss of benefit has led to rent arrears and cutbacks in spending on food and heating.[61]

Iain Duncan Smith, then Secretary of State for Work and Pensions, justified the bedroom tax as follows:

We need to put an end to the unfair situation where the taxpayer is subsidizing people to have homes, paid for by the state, with spare rooms they do not need. This is effectively a spare room subsidy. Britain cannot afford it and nor can the taxpayer.[62]

At the time, he and his wife were receiving a vastly greater subsidy (£160,000 in 2014) from the EU on 1,500 acres inherited by his wife, for which he had done no work whatsoever. When the EU proposed to cap the amount large-scale landowners could receive in such subsidies, he and his government colleagues vetoed the proposal. The hypocrisy is incredible.

In 2016, despite court rulings that the existing policy was discriminatory and unlawful, the government proposed extending the bedroom tax to the elderly, only to backtrack after a huge public outcry. As the head of the charity Age Concern retorted, 'Imposing a cap on older tenants will not only cause them anxiety and distress. It is also pointless, given the lack of affordable housing options available to them.' Perhaps 'pointless' was the wrong word. It was designed to fit with the austerity strategy, imposing yet more financial burden on those least able to bear it.

The bedroom tax is just one of the ways by which government has cut benefits for lower-income commoners. The overwhelming majority of those hit by it have been unable to move to smaller homes, partly because of government-imposed cuts in the supply of affordable social housing. They have simply had to manage (or not) with reduced benefits.

## Undocumenting migrants

Every commoner, as a member of a given community, should be treated equally and with respect for the legal principles of substantive and procedural justice. Procedural justice requires fair procedures that respect due process. Substantive justice requires people to be treated fairly in law.

In both respects migrants have been particularly targeted for exclusion from the civil commons. One glaring instance has been the mistreatment of the Windrush generation of migrants from the Caribbean, named after the ship that brought the first group from Jamaica in 1948.

In 2012, the Home Office minister, Theresa May, set up what she called, officially, the 'Hostile Environment Working Group' to design policies aimed at making life difficult for supposedly illegal migrants. After private protest from Liberal Democrats in the Coalition government, the name was changed to the equally revealing Inter-Ministerial Group on Migrants' Access to Benefits and Public Services. Some years before, Home Office officials had decided to destroy landing cards and related evidence of immigration of the Windrush generation, apparently because the documents were taking up too much space and were deemed unnecessary. But the new 'get tough' regime used the fact that there was no longer corroborating evidence of legal migration to hound people who had been living legally in Britain for decades.

The cruel consequences only came to public attention six years later, when a sixty-three-year-old man was denied free medical treatment for cancer under the National Health Service and was told to pay £54,000, a 'death sentence' as he rightly called it. Other cases then came to light. The new requirement to produce a host of documents to prove legal status had left many Windrush and other immigrants 'undocumented' and by implication illegal. Landlords, doctors and others, required by the 'hostile environment' policy to check migrants' legal status, erred on the side of caution by denying services in case of doubt, with no right of appeal. People lost their jobs, their homes, were denied benefits and medical treatment; some were deported, and others were refused re-entry to the UK after visits abroad.

Although the government was forced to apologize and claimed the treatment of the Windrush migrants had been an unintended mistake, internal memos made clear that this treatment was a direct consequence of a policy designed to harass migrants and increase deportations. The government had abandoned due process, without regard for the human consequences. Eventually, Amber Rudd, the Home Secretary, was forced to resign, but only because she falsely claimed that there were no 'targets' for deportations. Her own memos showed that there were, and that she was complicit in making and adhering to them.

Theresa May's 'hostile environment' policy also introduced a steep rise in charges for immigration or naturalization applications, far above processing costs. The fee for a settlement visa for an adult dependent relative rose more than five-fold, from £585 in 2008–9 to £3,250 in 2017–18, while the fee for adult naturalization almost doubled from £700 in 2011 to £1,330, against a processing cost of £372.[63] The registration fee for children has doubled since 2011 to over £1,000, registration being the process where someone who has a right to British citizenship applies to obtain it. These charges are highly regressive; lower-income people may renounce their applications or struggle to pay, perhaps going into debt to do so. Ability to pay is not an equitable rule for deciding whether someone is granted citizenship.

Another regressive act was to insist that any British citizen or legal resident wanting a non-European spouse to join them had to have an assured annual income of more than £18,600. Government ministers had argued for an income above £40,000, which would have barred all but the richest migrants from bringing their foreign spouse to live with them. But they were persuaded to be less mean.

Meanwhile, those applying for refugee status are being left in limbo for years, treated as a minority that can safely be ignored as having no political role. They are housed in substandard accommodation, given a pittance (£5.39 a day in 2018) to spend on food, clothes, transport and other necessities, and refused permission to take jobs. If they are granted asylum – Britain has one of the lowest acceptance rates in Europe – they are quickly pushed out of their provided accommodation and lose their daily allowance, leaving them to face the bureaucratic challenges of applying for welfare benefits and council housing. Unsurprisingly, many have ended up on the streets.[64]

## POPS and private justice

Privately owned public spaces (POPS) hark back to the nineteenth century when large parts of central London were gated communities, barred to the general public and policed by private groups. Rolled back in the twentieth century, private regulations and private policing have returned.

Today, an action that would be perfectly legal in a public road or square may be banned because the space has been privatized. Often there is no way of knowing what is and is not allowed, let alone what penalty might be applied or by whom. In 2017, when asked by *The Guardian* what private regulations applied to their POPS, forty-eight out of fifty owners refused to answer.[65] One homeless man told the newspaper of his experience in one POPS, Pancras Square: 'I'm allowed to lie down on the grass, but not to close my eyes. I tried to take a nap the other morning, just for an hour or two, and every time my eyes began to shut I was woken up by security guards.' Freedom has been lost in what had been the commons, and is now suddenly a zone of trespass.

Private companies owning what used to be urban commons or public space are using private security guards to enforce privately defined rules that have chipped away at common freedoms, often without commoners being aware (unless they inadvertently breach them) of what those rules are, or even that any such rules exist. While on principle private owners of public spaces should not be allowed to impose restrictions and penalties that are not in force in publicly owned public spaces, at a minimum the rules should be made clear.

## The erosion of civil commons in jobs

In a particularly petty action, George Osborne as Chancellor of the Exchequer offered employees tax relief if, in return for receiving tax-exempt shares worth between £2,000 and £50,000 from their employer, they gave up employment rights under UK law on unfair dismissal, redundancy and

the right to request flexible working or time off for training. Women were obliged to give sixteen weeks' notice of the
date of return from maternity leave, double the normal eight
weeks. This measure, introduced in April 2013, eroded the
quasi-universality of standard employment entitlements and
provided a subsidy to a relatively privileged group of workers. The scheme was scrapped in November 2016 after it was
found, predictably enough, to have enabled a few rich people
to avoid tax. It had been a handy subsidy used in tax planning, mainly by hedge funds, to reduce income tax and national insurance contributions.[66]

The erosion of once-established employment protection
has been a prolonged process. It is an international trend,
perhaps most developed in the United States, where millions
of employees, often without realizing it, must rely on private
arbitration rather than on the courts to obtain what is due
to them.[67] The growing number of employers and contractors using flexible labour can make deductions from wages
or payments with impunity, docking pay on grounds of inef-
ficiency, tardiness or similar.

Although this has always been a tendency, it is much easier
to do and harder to detect with casual indirect labour. Outside
standardized and unionized employment it is more difficult
and more expensive to obtain redress against arbitrary deductions. The personal consequences for trying to do so can be
severe, marking down the individual as a 'troublemaker'. Over
2 million workers in Britain have been cheated of wages due
to them, amounting to about £3 billion each year.[68]

The cost to the precariat only intensified when rules were
introduced in 2013 requiring workers to pay up to £1,500 to

take a case to the employment tribunal. This was ruled unlawful by the Supreme Court in 2017. But workers are still charged to take subsequent actions if an employer does not pay up when an award is made. It is another way of reducing access to justice for commoners, especially those on low incomes.

## Policy by algorithm

Companies, government agencies, financial institutions, the National Health Service, schools, police forces, welfare agencies, security services and others are increasingly relying on sophisticated algorithms embodied in assessment systems to make judgements on people that materially affect their lives. Many of these algorithms now use rules set not by human coders but by the machine itself, using artificial intelligence to crunch vast quantities of data to detect patterns and outcomes. AI can vastly improve decision-making, as in medical diagnosis, by spotting patterns that humans cannot. But it has also created a situation in which decisions can be taken on the basis of rules that no one can identify and on data that may be skewed or biased, for example, against racial minorities or people from poor neighbourhoods.

Someone can be denied a loan, a job, even parole, because an algorithm judges they are a bad risk even when they are not. This is a refined form of statistical discrimination. In one documented case in the United States, a man was given a longer prison sentence than his crime would normally warrant, because the computer algorithm judged he was at high risk of reoffending. Algorithmic mistakes have wrongly identified innocent people as terrorists, sent sick patients home from hospital, lost people their jobs and car licences, had people removed from the electoral register, and resulted in the wrong men being chased for child support.[69]

All of this is an incursion into the civil commons. Even the cleverest AI algorithm is based on probabilities, not certainty, let alone respect for due process. The individuals being assessed do not know the criteria being used, and as things stand have no means of finding out. Companies usually protect their algorithms as trade secrets, barring access by outsiders, which can include the organizations making use of them. But even insiders may not be able to identify the rules that AI has created. New York University's AI Now Institute says public agencies responsible for criminal justice, healthcare, welfare and education should ban use of 'black box AIs' because their decisions cannot be explained, thus flouting due process.

Decisions by algorithm are also inequitable, since lower-income people are more likely to be assessed by AI programmes and less able to combat them. In her book, *Automating Inequality*,[70] Virginia Eubanks describes the use of algorithms and 'big data' in US welfare and child protection programmes as creating a 'digital poorhouse' – a new regime of surveillance, profiling, punishment, containment and exclusion that is worsening inequality. She documents how computerized decisions have led to refusal of welfare benefits and the wrongful removal of children from their parents, and how difficult it is to challenge these decisions, especially for vulnerable, less educated or lower-income people without the know-how or means to do so.

It is not just the USA, of course. The use of algorithms

in decision-making is spreading all over the world. Another example is Australia's privatization of debt collection from people receiving means-tested benefits. It has commissioned private firms to build and operate an algorithm-based system that mines individuals' financial records and accuses them of fraud on the basis of its findings. The private firms collect the penalties and are paid commission based on how much money they extract from welfare claimants.[71]

Justice by algorithm, based on probabilities, is a denial of due process in all respects. It judges an individual based on data collected from others, not on the evidence for that person, and makes it difficult, if not impossible, for decisions to be challenged. In addition, because of its growing use in the welfare and criminal justice systems, it disproportionately affects the lives and livelihoods of lower-income people, a further erosion of the civil commons in which all commoners are due equal rights and equal treatment.

\*

The privatization and neglect of the civil commons has been profoundly regressive. It has affected the worst-off most of all, sharply increasing social income inequality. Those in the precariat have lost assured state benefits – they are less likely to receive anything and if they do it is worth less than before. They are more likely to be sanctioned and more likely to have to appeal against incorrect denials of entitlement. It is wrong, as some do, to calculate the degree of inequality by assuming everybody entitled to receive a benefit is actually doing so. The erosion of due process also mostly hits the precariat, whether they are seeking benefits, or finding themselves enmeshed in legal processes.

The government has turned itself into an agent of plunder of the civil commons, rather than acting as its steward, and it has weakened potential gatekeepers, as with the abolition of the Audit Commission.

One irony of the era, globally, is the 'enclosure' of common law: complex legal rules have proliferated and have become *more* regulatory, directive and restrictive. Neo-liberals boast of favouring deregulation, yet the scope of written law and contractualization of so many aspects of life have actually strengthened regulation. This has weakened the sphere of common law that depends on flexible norms, precedent and codes of reciprocity, bringing to mind Aristotle's idea of *philia*, civic friendship. He captured it beautifully for all time: 'When men are friends they have no need for justice, while when they are just they need friendship as well, and the truest form of justice is thought to be a friendly quality.' A legal system that does not respect the civil commons shreds justice and generates more inequality in its wake.

Successive governments have ignored the basic principles laid out in the Magna Carta, that punishment should be proportional to the offence, be imposed only after a fair hearing, and should not deprive someone of their livelihood. What should be done to revive the civil commons?

Article 30: Private owners of public spaces should
    be required to display prominent notices of any
    restrictions on use of the space and what, if any,
    'penalties' exist for contravening them. But private

owners of public spaces should not be allowed to impose restrictions and penalties that are not in force in publicly owned public spaces.

Article 31: Legal aid as a right must be granted for both criminal and civil cases. This should include cases brought against the alleged unlawful plunder of the commons by corporations or individuals, who can otherwise exert legal advantage by hiring expensive lawyers and indulging in costly litigation.

Article 32: The probation service must be restored as a common public service. The privatization of prisons and policing must be reversed.

Article 33: If any private social policy provider wrongly denies a claimant some benefit or service to which they are entitled, the provider should be fined, with part going to compensate the wronged claimant. Claimants should not be sanctioned without a fair hearing; there must be no sanctions without due process.

CHAPTER 6
# The Cultural Commons

> During a little over half a century the town has been
> transformed and ennobled. Rookeries and squalid courts
> have given way to fine streets and open places. Baths and
> washhouses are provided at a nominal cost to the users.
> Free libraries and museums of art are open to all the
> inhabitants; free schools and a school of art are provided
> for their education.
>
> — Joseph Chamberlain, Mayor of Birmingham, 1873–6

Joseph Chamberlain is a legendary figure in the development
of the urban commons of Britain. As Mayor of Birmingham,
he transformed Britain's second largest city, demolishing
slums, creating new streets and parks, building schools, municipal baths and libraries, and establishing communal gas
and water supplies. And he was a nineteenth-century pioneer
in recognizing the value of the cultural commons – hence his
emphasis on access for all to the institutions that embody the
artistic and creative sides of life. His like, and the resources
he was able to call upon, are desperately needed today, to
save the cultural tradition that he represented so strongly.

The arts, sport, the mass media, public libraries, art galleries,
museums, concert halls and public places for performances

are all part of our cultural commons. Public architecture, townscapes and landscapes also shape and constitute a country's cultural commons, which exists in a localized and historical context of embeddedness in society.

All the arts – music, literature, poetry, drama, painting, sculpture and so on – express part of our collective human culture and need to be accessible to all. Imagine a world in which Michelangelo's sculptures were concealed by private owners. We would all be culturally impoverished. Access to culture is a common right. As playwright David Edgar has written, the arts can widen horizons, expand perceptions, question presumptions and encourage empathy, as well as give pleasure and delight.[1] Similarly, writer and academic Robert Hewison has argued that the arts provide people with a collective experience that increases mutual tolerance, encourages cooperation and engenders trust.[2]

Cultural institutions embody custom and a sense of historical connection, reminding us of our shared existence. In Britain, generations of local politicians and social activists have erected the fabric of cultural commons, giving civic pride to millions of people. As one civic leader said of Glasgow, 'The modern ratepayer has the satisfaction of knowing that, while he pays for the support of museum and art gallery, the institutions are his property and dedicated to his service.'[3] However, the depletion of the cultural commons in the twenty-first century has been extensive and devastating, accelerated by the prolonged period of austerity. The origins of that depletion can be traced, as so often, to the philistine excesses of the Thatcher era.

A defining act of the Thatcher government was the sale of

sports grounds attached to state schools – land that had long belonged to the public, paid for by generations of taxpayers. This mass sale not only deprived youngsters of accessible space to play sports, helping to keep them fit, healthy and off the streets, but intentionally extended opportunities for property developers to profit from what had been the commons. The cultural loss was treated as unimportant.

Public spaces that have been created for community activity – commoning – reflect and reinforce the community's culture. Selling them to private interests is not simply a commercial transaction to raise money for the government. It vandalizes society. And since the 1980s the erosion of all spheres of the cultural commons has gone way beyond what Thatcher started.

## Public architecture

One of the least appreciated forms of privatization has had a profound effect on the cultural commons. Post-war cities and towns had their own architects' departments, responsible for designing and commissioning a vast range of public buildings as well as social housing. In 1976 half of all British architects worked in the public domain. In London, the architects employed by the Greater London Council and its predecessor, the London County Council, were responsible for planning, designing and building huge swathes of the capital, including some of the greatest testaments to the country's cultural commons, from the Festival Hall built in 1951 to the National Theatre in the 1970s. The architects and their colleagues were stewards of the urban landscape, setting and maintaining standards of public safety and comfort, and the aesthetics of city development. The aesthetics were not always to everyone's taste. Mistakes were made. But the stewards were accountable to the public, the commoners.

In the 1980s, those departments began to disappear. Architectural work was increasingly outsourced to private firms or dispensed with altogether as local authorities sold off public land and buildings to private developers. Less than 1 per cent of architects today work in the public sector. The resultant reshaping of cities has given little attention to the needs and tastes of commoners.

A more subtle threat to the cultural commons is 'investment' in public arts infrastructure intended to help regenerate depressed urban areas. Planting the huge modernist Guggenheim museum in Bilbao, in Spain's Basque Country, has succeeded in attracting millions of tourists, but it has not enriched the city's cultural commons. Indeed, such an externally imposed gigantic structure risks alienating art from the commons. Anyone who sees it should understand how discordant it is in that venerable old Basque port and industrial city.

Similar trends can be seen in Britain. While a number of successful venues have been created, including the Tate Modern in London and Sage in Gateshead, others have been artistic flops and financial disasters. The £15 million National Centre for Popular Music in Sheffield closed after little more than a year for lack of visitors and is now part of Sheffield Hallam University. The Public in West Bromwich, costing £60 million and dubbed by locals the 'pink elephant', was intended as a space for 'interactive digital art'. It lasted five years before being turned into classrooms for a sixth-form college. Both these projects lacked the embeddedness in local cultural traditions and activities that make a cultural commons. Dependent for revenue on attracting visitors from outside, they went with the grain of commodification, not against it.

London has seen its cultural commons destroyed by privatization and colonization. Renzo Piano's Shard in Bermondsey has been described as a 'giant middle finger presented to us all'. The race to build and profit from huge towers has been a cross between a gold rush and an invading horde, fuelled by foreign investment. One enraged commentator characterized what has been happening as the erection (pun intended) of 'a set of improbable sex toys poking gormlessly into the air'.[4] In 2000, there were thirty towers of over twenty storeys in the metropolis, already well up from the number in the 1980s at the outset of the neo-liberal age. In 2017, 115 were under construction, from 91 in 2016, and 510 such buildings were in the pipeline, from 455 a year earlier.[5] This is an astonishing transformation. There has never been a democratic decision to change London so dramatically. Many of those giant towers may come to symbolize a hubristic era of plutocratic zeal for property, a City in thrall to global finance and its own unique role in it.

## Public libraries

The library has been seen as the depository of popular culture at least since the establishment of the Great Library of Alexandria, which was founded by Ptolemy I, friend and successor of Alexander the Great, in the fourth century BC. At its height it is said to have contained half a million scrolls.

In the history of the British commons, the oral assertion and legitimation of what were commons practices gradually moved to the written record, although for many generations written records were often ways of retaining the validity of oral understandings.[6] Parish churches took a prominent role in preserving these writings, sometimes against the wishes of manorial lords keen to deny what had long been commons. Subsequently, local libraries took over some of this role.

Public libraries have long been part of the social fabric, important for most social groups but more so for those without much money to spend on books and suitable space in which to read them. Today, in Britain and elsewhere, libraries also enable people without computers at home to access information and knowledge, and to participate as digital citizens, as more and more government and private services move online. They also act as venues for the arts, with exhibitions, concerts, film shows and poetry readings, as well as participative activities to introduce children and other users to culture of all kinds – not just books.

Although local authorities in Britain have a statutory obligation to provide 'a comprehensive and efficient library service', budget cuts have forced hundreds of libraries to close and others to restrict services and lay off staff. Between 2012 and 2017, 450 libraries in Great Britain shut their doors and many more were said to be under threat. From over 4,500 before the austerity era, the number had shrunk to 3,745 by the end of 2017.

Some early observers of the impending cull celebrated the prospect. Journalist Christopher Caldwell has said that libraries were imperilled because local councils felt they had better things to do with the money.[7] That is not the case. They have been imperilled because central government has slashed funds for local councils. Caldwell revealed his real prejudice when adding that 'libraries belong to a brief transitional period at the end of the nineteenth century' and were 'used disproportionately by the old, the affluent and the ambitious'. This is simply untrue. Libraries are used by people of all ages and are especially valuable to those in the precariat and on low incomes who would not be able to pay privately for the services libraries provide for free.

In October 2016, Walsall council announced plans to shut fifteen of its sixteen libraries, to save £2.9 million a year. This was not due to low use. The libraries estimated that they had had a million visits over the previous two years and had lent out 775,000 books.[8] In Walsall as elsewhere, the libraries were more than simply a means of obtaining books; they were a social institution for bringing people together. And they were part of the community's social income, used by children from low-income families. Faced with a deficit of £86 million, the council made clear that the closures were a result of funding cuts by central government: 'The council fully appreciates that the art gallery and libraries are much loved by those who use them. However, like many councils across the country, this authority can't ignore the fact that savings have to be made.'

Two years earlier, the government had commissioned what was called the Independent Library Report for England, written by a publisher, which recommended that libraries should be reinvigorated. It was published after 324 libraries had been closed in the previous three years and when about

400 others had been transferred to volunteer management, mostly surviving without local authority assistance. The report did nothing to halt the decline.

What Will Hutton has called the 'last hurrah' for the ambitions of civic Britain was the construction of the public Library of Birmingham, a very large costly building that opened in September 2013. It was commissioned in 2007, just before the financial crash. When it opened, the library's chief executive acknowledged that no local authority could contemplate such a project today.[9]

Libraries, surprisingly enough, foster reading, and reading fosters empathy, which fosters social solidarity.[10] Closing libraries does the reverse. You cannot put a monetary value on that, or at least you should not do so. As Neil Gaiman argued in his impassioned defence of the public library:

> Libraries are about freedom. Freedom to read, freedom
> of ideas, freedom of communication. They are about
> education (which is not a process that finishes the day we
> leave school or university), about entertainment, about
> making safe spaces, and about access to information.

Libraries also play an important role in enabling the still large number of people who do not have a personal internet connection to search for jobs or claim benefits, which the Department for Work and Pensions obliges them to do online. Closing libraries and Jobcentres makes it even harder for the precariat to function. One wonders just how many people have been helped by librarians to navigate in a society made cruelly complicated, and how many have lost their way as libraries have closed their doors.

## Museums and art galleries

Museums are the repository of our common heritage and the heritage of nature, the species and the many forms of inter-action that have shaped us today. In Britain, they flourished in the Victorian era. Today, there are thirteen national muse-ums and art galleries, and many regional or local ones. Most of us take them for granted, perhaps taking our children to them on rainy days to give them a sense of history, possibly sparking a curiosity that might start a process of personal discovery.

Museums have been another casualty of austerity, which is ironic given that the government of the day prides itself on being 'conservative'. By 2017 more than 40 per cent of 257 local authority museums had cut opening times by an aver-age of 20 per cent.[11] The poorer north-east of the country has been hit hardest. As the Labour Shadow Arts and Heri-tage Minister, Kevin Brennan, said, 'Local museums are like cultural food banks – along with theatres and other cultural provisions. They foster creativity where it's needed most.'

Lack of funding has prompted Britain's museums to move ever closer to the American model, with greater reliance on private donations and sponsorship.[12] This inevitably gives the tastes of the rich priority in what is preserved and what is lost or discarded.

Public museums and art galleries are also being privat-ized. In August 2015, 400 gallery staff working at the Nation-al Gallery, which houses one of the world's most important art collections, were outsourced to Securitas, a security company with no institutional knowledge of culture or art services. Following a lengthy strike, the transfer went ahead after the union negotiated certain conditions, including the reinstatement of its representative, who had been sacked during the dispute. More than half the gallery trustees, appointed by the government, were from the world of finance and business. They will have seen the institution's employees as just a cost, not as an integral part of a precious piece of the cultural commons.

This action was a form of enclosure. Those outsourced employees, many of whom had worked for the National Gallery for years, could be shifted to jobs anywhere in the company, which has contracts guarding ports and airports, shops and offices. They had lost their occupational security and some will have joined the precariat. Meanwhile, on its website, Securitas claimed that outsourcing lowered costs precisely because private companies could pay lower wages. It even boasted about it, stating: 'The view held by some that outsourcing is more expensive than running things in house is simply not so when private security companies are able to pay their staff a lower rate.'[13] So much for the claimed efficiency gains of privatization. Securitas subsequently reneged on its commitments to the union, and the National Gallery later de-recognized the union, on the grounds that most of its members were by then employed by Securitas and not by the gallery.

In 2013, the British Museum outsourced management and cleaning services to the multinational Carillion. After Carillion went spectacularly bankrupt in 2018, it was left to the official receiver to compensate the workers as best it could. The Imperial War Museum privatized its gallery services in 2014, only to see the private contractor Shield Guarding (owned by an Indian multinational Topsgrup) collapse two years later. Shield was then bought by Noonan, an Irish contract cleaning and facilities management company, now largely owned by a private equity group, Alchemy, leaving staff unsure of their jobs and the future of their pensions.

Outsourced and insecure workers cease to be custodians of the commons; they have no stake in caring for it. And since outsourcing is intended to cut costs, it inevitably leads to poorer services by reducing staff and worsening their working conditions.

There has also been creeping commercialization of museums and art galleries, with the growth of private sponsorship by multinational corporations keen to promote their brand and public image. Governments in many countries, including Britain, have encouraged such sponsorship, sometimes through tax reliefs, in the hope and expectation that commercial donors will take up some of the slack left by cuts in public funding.

But there is a social price to be paid. The corporate donors can become de facto arbiters of what is displayed in the public arena and what is not. Some observers are intensely relaxed about that, seeing the corporations as entirely altruistic.[14] But this is naïve. To give just one example, an investigation by *The Guardian* showed that Shell tried to influence the presentation of a climate change programme it was sponsoring at the Science Museum in London because of concerns that one part of the project risked encouraging criticism of Shell's operations.[15]

Even if sponsors do not intervene directly, reliance on

corporate philanthropy tends to constrain riskier, more experimental projects, giving a disproportionate focus to conservative or establishment taste. As one curator put it, 'Sponsors want exhibits that are popular. I am not saying that popular artists are bad artists but the choice is not as independent as it is when the money is there already. Most sponsors think very carefully about what they want to connect their names and logos to.'[16]

Another concern is that sponsorship can be used for what has been called 'art washing' – enabling corporations to embellish their reputations in a context where their actions as producers are controversial or worse. Another oil company, BP, has long sponsored events and displays in the National Portrait Gallery and the British Museum, among others, portraying itself as a benevolent force rather than as a major global polluter.

Corporate sponsorship may also give governments a spurious justification to cut spending on the arts, increasing their dependency on private donations and putting public institutions at risk. BP propped up the Tate art galleries for twenty-six years, but suddenly ended its sponsorship in 2017, attributing the decision to the 'extremely challenging business environment' rather than to years of protest by climate change activists against the sponsorship.

Most of those promoting the arts may be doing so with genuinely altruistic motives. But there is a need for a pro-commons bias to correct for market power. Otherwise, corporate interests will displace community interests, drop by drop.

## Public theatre: venues for empathy

> When the storytelling goes bad in a society, the result is decadence.
> — Aristotle

The ancient Greeks taught us the vital need for public theatre, and the value of public participation in the great tragedies. Aristotle said that these tragedies aroused in audiences the emotions of compassion and fear – compassion for people suffering through no fault of their own and fear that something similar could happen to them or someone dear to them. Through their complex human dilemmas, the plays developed empathy in the citizenry, reminding each generation not to be too moralistic and judgemental. A vital sentiment of a good society, empathy is the ability to put oneself imaginatively in the shoes of 'the other', whether or not one agrees with their predicament or actions. The dramas reinforced common-ness as the intrinsic human condition.

The audience in the Greek arenas were not just passive onlookers, they were participants. This dual role was handed down through the generations in most countries. In Britain it was vividly reproduced in the Elizabethan era and in the plays of Shakespeare, enacted in the Theatre playhouse and then in the Globe theatre, where audiences almost surrounded the stage. To see the Globe lovingly recreated has been a modern delight.

If the public space of the cultural commons is eroded, the learning and reinforcement of empathy is eroded too, resulting in a reduction of people's critical faculties. Budget cuts

CHAPTER 6

in the name of austerity for regional theatre, as well as for
museums and galleries, inevitably mean much more limited
access to the cultural commons. If commercialization leads
to entry charges for museums or higher ticket prices for
theatre, those on low incomes will be the first to stop their
participation.

Privatization of the cultural commons has been deliberate. It has accentuated the commercialization of art, fostering
easy passive entertainment rather than challenging, critical
and even subversive creations, the essence of art throughout history. Already, the arts have been transformed into the
'creative industries', with decisions on funding dictated by
whether or not something will yield a financial rate of return.
A business-oriented mindset will be reinforced.

## The mass media: the neo-liberal drift and vanities of plutocrats

> Whoever controls the media, controls the mind.
> — Jim Morrison

The mass media are a vital part of our cultural commons.
For meaningful democracy, and to ensure all perspectives
and groups are represented, publicly owned and accountable
media are essential. But the media are falling victim to commodifying forces and interests.

In the UK, the BBC has been a bulwark of the political and
cultural commons, committed from the outset to hosting a
diverse range of views and robust debates in line with the
public service principles laid down by its first director general, Lord Reith. It has not been a commons in every respect.

Its elitist governance, with a small group of highly paid executives, producers and editors deciding on what constitutes the public interest, has resulted in a rather patrician view. It is also dependent on government for funding through the licence fee, so cannot be said to be fully independent. And it has tended to side with conservative values, beginning with its support of the government against the workers during the General Strike of 1926. But there has been strong support, inside and outside the BBC, for it to retain and strengthen its commons ethos.

The formative designer of the BBC Archive, Tony Ageh, has said the BBC should treat the archive like a public library, protecting and preserving its assets for future generations and encouraging citizens to explore and reimagine material for their own creative ideas. 'The library is the one memory institution that lets you take the artists' work home. That means you can come back with your own ideas.'[17] But the dilution of the BBC as an emblem of the country's cultural commons is well underway.

Since the early years of Thatcherism, the BBC has been squeezed of funds and forced to become increasingly commercial. Structural reforms introduced in the 1980s required a quarter of non-news programming to come from the private sector and strengthened editorial control of news and current affairs by the BBC's top brass, who are subject to intense political pressures.

The BBC's new Charter, introduced in 2017, goes much further, opening up all BBC output to competition, with the exception of news and current affairs. It also created a new commercial subsidiary, BBC Studios, which must compete with better-funded private companies for BBC commissioning; it can also sell programmes to others. Critics claim that subjecting programme-making to the dictates of the market erodes creativity and innovation, while the parallel centralization of editorial authority in news and current affairs has curtailed journalistic freedom.[18]

For years the government has held down the TV licence fee, which provides the BBC with most of its revenue. In 2010, the Coalition government reduced funding for the BBC World Service, an arm of Britain's 'soft power'. This was later partially reversed, after the 2015 Strategic Defence Review admitted it had been a mistake. But, once again without public consultation, the BBC was told that as from 2020 it would have to absorb the £745 million annual loss of revenue from free licences for the over-seventy-fives, introduced in 2001, which the government was currently paying for. The corporation says it cannot meet this cost, equivalent to a fifth of its budget, without closing channels and slashing other services.

As a result of the cuts already made, the BBC has been increasingly forced to produce a narrower range of programmes and has lost coverage of many popular events to private TV companies that can afford to pay more. This is a classic example of the micro-politics of privatization – deliberately weakening a public service, then claiming that because it is not serving the public well, the private sector could do the job better. After the BBC threatened to close two television channels, BBC2 and BBC4, and all local radio stations to fill the hole in its finances, the government agreed some mitigating measures. But the threat to BBC services remains. And although privatization of Channel 4, launched in 1982 with a statutory public service remit, is now off the table, the government has forced it to move large parts of its business outside London. Channel 4 says this will damage its business model and reduce its investment in programming.

The privatization of the mass media in terms of the implications for the information commons is covered later in this book. But it has also had an impact on the cultural commons, particularly by extending 'colonization' in the form of a more standardized global output, with a predominance of American soap operas and 'sound-bite' news and debate programmes. These corrode the vernacular, the local ways of communicating, local political values and local cultures. The rapid growth of Netflix, the US-based video streaming service, whose output of TV programmes and films now dwarfs that of any TV network or Hollywood studio, has also raised fears that cultural power will be increasingly concentrated in the hands of a few content commissioners and algorithms.[19]

In a quirky example of colonization in the print media, a famous London newspaper, the *Evening Standard*, was bought by Alexander Lebedev, a billionaire and former Russian KGB spy. His co-owner son Evgeny, now a British citizen, appointed as editor the former Conservative Chancellor of the Exchequer, George Osborne, the principal author of austerity and of tax cuts for the very rich. One could not make up such a story – KGB spy employs austerity architect and heir to a baronetcy – outside a theatre of the absurd.

## Public art in diminished space

Art is too important not to share.
— Romero Britto, Brazilian artist

One form of cultural commons stems from the very earliest period of humanity. Caves uncovered in 1940 at Lascaux in south-west France display astounding paintings of animals, some beautifully coloured, created up to 20,000 years ago by our Palaeolithic ancestors. These are among the earliest examples of public art.

Today we would be rightly critical of carving onto trees or rocks, disfiguring and potentially destroying nature in a desire for immortality. Yet art intended for the public has an abiding value for society, enlivening desolate communities, strengthening a morality running against a suffocating conformity, subverting totalitarian regimes, ridiculing power.[20]

Graffiti today have a mixed but subversive set of roles, just as they must have done in the ancient cities of Pompeii and Herculaneum, where erotic sketches and bawdy graffiti testify to a liberality that was to disappear from public view in succeeding centuries. Graffiti could be said to be the natural form of art of the precariat today. A prominent representative is the supposedly anonymous Banksy, a street artist whose wall graffiti are now often sold as highly priced commodities. He has been called a vandal, but his provocative work has beautified many a public place. And much of it is subversive. One iconic example shows a forlorn bill poster with brush and glue-pot in hand, next to a daubed wall reading, 'Follow your dreams!' over-stamped by 'Cancelled'.

In modern times, graffiti, street art, busking and other performances in public places are a subtle but important part of our creative commons, alongside art commissioned or intended to decorate buildings, streets and squares for public enjoyment. But as privatization and commercialization of cities gathers pace, this people's commons is under siege.

Apart from their aesthetic appeal, the colourful mosaic murals created by Edward Paolozzi in the 1980s for London's Tottenham Court Road underground station blocked 1,000 square metres of wall from being used for adverts. The murals, many with musical references inspired by the cluster of electronics shops in the area, had stood the test of time that defines a commons. They were there, unopposed, for over three decades, defying the commodification of public walls. But in 2015 the murals were dismantled as part of the station's redevelopment.[21] After public protest, almost all were retained and reinstated. But the episode showed the constant vigilance required to save the cultural commons from plunder.

'Old Flo' is the affectionate title given by generations of residents of the borough of Tower Hamlets in east London to a masterpiece sculpted by Henry Moore in 1957. Formally called *Draped Seated Woman, 1957–58*, the sculpture depicts a woman in a ruched dress seated with her legs folded to the side and the hand opposite supporting her weight. Moore sold 'Old Flo', which is 2.5 metres high (8 feet) and weighs 1.6 tonnes, to London County Council in 1962 for a nominal price (£6,000), a fraction of its potential market value at the time, on condition that it be displayed in a commons area. He was delighted that the site chosen was in the Stifford housing estate amidst a group of tower blocks in Stepney. It gave a little beauty to an otherwise drab urban landscape.

In 1997 the estate was demolished, and Old Flo was moved 'temporarily' to Yorkshire Sculpture Park until a suitable public place could be identified in Tower Hamlets. The Mayor of Tower Hamlets later decided to sell the statue in a public auction, for an estimated £20 million, to help cover the council's budget deficit. This prompted a wave of popular protest. After the Mayor was forced to resign over evidence of electoral fraud, his successor promptly reversed the sale decision. In late 2017, the statue was brought back from Yorkshire. But there was a final irony. It was placed decoratively in a POPS (privately owned public space), among the glossy towers of Canary Wharf. Could it not have been placed in a still-existing social commons, as Henry Moore so passionately wanted? It would have added a little splendour to a low-income area, and given pleasure to many commoners, instead of adding to the privilege of an affluent one.

## The austerity hit

There have been extraordinary cuts in local government spending on all the arts since the beginning of the austerity era. Table 3 shows that between 2010 and 2020 local funding of statutory care services for children and adults, and waste disposal, to which local authorities are obliged to give priority, was set to increase significantly. But funding for non-statutory cultural and leisure services, including parks, museums, libraries, sports centres, swimming pools and theatres, represented a shrinking share of council tax by the end of the decade, with spending cut by over 50 per cent.

| Service area | Expenditure (£ billion) | | | Share of each £ of council tax | | |
|---|---|---|---|---|---|---|
| | 2010–11 | 2019–20 | % Change | 2010–11 | 2019–20 | % Change |
| Arts, museums, libraries, leisure and parks | 3.61 | 1.73 | −52 | 6.97 | 4.47 | −36 |
| Road repairs, street lighting | 3.58 | 2.04 | −43 | 6.91 | 5.27 | −24 |
| Bin collecting, recycling | 3.39 | 3.80 | +12 | 6.56 | 9.81 | +51 |
| Looking after children | 6.73 | 7.90 | +17 | 13.00 | 20.40 | +57 |
| Care for vulnerable adults | 14.53 | 15.44 | +6 | 23.08 | 39.89 | +42 |

**Table 3**

Local Government Expenditure in England, 2010–20

Source: *Local government expenditure in England*. Local Government Association media release, 23 March 2015.

In early 2015, when faced by further impending cuts, the chair of the Local Government Association observed sadly, 'It is likely that people will be paying similar levels of council tax over the next few years but most will see a lot less in return. People are rightly going to question why their streets and parks are less well kept, the local library is closing and bus services are being cut when they are still paying roughly the same council tax each month.'[22]

By early 2018 almost all local councils across Britain were in financial turmoil and Conservative-run Northamptonshire council had declared bankruptcy. Many councils reported that they were planning further cuts to services, with parks and leisure centres at the forefront, and many planned to raise money by investing in commercial property developments and commercializing services.[23] The cultural commons were under existential threat,[24] and local authorities in the most deprived areas had had the biggest cuts in spending power imposed on them.[25] The austerity-induced attack on the public cultural commons has proved to be another means of increasing social income inequality.

*

Shrinking the cultural commons – through austerity, privatization, colonization and outright neglect – has deleterious effects on society, including the loss of civic pride. The cultural commons is where and how we learn and refine our sense of sharing, our sense of empathy and our sense of humanity. Reflecting government's ideological priorities, cuts in funding for the cultural commons, directly and indirectly through slashing local authority budgets, have helped pay for tax cuts for the wealthy, corporations most of all.

The cultural commons has proved an easy target for cuts, partly because spending on it is discretionary and partly because most individual spheres of culture are of only minority interest. Providers of cultural services may not defend other parts of the cultural fabric out of a mistaken belief – or hope – that the attack will leave their own unscathed. However, a true cultural commons is one that supports a multiplicity of cultural traditions, so there is something for everyone: it gives commoners access to cultural activities that may be new to them, and it allows room for experimentation and development. Making the arts dependent on private and corporate philanthropy, or forcing them to raise revenue by commercializing their work, discourages diversity, depresses access by commoners, especially those on low incomes, and curbs experimentation.

The growth of income and wealth inequality has also contributed to the erosion of the cultural commons. The emergence of a global plutocracy has fuelled the amassing of private art collections by the very rich, who have been given added incentive to expand their ownership of art by favourable tax treatment. They have set up private museums and art galleries, and bought up major artworks, making it harder for public galleries to maintain standards.

Yet neo-liberal ideology has posed the biggest threat. While overseeing huge cuts in spending on the arts, Maria Miller, then Secretary of State for Culture, Media and Sport, wrote in 2013 that 'much of what we're hearing from the arts world is close to pure fiction. Accusations that this government neither likes nor supports the arts are disingenuous in the extreme.'[26] At that point, the budget had been cut by a quarter since 2010 and was about to be cut by much more. In the following year, under pressure from the Treasury to make further spending cuts, she tried to defend her domain by arguing that the arts were a valuable 'commodity' and a 'compelling product'.[27]

Depicting culture as a commodity reflects disdain for the cultural commons, which thrives because it is not a commodity. Seeing culture in terms of market value inevitably prompts thoughts of how to make more money from it, and thus debases its social role. Measuring the arts by narrow economic criteria of profit and loss belittles cultural aspects that have little or no market value and opens the way to treating culture and heritage as a commodity, for sale to the highest bidder.

Fortunately, society is fighting back against the philistine destruction of the cultural commons. Despite government cuts to public sector funding for protection of heritage sites and projects, there has been a growing number of public campaigns to protect them, some of which have been humble public properties that elites might disregard as cultural. Thus plans by the local council to demolish Preston bus station were stopped when public pressure led English Heritage to list the bus station as a heritage site.[28]

There are encouraging examples of commons movements in public culture elsewhere that could be emulated in Britain. In Italy, for example, a precariat group of actors, technicians, musicians and directors occupied the Teatro Valle in Rome in 2011 and argued for the legal right and power to manage a public resource. They had sufficient public support that the Rome authorities did not intervene, and for some considerable time they operated what was interpreted as an act of commoning. It was copied in Venice (Teatro Marinoni), Catania (Teatro Coppola), Naples (Asilo della creatività) and Palermo (Teatro Garibaldi).[29]

In the light of these examples, the following articles are suggested for a Commons Charter:

Article 34: The BBC has a unique role as a public service broadcaster. Its governance must be made more democratic and funding through the licence fee must be made independent of the government of the day.

Article 35: The erosion of the cultural commons represents a concealed form of impoverishment and inequality. The public sphere must be revived and funding for the cultural commons restored.

Article 36: To assist in the revival of commoning, in activities involving shared creative activity, fledgling cultural cooperatives should be supported.

These articles are more than gestures in the direction of reviving the cultural commons. They are an implicit recognition that the cultural commons cannot and should not be shaped and determined by government, local or national. Government should confine itself to helping create the space in which the cultural commons can flourish and even play a discomforting role in the public arena.

# CHAPTER 7

# The Knowledge Commons

> Broad dissemination of ideas and knowledge, based on the freest exchange and discussion, is essential to creative activity, the pursuit of truth and the development of the personality.
>
> — UNESCO Declaration of Principles of International Cultural Co-operation, Article VII.1, 1966

There are three distinct but overlapping aspects of the knowledge commons: informational (essentially news and facts), intellectual (ideas) and educational (learning processes). Together they go beyond the narrower idea of 'intellectual'.[1] A true knowledge commons would be one where ideas can be freely generated and shared, and where everybody can learn and develop their talents. In all these respects, the knowledge commons is shrinking.

## Information commons

Everybody should have equal access to adequate information on which to form an opinion or take action to the legitimate advantage of themselves, their family or their community, given the existing state of knowledge in society. But identifying and protecting the information commons is complex.

How do we deal with 'fake news' and manipulation by advertisers and software designers? We are saturated with information coming from all sides and lack the time and energy to sift through what is available. How do we ensure that information helps in acquiring knowledge, not reinforcing prejudice?

For centuries, the library was the base of the information commons. Today libraries are changing character, where they are not under deadly attack. Many universities are reforming their libraries explicitly as information commons, such as the University of Sheffield in Britain and Indiana University in the USA. However, public and scholarly libraries now represent only one source of information for citizens. With the advent of the internet, the World Wide Web and social media, they can call on a multiplicity of information sources.

For the most part, this has been beneficial. More people have access, at least in principle, to more and better information than in the past. Governments and local authorities in most democratic countries have become more transparent in their workings and more willing to put data they collect for their own purposes into the public domain for others to use. In 2015, the London-based Open Knowledge International estimated there were over 1 million datasets published on open-data portals.[2]

Wikipedia, now the fifth most visited website globally after Google, YouTube, Facebook and Baidu (the Chinese search engine), is part of the information commons, though it is subject to the biases and errors of its voluntary contributors. The internet itself is based on open standard protocols that are treated as a commons. According to Wikipedia:

> The internet took the information commons to another
> level. The internet age empowered consumers to become
> creators, producers and distributors of information.
> The internet facilitated a decentralized production and
> distribution of information. It bypasses the control of some
> of the more traditional publishing methods. These [sic]
> information are neither regulated by managers nor are they
> coordinated by price signals in the market. This result [sic]
> in a common-based production of knowledge that can be
> easily shared among individuals.[3]

This is a rosy interpretation, given that the internet has also made it easier to spread misinformation and malice. But, leaving that aside for the moment, the information commons is under threat – from enclosure, commodification, privatization and ideological capture.

The dominance of a handful of American technological leviathans – notably Alphabet (Google), Facebook and Amazon – in capturing, ordering and commodifying information is a form of enclosure.[4] Their global reach and monopolistic control are unprecedented. Apart from China, which is breeding its own global tech giants, Google has emerged as the dominant portal to knowledge, Amazon the dominant, information-based platform for online shopping, and Facebook the dominant channel of social media.

They have suppressed the competition by using their vast cash reserves as a financial war-chest, enabling them to buy any start-up firm that could become a rival or take their technological frontier in new directions. Over the decade to 2017, the Big Five tech corporations (Apple, Microsoft, Alphabet,

Facebook and Amazon) bought 519 smaller firms, vastly expanding their portfolio of intellectual property rights, snapping up scarce technological talent and extending the range of their production.[5] In the twenty years since its inception in 1998, Google (Alphabet since 2015) acquired over 200 firms, some of which, like Motorola, were very large entities just a few years previously.

This network stranglehold dwarfs the monopolistic control exerted by the 'robber barons' of the first Gilded Age in the late nineteenth and early twentieth centuries. The early barons each controlled one industry (oil, railways, steel). In this, a second Gilded Age, the new behemoths spread their tentacles widely and their ambitions seem unlimited. Alphabet is a hardware company, a software company, a car company, a commercial bazaar, a phone company, a home appliance company, an advertising agency, a social media company and a TV network.[6] It has also entered the sphere of mass schooling, buying schooling start-ups.

One similarity between the two Gilded Ages is open dismissal of 'free markets' and 'competition' by leading entrepreneurial figures. J. P. Morgan, the financier who at the beginning of the twentieth century played a pivotal role in establishing the supremacy of US finance, openly opposed free markets. Today, the mega-investor Peter Theil, co-founder of PayPal and in 2016 a major funder of Donald Trump's presidential campaign, dismisses competition as a 'relic of history'.

Big Tech undermines 'commons' democracy in asserting the supremacy of what has been called 'functional sovereignty' over the 'territorial sovereignty' of governments.[7]

The monopoly power of digital platforms in the functional markets where they operate – commerce (Amazon), transport (Uber), lettings (Airbnb) – means they can in effect dictate the terms on which others can sell goods and services in those markets. They have become regulators in all but name. And as their data-fuelled reach extends into new target areas – from dispute settlement to urban planning – so does their power to influence what happens in those areas, subjecting people to corporate rather than democratic control.

These corporations have become dominant through a unique combination of characteristics.[8] They benefit from 'network externalities' – the more users they have and so the larger their network, the more useful or attractive people find their services. This is particularly true of social media.[9] The more people they suck into their system, the harder it is for other firms to compete, and the harder it is to compete, the fewer are the competitors and the larger is the number of people who become dependent on their services.

They also benefit from 'scalability'. Economies of scale mean that the larger these corporations become, the lower the unit cost of providing the service and the greater the income they can extract from it. For 'pure' information services, such as Google search, access to information by one person does not prevent access by others, so the same information can be 'sold' multiple times. Information and data are not like lemons. If you sell a lemon to one person, you no longer have it to sell to anybody else.

Big Tech also gains from 'economies of scope'. It can use the vast amounts of personal data it collects from one service to bestow a competitive advantage in another, like self-driving cars or home speakers. For instance, the European Commission found that Google abused its dominance in search to boost its ranking in comparison shopping. All the leading tech companies are mobilizing data in this way as they set out to conquer new territory, giving them an inherent advantage over any potential rival.[10]

In another parallel with the first Gilded Age, it is sometimes claimed that data are to the early twenty-first century what oil was to the early twentieth century: the core commodity of the productive system.[11] Data are being used to create market value and new data-centric financial assets,[12] and a secondary data market has emerged. At least 270 data brokers worldwide, including Oracle Data Cloud, are already collecting and selling data of all kinds, mostly for the purposes of targeted advertising. These data are gleaned from public sources such as social media profiles or are bought from private companies such as corporate databases containing personal information about a company's customers.[13] Selling data can be a very profitable venture because, like other information, data are a quintessential 'public good'; since they do not disappear when transferred, the data can be sold over and over again without depleting their market value or their ultimate ownership.

Big Tech's products and services are designed to be addictive.[14] This is especially true of social media. The more that users are compulsively online and for longer periods, the higher the amount the firms can charge advertisers. Studies suggest use of social media triggers the production of dopamine, a chemical in the brain that affects the emotions. Our brains are being rewired to be less organized for deep thought and reflection, eroding our attention span, memory, sleep and happiness;[15] hence the flippant statement by Reed Hastings, CEO of Netflix, who said in 2017 that its main competitor was not Amazon Video or YouTube, but sleep.[16]

The glut of information (and misinformation) marshalled by Big Tech has led to saturation. Eric Schmidt, former CEO of Google, said in 2012 that every two days more information was being generated than was the case from the dawn of civilization until 2003. Paradoxically, the information flood induces a sense of knowledge scarcity, creating what David Foster Wallace has called 'Total Noise'.[17] In a famous quip, Herbert Simon, a Nobel prize-winning American economist, said, 'What information consumes is rather obvious. It consumes the attention of its recipients. Hence a wealth of information creates a poverty of attention.' In effect, the internet has spawned collective attention deficit disorder.

For help in navigating this mass of information, we rely on Big Tech to bring order to chaos. Google's mission statement is 'to organize the world's information and make it universally accessible and useful'. This is disingenuous. Information, even if it is not misinformation, is not neutral. It can be presented in different ways. Priority can be given to some aspects over others. Algorithms used to select and rank information for web search, digital assistants and so on build in the biases of the data they are trained on and those – conscious or unconscious – of their constructors. For example, if you search for 'Jerusalem' on Google, you are told that it is 'the capital of Israel'.[18] Yet the United Nations and all countries other than Israel (until Donald Trump's announcement in late 2017, followed subsequently by Guatemala and Brazil) have refused to recognize this. Palestinians regard it as their capital, and many countries do not recognize it as a capital city of anywhere. So, whatever one's view, Google is making a political statement, not simply providing information.

The Big Tech giants have already done more than just package and commodify information and knowledge much more extensively than at any time in history. They seek to de-common us and the way we live. Amazon, Facebook and Google are changing what we read, who we read and how we read. Over 60 per cent of Americans now obtain their news through social media, much of it via Facebook, while a third of all information on media sites comes through Google. The traditional print and broadcast media, with a reasonably diverse range of views and rooted in local communities and customs, the essence of the commons, are fading fast.

Their decline is being hastened by a concomitant loss of advertising revenue, which has migrated online. In the USA, between 2006 and 2017, spending on newspaper advertising fell by nearly 75 per cent, with most of the money redirected to Facebook and Google.[19] In 2017, these two corporations accounted for no less than 84 per cent of global spending on digital advertising, excluding China, making them a 'digital duopoly'.[20] Again excluding China, total global spending on digital advertising came to about $1,000 billion, almost all of it pure profit. The clever organization of user data, enabling advertisers to reach their target groups with amazing precision, has turned both companies into gigantic money machines.[21] Meanwhile, more newspapers are closing, and others are struggling. This has contributed to the consolidation of newspaper ownership and to takeovers by plutocrats with right-wing views and editorial policy, dangerously shrinking the range of political opinion being expressed.[22]

By far the biggest beast commercializing the information commons is Facebook. Set up in 2004, by late 2012 it had 1 billion users around the world each month, 55 per cent of whom used it every day. In 2018, it had 2.2 billion users, 66 per cent of whom used it every day. By then, Facebook also owned WhatsApp, with 1.5 billion users in early 2018; Messenger, with 1.3 billion users; and Instagram with 1 billion users. Others in the same league were YouTube, owned by Alphabet, with 1.8 billion monthly users, and the Chinese messaging and social media app WeChat, with 1 billion.

Facebook's original mission statement was 'making the world more open and connected'. By 2017, that had evolved into 'giving people the power to build community and bring the world closer together'. Yet, perversely, Facebook has reinforced separation or division, building communities of the like-minded by channelling information (or misinformation) streams to individual users that entrench their opinions and prejudices. Its financial interest lies, not in factual accuracy or disinterested impartiality, but in increasing the number of users and time spent on Facebook, so as to maximize income through targeted advertising. And by channelling different messages to different users based on their demographics, interests and habits, Facebook is helping to corrode the *agora*, the public space for deliberation and proper debate about issues and policies.

Other uses of data by Big Tech are also increasing enclosure and control, for instance, by granting exclusive access to data for research purposes. Facebook has launched a research project with a team at Stanford University to use its vast store of personal data to study US inequality.[23] Yet, contrary to normal ethical rules for such projects, the many millions of Americans who supplied that data for free were not made aware they could be used for subsequent research. News of the ongoing study coincided with an announcement that Facebook had patented a way of identifying people's socio-economic status from data on their hobbies and the internet devices they used.

One of Alphabet's acquired prodigies, London-based AI company DeepMind, has been using NHS data on 1.6 million patients to create an app to predict and detect acute kidney injury. In 2017 Britain's Information Commissioner ruled that London's Royal Free hospital had failed to comply with the 1988 Data Protection Act in handing over the data, because patients had not been adequately informed.[24] There was no question about the laudable motives behind the project, but the case highlights the risks for privacy in making personal data, even when anonymized, available for other uses. Experiments have shown that anonymized data, if sufficiently detailed, can be traced back to named individuals. Vigilant gatekeepers are needed to prevent abuse.

More worrying are data transfers with commercial intent. Experian, a UK-based consumer credit agency that partners with Facebook, has 850 million records on nearly 50 million British adults, with information on names, addresses, income levels, education, relationship status and everywhere the person has ever used a credit card. Those data, shared with Facebook's own, give the social media giant an extraordinary amount of information about identified individuals, for its own use and for use, permitted or illegitimate, by others.

There have also been instances of credit scoring agencies and other data harvesters 'losing' data on millions of people. While there is some protection under the 1988 Data Protection Act, that has not safeguarded British citizens from loss of data by foreign firms.

In 2017, Equifax, a consumer credit agency, revealed that it had 'lost' data it had amassed on 143 million people, sufficient to create fake identities for 40 per cent of the US population. It subsequently emerged that it had lost data on 44 million British citizens as well, in breach of the UK's Data Protection Act. The Equifax disclosure followed similar revelations by Yahoo that it had exposed personal details for 1 billion people in 2013 and 500 million people in 2014. In 2014 eBay confessed to leaking information on 145 million people.[25] Data breaches in 2018 included Google, Facebook, the Marriott hotel chain, airlines Delta, British Airways and Cathay Pacific, and retailers Best Buy, Sears and Saks Fifth Avenue.[26]

Since May 2018, firms losing data on EU citizens can be fined 4 per cent of global turnover, or €20 million, under the EU's General Data Protection Regulation (GDPR). The GDPR principles should be integrated into any post-Brexit trade deals Britain negotiates, especially with the United States where data protection is more lax. Most of the corporations profiting from use of personal data are US-owned and, so far, the USA has not adopted the GDPR concept of 'data creators owning their own data'. The GDPR is a complex regulatory device that is challenging for companies, especially smaller firms, to implement. It may even reduce the rate of growth of what has been dubbed the 'global datasphere', which is fore-cast to expand tenfold between 2016 and 2025.[27] But it is a start in regulating the plunder of the information commons.

Equifax, Experian and Callcredit, the three main credit reference agencies in the UK, also deal with 'identity ver-ification' for the British government, in its hunt to track down and prosecute 'benefit cheats'. They can check whether someone else is living at the claimant's address or if credit card records suggest the household is receiving other income. But their data may be open to misinterpretation or simply wrong. This has led to benefits being withdrawn from desperate people based on incorrect information they know nothing about.

A potentially transformational moment came in March 2018 with the revelation that Cambridge Analytica had used Facebook profiles, ostensibly gathered for a research project, to target political messages supporting Brexit, the latest in a series of data-based interventions by the company in polit-ical campaigns in various countries. Public disgust was wide-spread. Perhaps it may prove to be the moment that inspires serious measures to recover the informational commons.

If so, it is not a moment too soon. Big Tech has become central to 'surveillance capitalism'.[28] The vast surveillance operation run by the US National Security Agency, heroical-ly revealed by Edward Snowden, scoops up data on many millions of people from social media, email, messaging and phone records, breaching privacy rules. Meanwhile, Apple boasts about the strong encryption on its iPhones and states on its webpage: 'At Apple we believe privacy is a fundamental human right.' Yet in 2018, Apple made iCloud data from its users in China accessible to the Chinese government when it transferred data management to a Chinese company. That company, governed by Chinese law, is obliged to hand over user data if requested to do so.[29]

China has been perfecting a surveillance system called 'Social Credit' that, according to the authorities, will 'allow the trustworthy to roam everywhere under heaven while making it hard for the discredited to take a single step'.[30] Detailed information is being collected on every individual to rate them as creditworthy and as 'citizens'. Even having low-rated friends may lead to somebody being denied access to credit, to jobs, to travel visas, and so on. It is an Orwellian control system.

Similar techniques are being developed elsewhere. In 2015, Facebook patented a credit-rating system that takes into account the financial history of people's friends. So you can be denied a loan or have to pay more for one simply because one of your friends was a gambler or in debt. And insurance companies are replacing the pooled-risk system to determine premiums – charging standard premiums based on average risk – by highly targeted systems based on personal characteristics, including data drawn from social media. If you are deemed a bad risk, you will pay higher premiums or be denied insurance altogether. This is statistical discrimination designed to shape and control behaviour.

Preservation of the information commons, like other forms of commons, depends on the existence of commons-oriented gatekeepers. By controlling access and what constitutes proper behaviour and output, they can hold people to the ethics and boundaries of a commons, monitoring the stewards (owners) as well as commoners. A British Data Protection Agency stronger than the existing Information Commissioner's Office is needed to protect privacy, which the market will destroy if left to itself.

In the mass media, the gatekeepers of the information commons have always been the editors, responsible for deciding what constitutes 'news', what priority should be given to various topics, what taste to display, what statements should be checked, and what risk to take in making accusations about immoral behaviour by public figures. Over many generations, great newspaper editors have become honoured citizens, showered with tokens of recognition towards the end of their careers. Most have had political biases. But they have usually sought a balance between three interests – the stewards (formal owners), the commoners (journalists and other staff) and the reading public. Today the technocratic purveyors of information have little interest in balance, preferring to go where their financial interests take them.

Jeff Bezos, Amazon's American CEO with a fortune of $161 billion as of 2018, candidly told Amazon investors that he rejected the need for gatekeepers, since in his view they inhibited innovation. He claimed that information is so abundant that it can be allowed to flow without restraint, seeing Amazon as a great bazaar in which there is no need for himself, or anybody else, to be a guardian of the community. Instead, Amazon has taken the commercialization of culture to a new level, selling just about everything and giving priority to what makes the most money. By 2017, it was selling 65 per cent of all e-books and over 40 per cent of all print books sold in the world.[31] In the life-and-death struggle with traditional publishers (their death), Amazon holds by far the upper hand, setting the terms that publishers must accept or have their books excluded from its algorithms and promotions.

Facebook has been commodifying the media commons through its news feed, which CEO and co-founder Mark Zuckerberg has depicted as a 'personalized newspaper'. Like Bezos, he saw little need for gatekeepers to monitor the veracity or provenance of the information going to people's news feeds. (In 2015, 725 of Facebook's top 1,000 most viewed videos were identified as stolen from their originators.[32]) The result has been a flood of fake news and misinformation going unchecked into people's news feeds, targeted to their Facebook profiles, with the potential to influence momentous political events. Donald Trump's election in 2016 as President of the United States and before that the victory of the Leave campaign in the referendum on the UK's membership of the European Union are obvious examples.

If there is no check on truth, the concept of information is corrupted. Facebook has reinforced the trend for people to shrink into informational silos – opting for sources that reinforce their own views and excluding others that challenge them – and to dismiss all contrary information as opinion or 'fake'. This has opened the way for the rich and powerful, and those controlling the media, to manipulate what purports to be information to promote their own interests against those of the precariat and other commoners. Truth, democracy and equality are the victims.

Even where misinformation is not involved, for whoever

can pay, Big Tech is playing a growing role in determining political winners. Google has boasted about the use of Google Analytics in securing Barack Obama's election victory in 2012, enabling Obama's campaign to reach target groups of voters.[33] This is taking society further away from what might be called a commons-driven democracy.

The information commons is also destroyed when Big Tech acts as an ideological gatekeeper. To give just one example, Instagram, Facebook's photo-sharing platform, bowed to demands by the Russian government to remove videos showing Oleg Deripaska, a Russian oligarch, entertaining the deputy prime minister on a yacht in Norway which opposition leaders claimed was a bribe. Instagram said it was obliged to do this to comply with Russian law.

When evidence first emerged that Facebook had been used by Russian agents to influence the November 2016 US presidential election, Mark Zuckerberg simply denied fake news was a problem. 'More than 99 per cent of what people see is authentic. Only a very small amount is fake news and hoaxes,' he said in a Facebook post. Several commentators hastened to point out that, on their news feeds, his post ran next to stories that were demonstrably false and fraudulent.

Zuckerberg was in denial. In one horrific example of the role of fake news in stirring social tension, a video was posted on Facebook in Sri Lanka showing a Muslim chef apparently putting sterilization pills in food intended for Singhalese customers. It went viral across the country and provoked riots that resulted in two deaths and the destruction of homes and shops owned by Muslims. The video was an invention intended to incite religious hatred.

In 2018, an online petition called on Zuckerberg to protect democracy by exposing 'fake users and disinformation campaigns', banning 'all fake or imposter user accounts', notifying users each time they are exposed to fake or malicious content, and funding an independent army of fact-checkers 'big enough and fast enough to stem the spread of lies'.

As the revelations became incontrovertible, Zuckerberg changed his stance, expressing regret that 'my work was used to divide people'. In 2018, after being summoned to testify in the US Congress and the European Parliament, he announced the hiring of 10,000 additional 'moderators', doubling the number of gatekeepers to police not only fake news but other material deemed undesirable. YouTube and Twitter said they would add thousands of moderators for the same reason. But this is a stop-gap, public-relations move to placate public anger, since there is no way that even many thousands of moderators can screen the sheer volume of incoming material posted by users all over the world. And while social media platforms are working on artificial intelligence (AI) solutions, these are currently highly imperfect, for example, excluding pictures on breastfeeding sites as sexual images.

Nevertheless, as Guy Verhofstadt, the former Belgian Prime Minister, has written, 'The tech giants . . . will continue to claim that they are merely distributing information. In fact, they are acting as publishers, and should be regulated accordingly – and not just as publishers, but as near monopoly distributors.'[34]

Tim Berners-Lee, inventor of the World Wide Web, points out that allowing a handful of platforms to control which ideas and opinions are seen and shared has made it possible 'to weaponize the web at scale'. As a consequence, 'we've seen conspiracy theories trend on social media platforms, fake Twitter and Facebook accounts stoke social tensions, external actors interfere in elections, and criminals steal troves of personal data'.[35] He has founded the World Wide Web Foundation to fight for the web's future as a free, open and creative space for all.

If Big Tech makes information little more than incessant noise, that will further weaken people's ability, energy and concentration to sift truth from falsehood. And it will create even more fertile ground for populists to offer simplistic, superficial and prejudiced solutions to social tensions, in which blaming minorities (such as migrants) will be all too easy.

There is a place for satire and cartoons, but protection against gullibility and hate speech is alien to the disruptive intentions of Zuckerberg and his fellow innovators. Commoners need a commons gatekeeper, in the form of a regulatory agency charged with holding Big Tech to democratically decided standards. It cannot be left to powerful commercial corporations to regulate themselves in the common interest. They just will not do it.

Big Tech is postmodern: it implies that there is no such thing as truth, only opinion and emotion. Progress comes in the machine, in the engineering, not in the human being. Much is written about the ramifications of AI, including its potential threat to political stability and privacy.[36] But Silicon Valley's master project, epitomized by the notion of 'singularity' – the point when the artificial mind is equal to the human mind – is about trying to enclose thinking by inventing super-intelligent machines that can think for humans, better than humans. This is not just about technology: it is an ideology. If AI and 'deep learning' can identify patterns of thinking, they can also be used to shape information and the way humans think. 'Certainly, if you had all the world's information directly attached to your brain, or an artificial brain that was smarter than your brain, you'd be better off,' Sergey Brin, Google's co-founder, has said. 'Perhaps in the future, we can attach a little version of Google that you just plug into your brain.'[37] Of course, this would be information ordered by Google, driven by its commercial interests and all the biases built into its sprawling algorithms. The enclosure of the information commons is generating a colossal flow of income and power to a tiny plutocracy.

Some recommend nationalization of the data-accumulating technology corporations, on the basis that they are natural monopolies and so prime candidates for public ownership.[38] However, nationalization is not a practical option, given that the public good in question is global, not national in character. Instead, policy should emphasize greater democratic control, if necessary through regulation, curbs on monopolistic profits and measures to capture for commoners part of the income they generate in the information commons. How to do this is considered later.

Ownership and control of one's own data is another necessity. Tim Berners-Lee and Nigel Shadbolt claim that 'we are at the start of a personal asset revolution, in which our personal data, held by government agencies, banks and businesses, will be returned to us to store and manage as we think fit.'[39] The World Economic Forum has proposed creating data bank accounts to hold an individual's data, where they could be managed and sold.

Data portability, which would enable, say, Facebook users to switch to another social media service and take their data with them, is supported in the EU's GDPR, but has been little used so far. Some have suggested workers in the platform economy would benefit from portable ratings, so, for example, 'Master Worker' status bestowed by Amazon Mechanical Turk could be transferred to another platform.[40] However, it is well documented that worker 'ratings' are not objective and can be highly dubious and misleading. Poor ratings do not necessarily signify poor performance.

Finally, a true information commons must be available to all. Today more than half the world's population have access to the internet, but its ubiquity in all areas of life has worsened the 'digital divide' between those with access and those without. In 2016 the United Nations declared internet access to be a human right, on a par with clean water, electricity, shelter and food. The UN also adopted the Alliance for Affordable Internet's target threshold of affordability, a target that accessing the internet should cost less than 2 per cent of national average monthly income. The world is still a long way from reaching that goal, but it should surely be incorporated into foreign aid policy and anti-poverty policy at home.

Article 37: Data must be owned by the individuals who generate them and used only for purposes to which they agree.

Article 38: Regulation is needed to protect privacy and require tech companies to meet democratically decided standards, including removing and barring false or malicious content.

Article 39: The principles in the European Union's General
Data Protection Regulations should be integrated into
any UK post-Brexit trade deals.

## Intellectual commons

Inventions then cannot, in nature, be a subject of
property.
— Thomas Jefferson, 1813

Knowledge and ideas are public goods, or should be, since
one person having them does not prevent others having
them. They should be part of the intellectual commons,
available to all. Yet the global intellectual property regime
has instead diminished our intellectual commons, awarding
vast sums to wealthy corporations and individuals while depriving lower-income groups of access to knowledge and the
product of ideas.

There are exceptions, of course. Tim Berners-Lee refused
to take out a patent on the technology of the World Wide
Web, so that it could be a global resource to be developed
freely as users wanted. He has dedicated his professional
life ever since to the building of a global intellectual commons. Similarly, in 1955 Jonas Salk, who had just developed
the polio vaccine, was asked by the iconic American TV inter-
viewer, Ed Murrow, 'Who owns the patent on this vaccine?'
'Well,' Salk said, 'the people, I would say. There is no patent.
Could you patent the sun?'

The main defence of intellectual property rights derives
from John Locke's *Second Treatise of Government*, which influenced the US Constitution and bourgeois property law.[41]

His argument, based on the labour theory of value, was that ideas are the result of individual labour, which should be rewarded with property. The Lockean justification fails, however, if ideas are seen mainly as collective, piecemeal or due to luck, guesses or to previous privileged access to the ideas of others. Locke in the seventeenth century saw ideas as inventions, mainly drawn from hard, time-consuming manual labour. But ideas may also stem from having fun and may be a source of happiness, far removed from labour. Moreover, most ideas are derivative, based on a Lego castle of previous ideas. There is no justification for giving the person who lays the last brick the whole castle as a reward.

Turning ideas into intellectual property rights, so denying their use to others, contrives scarcity by limiting common access to information. Capturing information for privileged commercial use drives up the price, giving the right-holders extra income. And intellectual property rights have been strengthened worldwide by an elaborate network centred on the World Trade Organization (WTO) and the World Intellectual Property Organization (WIPO), both based in Geneva.[42]

Led and shaped by the USA, the Agreement on Trade-Related Aspects of Intellectual Property Rights (TRIPS) came into force in 1995 as part of the international accord creating the WTO. TRIPS extended existing property rights in ideas by making WIPO treaties on patents, copyright, industrial designs, trademarks (brands) and so on binding on all WTO members. It was the single biggest blow against the intellectual commons in history.

TRIPS globalized the American model of intellectual property, following a campaign led by US multinationals, notably pharmaceutical companies. As the CEO of Pfizer boasted, 'Our combined strength allowed us to establish a global private sector/government network to lay the ground for what became TRIPS.' At the time, the World Bank estimated that the USA would gain many billions of dollars of extra income, at huge cost to developing countries including China. It was an act of economic colonialism.

Take patents. An inventor – an individual, institute or, more usually, a company – can apply for a patent which, if granted by a national patent office, gives the 'owner' a monopoly income from use of the patent for twenty years. Drug patents can be extended for even longer by fiddling with the composition or presentation, or through data exclusivity rules that delay production of cheaper generic equivalents.

In 1995, fewer than 1 million patents were filed with national authorities. In 2017, 3.2 million were filed, and 13.7 million patents were in force worldwide. The Director General of WIPO has called for many more. While there are no estimates of the global income from patents, the revenue from patent licensing alone (excluding companies' exploitation of their own patents) was put at some $500 billion in 2009, since when it will certainly have risen further.[43]

Proponents of intellectual property protection claim that a monopoly income is a necessary reward for taking risks in spending money and ingenuity to develop something. If there were no prospective patent, companies would not invest in the research; innovation and the associated economic growth would be slowed, holding back social and economic 'progress'. There are three lines of retort to this. Why twenty years, and not ten or five? The length of the patent term is arbitrary and has been lengthened over time largely due to lobbying by industrial corporations. What about other ways of rewarding risky investment, such as national or sectoral prizes? A prize system would incentivize inventors without turning innovations into monopolistic property owners. And, most fundamentally, what is the evidence that patents stimulate ideas and innovation?

Many of the most lucrative patents stem from publicly funded research in publicly funded institutions. This means the public, the commoners, are shouldering all or part of the risk, especially since much company spending on R&D receives government subsidies, directly or in the form of generous tax breaks. In the USA, this was institutionalized by the Bayh–Dole Act (or Patent and Trademark Law Amendments Act) of 1980, which allowed firms to patent inventions derived from publicly funded research.

There is also, rather awkwardly for the defenders of the plunder of ideas, no evidence that intellectual property rights increase the pace of innovation.[44] Historically, nations with strong patent systems have not been more innovative than those without them, and nations with longer patent terms have not been more innovative than those with shorter patent terms.[45] A study in 2017 found no evidence that increased levels of intellectual property protection lead to faster economic growth.[46]

Many patents have no demonstrable societal benefit. Since 1998 there has been a huge growth in the number of, and revenue from patents relating to financial services, such as clever schemes for financial derivatives, filed by the largest financial institutions to boost their already enormous rental incomes.[47] Many patents are taken out simply to stop the production of a potential rival product or service, thus inhibiting production rather than stimulating it.

The intellectual property rights system has been further entrenched by over 3,000 bilateral, regional or multilateral trade and investment agreements. Many of these agreements incorporate ISDS (Investor-State Dispute Settlement), which enables corporations to sue governments for compensation in an international tribunal of three corporate lawyers if they think a policy change will affect their future profits. This un-democratic and opaque legal device has strengthened the ability of multinational corporations to oblige governments to enforce their intellectual property 'rights'.[48]

The patenting of genetic resources, which belong to us all as commoners, is particularly offensive. In one little-noticed development, since the 1990s there has been a remarkably rapid and extensive patenting of 'marine genetic resources' (MGR) for commercial applications,[49] in anticipation of an era of 'blue growth' dominated by resources from the oceans. Who controls them will matter.

The past two decades have seen a few firms rushing to file thousands of patents relating to hundreds of marine species. This enclosure and privatization of the 'blue commons' has also led to a striking, almost imperial, colonization of them and, as with Big Tech, to a dominant position by a single firm. Entities in just three countries account for three-quarters of all MGR patents: Germany (49 per cent), the USA (13 per cent) and Japan (12 per cent) – with seven others taking up almost all the remainder. And while patents have been filed by just over 200 companies, one has been pre-eminent. It is the Germany-based multinational BASF, the world's largest chemical producer, which 'owns' nearly half the patented marine sequences. BASF coexists with an even more hegemonic research company, Yeda, the commercial arm of the Weizmann Institute of Science in Israel, which has more MGR patents than all other research institutes and universities in the world put together. BASF, like Big Tech, is big enough to buy up any potential competitor and to force other firms to abide by rules it sets de facto. Commercial exploitation of the blue commons will in effect be controlled by one firm, one research company and three countries. Britain will be one of the countries paying them rental income on a colossal scale. The commons and commoners will be the losers.

Patents are only one way by which the intellectual commons are captured. Copyright, too, gives a right to monopoly income on literary and artistic works. It has existed for centuries, having started in fifteenth-century Venice, but has been extended and made global, notably by TRIPS. Again, Thomas Jefferson was an early critic, depicting it as a tax on knowledge. It may seem reasonable that writers, artists and other creatives should benefit if money is made from their work and should have some control over how their work is used. Less defensible is the longevity of this monopoly. Copyright for literary and artistic works now runs for the duration of the person's life plus seventy years after death.

In 1710, in the reign of Queen Anne, the world's first copyright Act granted copyright protection for publications for fourteen years, extendable, if the writer was still living, for another fourteen years. This was copied in the US Copyright Act of 1790, although it applied only to US citizens and residents. Gradually, protection was extended to music and much else during the nineteenth century. But the period of fourteen years has been swept aside, with much longer periods applying globally, enabling publishers, music companies, broadcasters and others to go on denying commoners free access to copyrighted works for many years.

To take just two examples, *Selma*, a film about Martin Luther King, was unable to use the actual words of his speeches, including the iconic 'I have a dream' address in 1963, because his estate denied permission. 'I have a dream' will not be in the public domain until 2039. Similarly, until 2015 when its copyright was overturned, Warner Chappell Music was able for many decades to recoup royalties for public performances of 'Happy Birthday', thought to be the most sung song in the world, and prevent others using it in films and broadcasts.

Journalist Paul Mason has claimed that, although corporations seek to restrict the supply of information, it remains abundant, since 'information goods are freely replicable'.[50] If this were the case, open access campaigners would have nothing to complain about. But powerful institutions and regulations promote the commercial capture of information as intellectual property, making much of it neither available, nor free, nor legally replicable.

Intellectual property accounts for a large part of 'intangible' assets in the modern production system. The imputed value of intangibles, which also includes the rather nebulous 'goodwill', is rising rapidly relative to tangible assets such as buildings, land and machines, and in the UK and the USA at least has already surpassed that of tangibles.[51] Admittedly, any calculation will be subject to substantial error, especially as many companies find it hard if not impossible to estimate the value of their own 'intellectual property', and some no doubt underestimate it for tax reasons.[52]

The main concern here is that value attributed to intellectual property is being sucked from the commons. What would happen if, by a stroke of a pen of a philosopher king, all time limits on intellectual property were halved (or more) – to ten years in the case of patents and perhaps back to the old rule of fourteen years in the case of copyright? That would be a good blow for the intellectual commons, and for citizenship and equality. Sadly, it is unlikely to happen.

While the USA has promoted intellectual property rights and trumpeted the virtues of free private markets, it has long largely socialized its R&D, albeit under other names. Most major innovations have come from places heavily subsidized by government. However, resolute in support of its big corporations, the US government has privatized the results. The federal authorities have directed most subsidies to research on what they believe will become the big areas of profit-making in decades to come, a strategy known as the 'Chomsky trade'. Noam Chomsky once said, tongue in cheek no doubt, that the way to make money was to see where federal research was going and then pitch money into those firms linked to it, to gain returns in thirty years.[53]

The public pays for the development of innovations and for the risks. In a just society it would be the public who gained all or most of the economic rewards. Instead, corporations that take up and patent those inventions gain all the profits, and in addition often manage to avoid tax on those profits. The intellectual commons are plundered, primarily by plutocratic corporations and the plutocrats and elite who hold shares in them.

Increasingly, the rewards are going to companies outside the USA, notably China. By 2011, China had overtaken the USA in patent applications, and in 2017 it filed more patent applications than the USA, Japan, South Korea and the European Patent Office combined. A similar shift is occurring with industrial designs and trademarks. But while US President Trump has denounced China in characteristically bellicose language for 'intellectual property theft', it is worth remembering that the USA once indulged in much the same practices vis-à-vis Europe.

Two centuries ago the US Treasury offered bounties to successful thieves of patented techniques. Samuel Slater, the Englishman said by US President Andrew Jackson to have been 'the Father of the American Industrial Revolution', was dubbed 'Slater the traitor' in England for taking textile manufacturing secrets across the Atlantic. The USA also refused to accept foreign copyright protection and did not sign the 1886 Berne Convention for the Protection of Literary and Artistic Works until 1988. Charles Dickens was the most well-known loser; he complained bitterly that his *Christmas Carol* was pirated and sold in the USA for about one-fortieth of the price in Britain.

Now China is insisting that American companies partnering with Chinese companies in China must share their intellectual property. Whether or not this constitutes 'theft', the reality is that China has overtaken the USA in the legitimate sphere. There are now two giants keen on extending the plunder of the intellectual commons and there seems little prospect of rolling back the system, even though it is increasingly clear that the neo-liberal economic rationale for it is fallacious and damaging. Privatizing and commodifying the intellectual commons does not promote faster or better innovation. It merely enriches private property holders at the commoners' expense.

The following articles for a Commons Charter should be regarded as skeleton commitments to help restore the intellectual commons.[54] They require coordinated international action since they run counter to TRIPS and the remit of the World Intellectual Property Organization.

> Article 40: Intellectual property rights are too strong and are depleting the knowledge commons. Patent applications should be more strictly vetted and their duration shortened.
>
> Article 41: Copyright protection should end with the death of the author or artist or, reverting to the old rule, last for fourteen years after creation of the work if the author or artist dies within that period.

## The educational commons

The educational commons are the physical facilities, the institutional fabric and the people that enable learning, available to all. Teachers should be integrated into the community, passing on the wisdom of time and place. Commons-based education involves learning how to survive and flourish in the communities we inhabit and gaining empathy and understanding, in the context of local customs forged 'in time immemorial'.

Education is a natural 'public good', since one person having more of it does not prevent another from having more of it as well. We can all gain from more education. But the modern commercialization of the education 'industry' has turned more of what purports to be education into a commodity. If I have more than you, I am more competitive than you and thus can expect to earn more than you. Almost everything on education that appears in the mass media these days seems to put most emphasis on income and job effects.

Education should be liberating, a process of self-discovery and the pursuit of truth, knowledge and creativity. A famous statement misattributed to Thomas Jefferson but said to reflect his views is that the primary purpose of education should be to teach someone to be a good citizen. John Stuart Mill put it even better in a defence of liberal education in a speech on being installed as Rector of St Andrew's University in 1867. It still resonates:

> At least there is tolerably general agreement about what an
> university is not. It is not a place of professional education.
> Universities are not intended to teach the knowledge
> required to fit men for some special mode of gaining their
> livelihood. Their object is not to make skilful lawyers,
> or physicians or engineers, but capable and cultivated
> human beings . . . Men are men before they are lawyers,
> or physicians, or merchants, or manufacturers; and if
> you make them capable and sensible men, they will make
> themselves capable and sensible lawyers or physicians.[55]

One can quibble and scoff that, back in the Victorian era, universities were class-bound and zones of privilege, reserved for a tiny minority. But the ethos went back to the origins of universities in giving a prominent role to the creation and refinement of character. Education loses its integrity once it becomes little more than a sphere of market forces, property rights and rent-seeking. Institutions should also have character. St Andrews should not be expected to be the same as Cambridge or Yale or any other university. Universities, colleges and schools should reflect and even celebrate the local, the vernacular. This is an essential attribute of an educational commons. Standardized schooling is a form of enclosure.

The ethos represented by Jefferson and Mill was reflected in the Robbins Report of 1963, probably the most influential report on tertiary education in Britain's history. It reiterated the functions of universities as perceived before the onset of the neo-liberal era: the 'instruction of skills', combined with 'the promotion of the general powers of the mind so as to produce not mere specialists but rather cultivated men and women'; 'the search for truth'; and the transmission of a common culture and common standards of citizenship. That seems a fair benchmark by which to judge the commodifying reforms of recent years. They have not adhered to those aspirations.

State (public) schools freely available to all should be the rock on which a commons-based system is constructed. As the United Nations' Special Rapporteur on the right to education said in 2015, 'Privatization in education negatively affects the right to education both as entitlement and as empowerment.'[56] But in recent years budgets for state schools have been squeezed in many countries, including Britain, while private schooling – including schools run by religious or ideologically motivated organizations – has been boosted by subsidies and grants.

In the USA, some state school boards face bankruptcy, having borrowed heavily to fund their schools in the face of shrinking tax revenues. In the UK, state schools have been laying off staff, and school buildings have been falling into disrepair. With state schools under stress, barely holding on to their commons orientation, privatization of schooling has been developing fast. Successive British governments have matched US charter schools by expanding quasi-private 'academies' and 'free schools', publicly subsidized, private-ly run schools. In addition, despite charging astronomic-al fees, more than half the 2,707 so-called 'public' (private fee-paying) schools, such as Eton and Harrow, have charity status entitling them to substantial tax breaks.

State schools pay full business rates to local councils while private schools receive 80 per cent rate relief, amounting to over £100 million a year in lost public revenue.[57] Fee-paying schools take only 7 per cent of all pupils, who by definition come from affluent families, so these subsidies privilege priv-ilege and are paid for by taxpayers, most of whom could not dream of sending their children to such schools.

The government has also encouraged privatization by giving 'free schools' 60 per cent more funding per pupil than local authority state schools. A quarter of free schools re-ceived twice as much or more in 2013–4, while a primary school that was part of the Future Academies chain run by the government's then academies minister, Lord Nash, and his wife received four times as much for each of its twenty-six pupils.[58]

Academies and free schools have generated a predictable spate of amoral opportunistic actions that have nevertheless failed to divert the government from its disastrous privatization course. In 2015, the Griffin Schools Trust, a small academy schools chain, was shown to have paid more than £700,000 in two years to consulting companies owned by the trust's two joint chief executives, and about £100,000 to three other consultancies in which the trustees had a majority interest.[59] An investigation by *The Guardian* a year earlier revealed that the largest such chain in the country, Academies Enterprise Trust (AET), had paid nearly £500,000 in three years to the private business interests of its trustees and executives.

The Perry Beeches Academy Trust was lauded by then Prime Minister David Cameron as among the best in the country, and its CEO appeared to much applause at the Conservative Party's annual conference in 2012. Just over three years later, he had to resign following an investigation into financial mismanagement, leaving the five schools the trust managed in a parlous financial state.[60] He had been arranging payments to his companies without contracts, and over £2.5 million in funding for free school meals could not be checked because eligibility records had been destroyed.

In another case, taxpayers were paying £468,000 a year so that a 'free' primary school could rent land and buildings from an investment fund, Legal and General Property. This payment, index-linked to inflation, was guaranteed for twenty-five years. The investment fund issued a press release saying its purchase of the school 'represents an attractive opportunity to access a long-term secure income stream, backed by the government'.[61]

Schooling has become a profitable commodity for private investors, a negation of an educational commons. Introducing a corporate model to primary and secondary schooling transfers what should be a public good into a commercial zone, except that instead of profits rewarding a risk taken by a private company, the risk is ultimately borne by the public. If an academy trust or chain goes bankrupt or decides to pull out, the schools are left without funds, leaving the Department for Education to find the money while it considers applicant firms offering to take over the 'business'.[62] The risks and uncertainty are borne by the parents and children, and the obligatory rescue costs are borne by taxpayers.

In September 2017, the Wakefield City Academies Trust, which ran twenty-one schools across Yorkshire, declared just after the start of the school term that it was disbanding. This was after the trust had syphoned off millions of pounds to its own accounts from school reserves, some of which had been raised by local parents and other volunteers for school improvements and equipment.[63] Pupils were left recycling old exercise books. Meanwhile, the chief executive of the trust had paid himself handsomely and ensured that payments to his information technology and clerking companies were made before disbanding. It then came to light that, only a year earlier, the government had instructed a failing school to join the trust, thereby obliging it to hand over its surplus funds. Shortly afterwards, a leaked internal report by the Department for Education concluded that the trust was in an 'extremely vulnerable position as a result of inadequate governance, leadership and overall financial management'. By allowing the situation to continue for almost a year, the government was partly responsible for what transpired. It gives the lie to its 'gatekeeper' claim that 'we will not hesitate to take swift action' if problems arise.[64]

After the Wakefield Trust collapsed, the Department for Education named eight preferred new sponsors, one of which had already been stripped of three of its schools because of low standards. A National Education Union activist told the media in frustration, 'We are not football teams. We are not part of the transfer market, where we can be transferred from one multi-academy trust to another.' But this is precisely what schooling has been reduced to.

The two models of commons and capitalism do not function together. Once privatization of the educational commons is undertaken, asset stripping is inevitable. Those who set up or manage academy trusts, which are notionally non-profit, are geared to making money and minimizing losses, whatever gloss is put on their 'mission statements'. By early 2018, reflecting the strains of austerity, many of the multi-academy trusts were reported to be in financial difficulty and reacting by overcrowding schools and curbing teacher numbers and pay.[65] At the end of 2017, over sixty academy schools and their students were in limbo because the trusts responsible for them had gone out of business or relinquished the schools.

The commercialization of public education began under Thatcher and continued under New Labour and subsequent Conservative-led governments. The stepping-stone to privatization was state subsidization of private provision and the encouragement of partnerships with commercial interests. Many state schools have been lured into 'school–business partnerships' that epitomize the surrender of a commons.

In 1998, in the London Borough of Tower Hamlets, home to the Canary Wharf financial district and close to the City of London, a large well-established state secondary school linked up with an American bank to run the school. In a developing country, this might have been decried as an act of colonialism. The bank 'invested' £500,000 in the school over a decade, while its executives chaired the school's governing body, and bank staff helped in classes. Pupils were said to talk about the bank 'as though they were a department at the end of the corridor'.[66]

The headmistress claimed that for a school–business partnership to work it was necessary to have a 'shared culture'. Surely, a state school should not share the culture (if that is the right word) of any particular interest, and certainly not that of an American investment bank. The bank in question was Lehman Brothers, whose later ignominious collapse due to reckless speculation and unethical practices led the world into the financial crisis of 2008. The school was converted into an instrument of commerce, a far cry from preserving the commons and the values enshrined in it.

Nomura, the Japanese bank that took over Lehman's remnants, decided to continue the partnership with the school. About fifty other businesses have formed partnerships with schools in Tower Hamlets, including multinationals and banks, all presumably trying to embellish their corporate reputations. This pattern has spread across Britain.

Even presuming that the motives of these companies are

altruistic, we should feel uncomfortable about the influence of commercial interests in schools. Suppose a local trade union were partnering with a school, with an office at the end of the corridor. Very different cultural values would be imparted. It would also be inappropriate. Favouring any special interest is a threat to principles of universalism and autonomy. Having a commercial partner, especially one on the school board, is likely to influence the approach of at least some of the teachers in deciding what is taught.

In 2018 more than a third of senior government ministers were privately educated (though not Prime Minister Theresa May), and it is not surprising that a Conservative government is running down the state sector while channelling funds to private alternatives. But for a long time, the opposition Labour Party did little more than complain that the government's failure to invest in young people was 'holding the economy back'. What an alienated view! Education is for developing knowledge and understanding, not for making money. That is the foundational principle on which the public, or state school system should be based.

There has also been increased 'enclosure' of schooling by centralizing government control of content, standards and efficiency. This cements a norm-driven orthodoxy rather than a diverse, commons-driven flourishing of ideas and creativity, and sits oddly with the government's rhetoric of choice and independence. Not only have governments encouraged privatization, they have also promoted particular types of choice, as in the case of faith-based schools. Such schools encourage division based on religion and may run curricula that give religious beliefs priority, to the detriment of students – for example, teaching creationism as an alternative to evolution or banning girls from taking swimming or gym classes. Similarly, when a government encourages school–business partnerships, it is shaping the choice, putting commerce-oriented gatekeepers in schools in a position to influence appointments of teachers and the values expressed.

The choice of how and what is taught and learned is curtailed if a narrow curriculum is set at national level. As George Monbiot fumed, 'The best teachers use their character, creativity and inspiration to trigger children's instinct to learn. So why are character, creativity and inspiration suppressed by a stifling regime of micro-management?'[67] The government's claims on choice are contradicted by its insistence, backed by constant checks, that teachers conform to a singular model of teaching. This has led to strains within the teaching community, leading to rising rates of resignations and breakdowns.

To these incursions on the education commons must be added the impact of austerity in slashing spending by local authorities. This has hit the creative and empathy-strengthening character of learning that the educational commons should be promoting. Consider the teaching of music, deeply embedded in British history and the commons, which has always been a central feature of public schooling – until now. State schools traditionally employed music teachers and, from the 1950s until the 1990s, most councils also paid for a music service, hiring peripatetic teachers to give one-to-one or small-group instrumental tuition. And schools and councils organized bands, choirs and concerts.

Faced with swingeing budget cuts by central government, many councils have slashed their budgets for music services.[68] In Wales, where musical traditions run deep, only seven of the twenty-two Welsh councils still pay for a music service, and some councils in England and Wales have restricted lessons to a minimum. In Scotland, by 2018 twenty-two of the thirty-two councils were charging pupils for learning an instrument.

The 'English Baccalaureate', the centralized evaluation system that the government introduced in 2010, judges schools on the proportion of pupils who obtain good grades in English, maths, history and geography, the sciences and a language, but not any of the arts. Music and other arts help define a society and help to evolve the customs, ethics and social solidarity epitomized by the commons. Music is in danger of becoming the sole preserve of the rich. Between 2008 and 2018, there was a 39 per cent fall in the number of A-level candidates in music. Fewer music students will soon lead to fewer music teachers. Many schools have already been denied funds for maintaining and repairing instruments by the austerity logic. The public educational commons is being converted into a vehicle of inequality.

Commercial intrusion into schools has been a form of enclosure. What has happened in Sweden is indicative of where that can lead. Although long perceived as the home of social democracy, Sweden has drifted towards privatization in recent years. There, a commercial for-profit chain, Kunskapsskolan ('Knowledge School'), has created a highly standardized and automated secondary school system.[69] Pupils are required to use an online Learning Portal containing the syllabus, exercises, texts and other resources, and do a lot of studying on their own. Each subject is divided into steps, which determine whether a pupil has passed the course or earned a merit grade, while electronic performance monitoring tracks the efficiency of teachers.

In early 2018, Kunskapsskolan claimed to have over 100 schools operating its system around the world, including in the UK. Its admirers have included Tony Blair and Michael Gove, the Secretary of State for Education in the Coalition government after 2010. However, three of the four secondary schools in England that adopted the system, lauded by Gove as the model of schooling he wished to see adopted across the country, were subsequently rated on evaluation as 'poor' and all four were transferred to other trusts. The Learning Schools Trust that had been responsible for them packed up shop in 2016.

All these models of privatization raise questions about the quality and authority of the gatekeepers, those who should be ensuring a smooth public service. For the academy schools in England and Wales, the gatekeeper role is played by Ofsted, the schools inspectorate. Since 2016 Ofsted has been headed by someone with no teaching experience: she had a career background in banking and management consultancy before her association with an academy chain founded and run by hedge-fund financiers.[70] For these reasons, her appointment by the Education Secretary was opposed by the House of Commons Education Committee, to no avail.

More systemically, Ofsted does not have the legal power to inspect all the schools run by academy chains at any one time as its brief is only to inspect individual schools. The government rejected amendments to the 2015 Education Act that would have extended Ofsted's role, preventing the gate-keeper from ensuring the commercial stewards of the education commons properly met their responsibilities.

Internationally, all the evidence shows that privatized, selective schooling performs worse than schools run by national or local governments that, at least in principle, respect the commons, not commercial interests.[71] In England, academy schools on average perform no better than local council-run schools in terms of results, despite better funding, and multi-academy trusts running at least five schools performed worse.[72] They have been accused of failing lower-achieving children by excluding them from exams to boost rankings, contrary to the commons principle of equal rights. They are undemocratic; parents have little say. And they have commodified and privatized schools and schooling, all too often channelling funds to head teachers and trustees rather than to providing the best possible education for their students.

Tertiary education, too, has abandoned the educational commons. One facet has been the acceptance of money from plutocratic donors who may wish to aggrandize their reputations or shape the ideological direction of teaching. When a former wealthy arms deal broker pays Oxford University to create a college in his name, the Saïd Business School, the university not only besmirches moral principles but bows to the basest form of commercialism. When American universities accept large grants from the Koch brothers – right-wing billionaires – that allow them to shape course content and determine faculty appointments, those universities are betraying the educational commons.[73]

In Britain, the tertiary educational commons has been hard hit by financing reforms for students and institutions. From 1962 until 1990 all full-time undergraduates at British universities and colleges were entitled to both a means-tested maintenance grant that covered their basic financial needs, and payment of tuition fees. However, tuition fees were low because the institutions also received considerable direct funding from central government. Students from low-income families thus had broad financial equality with those from affluent families.

Student loans were introduced in the 1990–91 academic year and gradually replaced grants for living costs until, in 2015, maintenance grants were abolished altogether, including for the poorest students. Students were also required to take out loans to pay much higher tuition fees – £9,250 a year in 2018–19, a rise from £1,000 in 1998 – as the burden of funding an expanded higher education system has shifted from government to students and their families.

Higher fees and student loans intensify social income inequality. Students from low-income families need larger loans than those whose families can afford to pay some or all of the costs. A nurse's children in effect pay much more than a banker's. It is a further erosion of the educational commons as an equally shared experience in a community of equals. Cuts in government funding have also led to increased commercialization of higher education institutions, to attract non-European Union students, who pay even higher fees, and to raise donations from industry and rich individuals for research and facilities.[74] These moves tend to compromise academic integrity and standards because donors can insist on what they want.

The development of Massive Open Online Courses (MOOCs) represents a powerful trend towards standardization and commodification of teaching. Led by US-based corporate ventures Coursera and Udacity (which operates in 119 countries, once described by its founder as providing a 'lousy product'), and UK-based FutureLearn, they have spread rapidly around the world. These companies are colonizing the educational commons everywhere they go. The Khan Academy, which produces short online courses aimed at schoolchildren, claimed to have 10 million unique users a month in 2018. Coursera, which claimed over 30 million users in 2018, now offers a fully online bachelor's degree.[75] Udemy, backed by huge venture-capital investment, offers over 22,000 courses. Google, in partnership with edX, an online-education 'non-profit' company started by Harvard University and MIT, has set up a platform called MOOC.org that will let anyone teach 'YouTube for courses'.[76]

All these variants are presented as 'open-access, free university education'.[77] In reality, for all their pretensions, they are a denial of the educational commons, which is built on local custom, inherited wisdom, shared experience and contested domains. None of these can be compressed into a standardized video, whose estimated optimal duration is six minutes, or a course of four weeks, said to be the optimal length. MOOCs represent a commodification of knowledge. The thinking of all interesting and educated minds evolves through personal interactions. To 'can' a Harvard or Oxford professor's words at a single moment, compressed as the wisdom to be bestowed on and passively received by a global student audience, is an insult to the ethos of teaching, education and thinking. This is not to deny the potential of technology to aid and improve formal teaching. But allowing commercial interests free rein risks ignoring what is lost or sidelined.

Enthusiasts for MOOCs and the use of IT more generally claim they are disrupting education in the same way that Uber and its rivals are disrupting taxi services and Airbnb is disrupting the hotel sector. But that is disingenuous, since it is shaping how people think. For instance, there is a related trend towards modular teaching, nano-degrees and micro-credentials, leading to 'stackable credentials', with marketable qualifications built up brick by brick over years.[78]

This represents a commodification of teaching and learning geared to the labour market and serving to entrench 'credentialism' – the tendency for employers to demand ever more qualifications for jobs as an applicant-sifting device. This is undesirable because it further tilts the education system towards narrow commercial criteria. A secondary market is emerging, with start-ups offering MOOCs automated assessment systems, post-course skills evaluation and standardization of grading.

The Conservative government in 2017 announced plans to introduce two-year degrees instead of the standard three-year version,[79] described by a government minister as 'the most important legislation for the sector in twenty-five years'.[80] The avowed intention of two-year degrees was to reduce the costs of providing and obtaining qualifications. The Department for Education stated that the fast-track degree would carry the same weight as three-year degrees.[81]

The general secretary of the University and College

Union complained in vain, 'Our universities must remain places of learning, not academic sweatshops, and the government needs to resist the pile 'em high and teach 'em cheap approach to students' education.'[82] Universities will become 'learning factories' with a reliance on teaching by rote rather than the more time-intensive and intellectually challenging imparting of critical thinking.

Education is, or should be, much more than about gaining credentials and an entry-level job ticket. Commodification and standardization squeeze out the cultural and vernacular parts of learning. And 'accelerated degrees' (the new two-year variety) will also intensify regressive trends in education. Those destined for the precariat are likely to be directed into two-year degrees and MOOCs, while the privileged continue to go for more culturally enriching and non-standardized avenues of learning.

The 2017 legislation also increased centralization of control over the content of teaching in universities, through creation of a new regulator, the Office for Students, whose remit is to 'increase competition and choice in higher education', and an assessment device branded as the Teaching Excellence and Student Outcomes Framework (TEF), by which universities are to be rated Gold, Silver or Bronze. Yet the government's expressed commitment to more choice is in contradiction to its imposition of centralized control over the content and evaluation of teaching. The essence of a university is respect for local traditions and the autonomy of intellectual development.

The commodification of tertiary education in many countries, including the UK and USA, has also seen the turfing out of traditional gatekeepers of the educational commons.

Those appointed to positions of administrative authority are increasingly selected from the financial sector, often with little or no experience of climbing the academic ladder and thereby learning the oral and literary traditions that go to define a commons. One of a gatekeeper's main roles is to determine who has entry to the commons. The commercial mind is likely to ask of potential recruits to their staff, 'Are they going to bring in money and reputation with potential donors and students?' The traditional academic gatekeeper is more likely to ask, 'Will they be competent scholars, community colleagues and dispassionate searchers for truth?'

Another aspect of the educational commons relates to the methods for recognizing and disseminating knowledge and research. Since the seventeenth century, the main vehicle has been the academic or scientific journal, an instrument for legitimation, scientific advance and community building and preservation. Beginning with the *Philosophical Transactions of the Royal Society*, journals have given published authors prestige and assisted their career prospects, lifetime income and security. In principle, submitted articles are subject to peer review, evaluated for quality and validity by anonymous independent experts, before they can be published. In practice, the system has come in for growing criticism. The cost to libraries and individual subscribers can be prohibitive and critics argue that it is wrong to make people pay to read the results of research that is publicly funded. Many journals charge authors to have their articles considered for publication, or to make them freely available online. Journals may be captured by a particular strand of thinking, a defect that has been particularly striking in economics and other quasi-political sciences, but also in certain physical sciences embroiled in bitter disputes over key assumptions or methodologies. Critics also claim the process takes too long.

In the United States, there is a move to disseminate research results more quickly and speculatively, partly through 'pre-prints' (finished articles that have not gone through a protracted peer-review process by a prestigious journal) that are then subject to comment and criticism by the wider scientific community.[83] The Bill and Melinda Gates Foundation, the largest medical research charity in the world after the Wellcome Trust, is backing the free dissemination of research it has funded and is barring publication in journals that charge for access. This sounds democratic and even supportive of a wider knowledge commons. However, the process is driven by private entities, not by disinterested gatekeepers of the knowledge community.

The commodification of tertiary education has been accompanied by a linguistic rejigging that reflects the dominant commercial mentality. Government ministers, civil servants and university administrators unashamedly refer to 'the education industry'. In 2017, a government minister even proposed that students studying subjects that were not oriented to jobs, including history and arts, should not receive student loans. Over two-thirds of all British universities (and in this they are far from alone) now employ more administrative and support staff than academic faculty.[84] Administrative staff thrive on commercial criteria, epitomized by words, concepts and concerns that keep them active, such as 'competition', 'efficiency gains', 'deliverable outcomes', 'choice' and 'rankings'. Universities are selling themselves as commodities, as attractive items of consumption by customers or clients – the potential students. The gentrification of student accommodation is just one aspect of the attempt by many universities to make themselves centres of consumption increasingly divorced from local roots and values. Universities now spend millions of pounds on agents to go around the world selling the brand in competition with other universities from the UK and abroad.[85]

Spending so much money, time and energy on selling the brand, and the fancy facilities on offer to potential students and faculty, diverts resources that could be devoted to learning and teaching. Commodification has also strengthened class fragmentation within what was once the academic 'community'. At the top is a tiny elite of remarkably high-paid administrators and vice-chancellors, some receiving over half a million pounds a year, plus perks.[86]

Among academics, the elite attract huge salaries and are subject to transfer fees like football stars, some holding lucrative appointments at several universities. Their names are expected to bring in student clients and possibly research funds, but they have little to do with reproducing the vernacular values of a particular university. Below them is the academic salariat, tenured fellows and professors, many of whom expect to stay at their university or college for the whole of their careers. They have prospective pensions, bonuses and sabbaticals. Some do well financially, but many have experienced a gradual decline in their inflation-adjusted earnings, and certainly a big decline relative to the stars and administrative elite above them in the hierarchy. Some will be joining the elite, or aspiring to do so, by selling themselves to the MOOC providers, a potentially lucrative sideline that could become the primary source of income.

It is below the salariat where the main commodification has been taking place, in the remorseless growth of an academic precariat.[87] The Higher Education Statistics Agency suggests that a majority of front-line teachers are now on short-term, zero-hours, hourly-paid or fractional contracts. At the University of Birmingham, for example, the proportion was 70 per cent in 2016 and at Warwick 68 per cent.

This trend is not unique to Britain but is a worldwide phenomenon. The growth of the academic precariat is bound to diminish the quality of teaching. Someone who does not know when, how much and even what they will be required to teach, is hardly likely to focus on keeping subject knowledge up to date, or to dedicate more than perfunctory time and energy to it. There will also be little opportunity for teachers to bond with students in what should be a two-way learning experience. A chronically insecure teacher is unlikely to be or to remain a good teacher.

Besides schools and universities, the education commons should include the institutions by which individuals join and remain in occupational communities. For hundreds of years, these were the professional and craft guilds, whose name derives from *geld*, meaning an association of persons contributing to a set of common purposes. This extended to the transmission of knowledge. An ancient code of ethics required professionals handling knowledge 'to treat their cargo as if the world depended on its safe transit through the generations'.[88] That beautifully captures an ethical principle of the educational commons, conveying so much more than the ugly neo-liberal concept of 'human capital'. A young person entered a craft or professional fraternity and learned the mysteries of the craft, trade or profession, and was expected to pass on the learning and mastery to future generations. In a well-functioning occupational commons, if there was competition it was expected to be one of craftsmanship.

In the modern era of 'deregulation', such guild regulation of what is acceptable and what is not has been largely replaced by state licensing, where a government-sponsored or approved board grants the right to practise in a particular craft or profession. Ethical codes are being displaced by 'customer satisfaction' as the main indicator of competence. The resultant erosion of ethics and empathy is a modern tragedy of the commons. And online rating systems could displace occupational licensing in the future, which would take the shaping of occupations even further from the commons traditions of the guilds.

Throughout history, guilds have provided institutional resistance to commodification, even though they have also been prone to rent-seeking.[89] Today, perhaps more than ever, with appropriate regulations, the model of living and working that the guilds have always embodied should draw support from a wide political spectrum. Those on the left should be drawn primarily to their potential to protect members from exploitation; those on the right should welcome them primarily as a means of protecting individuals and groups against a centralized state.

Education is and should be part of our national public wealth and commonality. A commons-based educational system would give proper place to the reproduction of the best values and traditions of the local community and would foster a governance structure that gives a voice to all those involved in education and directly affected by what takes place. A multi-stakeholder cooperative model would enable all proper interests to be represented in the management and development of education, led by teachers and students rather than by administrators and government officials. This model should build on the experience of the hundreds of schools in the UK that have operated something similar, in which membership is drawn from staff, teachers, pupils and the local community.[90]

Accordingly, the following article should be included in a Commons Charter:

> Article 42: The privatization and commodification of all levels of schooling and education should be reversed. All stakeholders, including students, teachers, parents and the local community, should have a governance role, along the lines of the multi-stakeholder cooperative model.

*

Everything, according to Big Tech, can be solved by technology, if only those at the frontier could plough ahead unhindered by politics and conventional market forces. It is salutary to recall that this perspective last came into prominence in the 1930s, as a political movement, to sweep aside politicians. One of the most prominent leaders of that movement was the grandfather of Elon Musk, whose ambitions in outer space are taking the colonization of the commons into uncharted territory.[91]

To the extent that corporations plunder the information-al and intellectual commons, they can set up winner-takes-all markets. The combination of Big Tech (and Big Pharma) with a greatly strengthened intellectual property rights system, and a neo-liberal state eager to back commercial winners, has buttressed rentier capitalism and left the knowledge com-mons depleted and defenceless.

The plunder of the intellectual commons has also contrib-uted to the erosion of the educational commons. For instance, the intellectual property system has accelerated the margin-alization of the arts and humanities in universities; those areas are unlikely to yield patentable outputs and thus income flows back to the university or to corporations associated with them.[92] Ignoring those trends in analyses of income distribu-tion conceals the extent to which inequality has been growing, and underestimates the incipient anger and bitterness among those losing out. It is morally inexcusable.

CHAPTER 8

# A Commons Fund for Common Dividends

> Distribution should undo excess,
> And each man have enough.
> — William Shakespeare, *King Lear*

Society is defined by its commons or, to echo the Earl of Lauderdale's words in 1804, by whether public wealth takes precedence over private riches. Over the past thousand years, Britain's commoners, including all those who came to these shores to enrich society with their energy, culture and intellect, have bequeathed to us a rich and intricate tapestry of natural, social, civil, cultural and knowledge commons. They belong to every member of society. But our public wealth has been plundered by encroachment, enclosure, commercialization, privatization and colonization of Britain's commons, accelerated by neglect and downright sabotage in the austerity era.[1] What should be done?

This chapter proposes two concluding articles of a Charter of the Commons that, if implemented properly, have the transformative potential to compensate commoners and to promote an ecologically sustainable society in which security, freedom and equality can flourish.

In thinking of society afresh, we should reflect that the wealth of all of us is far more to do with the efforts, achievements and luck of those who came before us than what we do ourselves. Morally, we should all have a fair share of that collective wealth, since we cannot know whose ancestors contributed more or less.

All forms of 'rentier' income – income arising from private ownership of physical, financial and 'intellectual' property – should be shared. These assets not only derive from enclosure and capture of the commons; their value and the income from them ultimately reflect the laws, regulations, fiscal policies and other measures that governments have put in place, in our name.

In the past three decades financiers have made vastly more money than the generation of financiers before them. This is not because they are vastly more clever or hard-working, but because they have benefited from the financial deregulation of the Thatcher–Reagan era. Similarly, those striding atop Big Tech today are making vastly more than their predecessors largely because, in the 1990s, intellectual property rights were globalized and strengthened. There are many other examples. The key point is that private riches owe much to the existence and plunder of the commons, for which commoners should be compensated. This leads to what is surely the most transformative article in the Charter of the Commons.

Article 43: A Commons Fund should be set up, primarily sourced by levies on the commercial use or exploitation of the commons. The Fund should invest to generate and preserve ecologically sustainable common wealth, and Common Dividends should be paid out equally to all commoners.

As a matter of social justice, all forms of rentier income – representing a tangible loss to commoners – should be subject to a levy paid into a Commons Fund.[2] The Fund's primary revenue would come from levies on the commercial use of the commons, as due compensation for commoners, the ultimate 'owners'.[3] Its primary investment objective should be the promotion of common wealth, rather than GDP growth. Producing more weapons increases GDP growth; so does converting a park into a commercial venture or using up resources as quickly as possible. By contrast, improving a commons does not. This is why the Fund's objective should not be focused on increasing GDP. A Commons Fund should restrict investment to firms and projects that would enhance or at least not threaten the commons.

The proposed Fund would be built up from levies relating to three types of commons: exhaustible (non-renewable) resources, such as oil, natural gas and minerals, which should be treated as capital assets; replenishable commons, such as forests, for which resources must be put aside to cover replenishment costs; and non-exhaustible commons, such as the air, water and ideas, levies on which could be made available for current distribution.

There could also be a higher levy rate for foreign capital ownership of commons and commercial advantage gained from their use, on the grounds that – as with foreign ownership of English water – foreign capital has no real accountability to the country's commoners. An extra levy could be construed as a form of insurance against neglect.

The Fund would be an instrument for preserving the capital value of exhaustible commons resources and for compensating commoners for loss of their commons. The proceeds of levies on exhaustible common resources should be treated differently from those on non-exhaustible and replenishable commons. If they belong to society, to be shared, then allowing commercial interests to deplete them deprives society of that asset. It also deprives future generations of that asset and any income from it.

Treating exhaustible commons resources as assets belonging to commoners means that selling them amounts to asset depreciation and proceeds from that sale gained by the state should be treated as public wealth, not as current revenue.[4] For example, the revenue from extracting and selling our oil and gas reserves should not be regarded as income from production but as proceeds from selling the proverbial 'family silver'. Applying the Hartwick Rule of intergenerational equity, as far as possible the capital value of the depleting resource should be preserved so that future generations as well as current generations will benefit from it.

The proposed Commons Fund would also promote a more ecologically sustainable economy by applying levies to all polluters for their actions in imposing costs on commoners. Besides contributing to the Fund, the levies would ensure polluters faced the proper social costs of those intrusions into the commons, acting as a fiscal deterrent to ecologically and socially destructive practices.

Another attractive feature of a Commons Fund is that

it would give all citizens a sense of common ownership. It would indicate that the levies, including some that might raise costs for them personally, would be going into a Fund designed to benefit all commoners. The Commons Fund would be a variant of sovereign wealth funds that now exist in over sixty countries. The closest to what is proposed here are the Alaska Permanent Fund and the Norwegian Government Pension Fund Global, better known as the Norwegian Oil Fund. Alaska's Fund was established in 1976 and has been built up from levies (royalties) on the oil industry. By 2018, it was worth 113 per cent of Alaska's GDP and its diversified portfolio had been yielding annual returns of nearly 10 per cent.[5] However, after many years of success and popularity in the state, the Fund proved susceptible to political meddling; the Republican party previously having abolished the state income tax, the state governor cut the dividend in 2016, 2017 and 2018, and planned to raid the Fund to fix a fiscal deficit. He was forced to withdraw from his 2018 re-election campaign amidst a wave of unpopularity, but his elected successor, a Republican, has stated an intention to go in the opposite direction, boosting the dividend to unsustainable levels that threaten to deplete the Fund.

The Norwegian Fund was set up in the 1970s when Norway wisely decided to retain government stakes in its share of the North Sea oil reserves and deposit revenues in the Fund. The Norwegian Fund, which now controls about 60 per cent of the country's recorded wealth, has been described by *The Economist* as 'perhaps the most impressive example of long-term thinking by any Western government'.[6] By contrast with the Alaska Fund, the Norwegian Fund is immunized against political manipulation; it is independent of central government and run by a board overseen by the central bank. Respecting the Hartwick Rule, the Fund protects its capital while distributing money annually, based on the average annual return on its investments over the previous five years.

Several other examples have shown the compatibility of such funds with a market economy, although their pitfalls have salutary lessons for the design of a Commons Fund. One such is the Wyoming Mineral Trust Fund, with assets of over $7 billion built up from licensing mineral extraction. But commons principles have been ignored. The revenue has been used to eliminate state income tax, not for maintaining the capital value of the Fund. So the wealthy who would have paid a lot of income tax have gained, while the precariat and others on lower incomes have lost. Inter-generational equity has been ignored altogether.

Another example is the Texas Permanent School Fund, set up in 1854 by the state legislature to benefit Texan public schools. Later the Fund was granted control of half the state's land and the mineral rights that were still in the public domain. In 1953, the Fund added coastal 'submerged lands', extending three miles offshore, after the US Congress passed legislation returning control to the states. It was a fortuitous rescue of the commons. Today the Fund distributes over $800 million a year to Texan public schools, operating alongside a $17.5 billion Permanent University Fund, which is effectively the steward for over 2 million acres and uses the proceeds to support the state's university system. The Texan funds show the transformative potential of a Commons

Fund, although they have benefited only a selected group – in the case of the University Fund a relatively privileged one.

There are also examples of funds that have mistakenly treated revenue gained from commodifying natural resources as windfall income, to be spent immediately. In 1956, in what is now Kiribati, the British colonial administration set up the Revenue Equalization Reserve Fund to receive and invest revenue from the sale of guano (phosphate) deposits. These deposits were exhausted in 1979, but the Fund continued to be topped up by revenues from the sale of fishing licences. It proved highly profitable, reaching 800 per cent of GDP by 2000. But poor investment decisions and excessive withdrawals by the government for current spending subsequently halved its real value. Respect for inter-generational equity and common rights was lost.

Another Pacific island, Nauru, established a phosphate-based fund in the 1970s intended to provide a continuing revenue stream after the mines closed. But its government too splurged the savings on current spending, which soon exhausted the fund and left the economy almost entirely dependent on hosting a refugee processing centre for Australia. These are small-scale examples of how commons can be dissipated. They underscore the need for a capital fund to be set up as an independent entity and as a 'permanent fund', charged with maintaining the capital while distributing only the net returns from investment.

A more encouraging example is the Shetland Charitable Trust, set up in the mid-1970s. The local council negotiated with companies expanding oil and gas extraction from the North Sea to give the community 'disturbance payments', which were deposited in a charitable trust managed by the council. In 2003, the trust became independent and by 2018 had assets of £232 million, having already disbursed about £300 million. It is a permanent fund, spending the investment returns but keeping the capital intact. The Shetland Islands have a population of 23,000, and they are the intended beneficiaries. The trust has tried to reduce inequality as well as improve living standards, giving millions of pounds to civil society organizations and initiatives, including Citizens Advice, the Shetland Disability Recreation Club, and buses for the elderly and disabled. Perhaps the money could have been spread more widely, but the trust's success again indicates the potential of capital sharing from minerals.

As these examples suggest, most capital funds have been based on a single commons resource. But they could be built with the proceeds from any and all commons. There have been at least four missed opportunities to do this in Britain. Had Thatcher and her Chancellor of the Exchequer, Nigel Lawson, followed the example of the Norwegians in the early 1980s, and used tax receipts from North Sea oil and gas fields to build a capital wealth fund, it would today have more than £450 billion in assets, bigger than the sovereign wealth funds of Kuwait, Qatar and Russia combined.[7] Some believe the fund would have been even larger. It was one of the worst economic mistakes ever made by a British government. Norway has generated twice the revenue gained by the UK from every barrel of North Sea oil produced.[8]

Three other missed opportunities were: the sale of public land worth an estimated £400 billion; the sale of council housing at well below market value, amounting to between

£75 billion and £100 billion; and the sale of state-owned enterprises, worth about £126 billion. The proceeds from those cuts to the commons could have been used to preserve their value for commoners now and in the future. Instead, they have been dissipated.

The proposal here is to build up a Commons Fund from levies on the use of all commons and to use the Fund to pay Common Dividends to all. In the United States, entrepreneur Peter Barnes has called for dividends to be paid to all citizens from a Sky Trust funded by taxes on carbon emissions; use by companies of natural resources (air, minerals, water) and the legal and financial infrastructure, including the intellectual property system; a financial transactions tax; and use of the electro-magnetic spectrum.[9]

In the UK, the Institute for Public Policy Research has proposed a citizens' wealth fund worth £186 billion to pay, from 2030, a £10,000 'universal minimum inheritance' at age twenty-five.[10] This would be financed by a mixture of asset sales, including the public stake in the Royal Bank of Scotland; capital transfers including the transfer to the fund of the Crown Estate; reformed wealth taxes, including a gift or accessions tax to replace inheritance tax; new revenue streams such as a 'scrip' tax of up to 3 per cent requiring major businesses to issue equity to the fund; plus a small amount of borrowing and returns reinvested through the prior decade.

The Royal Society of Arts has argued for a 'universal basic opportunity fund' to provide every citizen under the age of fifty-five with a £5,000 'opportunity dividend', which they could spend on retraining, starting a business or anything else as they pleased.[11] This fund too might be financed in part by levies on the use of common assets.

Another group has proposed establishing three national funds – a Citizens Dividend Fund, a Social Care Trust Fund and an Urban Land Trust – as part of a 'remodelling capitalism' strategy.[12] This risks 'salami slicing' what would be limited financial resources too thinly, so that none of the funds would be adequate. But the proposal is financially feasible. And a report for Compass envisages a three-step approach for phasing in a full basic income. The first step would be to convert the existing personal tax allowance into a payment to everybody of £25 a week in the first year. This would be followed by a series of up-ratings over the next nine years, followed by payments from the creation of a citizens' wealth fund.[13]

How should the Commons Fund be constructed? The governance of the Fund should be similar to that of the Norwegian Fund, with an independent Board and executive to prevent manipulation for electoral advantage by the government of the day. The Board should be chosen democratically and include representatives of the commons. The Fund should be required to invest in ways that strengthen the commons, and to respect three basic principles: the Precautionary Principle, the Public Trust doctrine and the Hartwick Rule. The Precautionary Principle, which is widely used in environmental and other risk assessments, would require the Fund to minimize ecological risk in its investment policy. The Public Trust doctrine, the principle that the state holds assets in trust for its citizens and has a duty to protect them, would require preservation of the capital value of depletable commons assets. And the Hartwick Rule would require a distribution policy ensuring that future generations gain as much as today's.

Building the Commons Fund should start with wealth. No private wealth of substance has been gained without public contributions, including the physical, financial and legal infrastructure that has made accumulation possible. It is a conceit for those possessing great wealth to imagine this is due solely to their own efforts and wisdom. And as the rich can transfer their estates to their offspring, private riches have become more unequal over time, especially as wealth has grown much faster than incomes in the modern era.

Since 1970 private wealth has risen from 300 per cent of the economy to over 600 per cent, while net public wealth (assets minus debt) has fallen from 50 per cent of GDP to being negative today.[14] The growth of private wealth may have been much more than that, since concealing wealth for tax avoidance and evasion has become a very profitable global industry. As the Panama Papers showed in 2016, thousands of rich and politically prominent people were using tax havens to avoid tax on their assets, including the then British prime minister's father and for a time the prime minister himself.[15]

Private wealth in the UK is more concentrated than income – a tenth of all households own 45 per cent of the nation's wealth, while the bottom half of households own just 9 per cent. When it comes to financial wealth, such as shares, the top tenth owns 70 per cent.[16] Yet tax revenue from wealth represents only 4 per cent of all tax revenue.[17] So, there are strong prima facie grounds for placing more of the tax burden on wealth, especially as rising wealth inequality has been partly due to the shift from public to private wealth. Reducing inequality requires a strategy to raise the share of public wealth in national wealth. A Common Wealth Levy would be a good start for the Commons Fund, the name recognizing that private wealth owes much to use and appropriation of the commons. The levy should target the inter-generational transfer of wealth.

Throughout history the tendency for great wealth to beget even greater wealth through inter-generational transfer has been checked by inheritance tax, which was first introduced in ancient Rome more than 2,000 years ago and in Britain in 1694. Economists have traditionally supported it. Adam Smith, generally regarded as the father of mainstream economics, said that 'a power to dispose of estates forever is manifestly absurd'. Inherited wealth also leads recipients to reduce their economic activity and clearly gives 'something for nothing' to a minority.

Yet inheritance tax seems to be dying. Conservatives, neoclassical economists and libertarians have rebranded it 'the death tax' and condemned it as 'double taxation', since in their view wealth derives from earned income that has already been taxed.[18] But this is generally not the case; much wealth derives from financial investments and the rise in market value of land and property that reflects, in part at least, their scarcity value.

Revenue from inheritance tax has declined dramatically. Across the OECD, since the 1960s it has fallen on average by three-fifths as a share of national income. US President George W. Bush declared his desire to be rid of it altogether and President Trump has said he intends to do so. Perhaps

more surprisingly, Sweden was the first country to end inheritance tax, under a conservative government, an action which
was not reversed by its social democratic successor.

In the UK, where property prices and values have risen
rapidly, inheritance tax has been slashed. In 2015, the Chancellor of the Exchequer raised the threshold for the onset of
40 per cent inheritance tax (IHT) for home-owners from an
estate of £650,000 for a couple to £850,000 in 2017–18, rising
to £1 million by 2020. This was class-based fiscal policy favouring the wealthiest. It has no economic or moral justification, especially as the lost public revenue – forecast to be
nearly £1 billion in 2020 – will boost the public budget deficit,
cited as the reason for cutting welfare benefits. This should
be reversed.

One option would be to introduce a more progressive
tax on inherited wealth, starting at a modest rate of, say, 10
per cent on wealth from £50,000, rising to 40 per cent at
£300,000 and 50 per cent beyond £500,000. Within this, a
levy of, say, 2 per cent on inherited wealth should go into
the Commons Fund. An alternative would be to end inheritance tax in its present form and introduce a general wealth
tax, as exists in several European countries, including the
Netherlands, Portugal, Spain and Switzerland. Their wealth
tax structure varies, but most impose a low rate of tax, of between 0.5 per cent and 3 per cent, on wealth above a certain
threshold.

Inheritance tax raised just over £5 billion in 2017–18 – a
record, but small in relation to the potential revenue from a
wealth tax. Wealth in the UK, including property and financial assets, amounted to £12,800 billion as of 2016.[19] So, for

the sake of illustration, if all wealth was taxed, a 1 per cent Common Wealth Levy could raise £128 billion. And as the top 10 per cent of households owns nearly half the country's wealth, even a threshold of £300,000 before the tax applied, which would exempt half of British households, would still provide considerable revenue for the Commons Fund. In the USA, estimates suggest that a 2 per cent tax on US-held financial wealth alone ($77 trillion in early 2018) could generate enough revenue to provide $12,000 annually to every household.

There should also be a Wealth Transfer Levy, to overcome the widespread practice of transferring ownership in advance of death. It would not capture all wealth transfers but would be more effective than the existing system.

The other foundational levies for the Commons Fund should be on land. A land value tax (LVT) would be a levy on the commons lost to enclosure, privatization and commercialization. Land is a capital asset and should be used to benefit future generations as well as those living now. The taxation of land has been advocated since the eighteenth century, from across the political spectrum. As Thomas Paine put it in his great *Agrarian Justice* in 1797:

> Man did not make the earth . . . It is the value of the improvements only, and not the earth itself, that is the individual property . . . Every proprietor owes to the community a ground rent for the land which he holds.

Thomas Jefferson was even more adamant, saying, 'The earth belongs in usufruct to the living' and should revert to society on a landholder's death. Adam Smith in 1776 saw that taxing land would temper greed and protect the commons; David Ricardo, perhaps the greatest classical political economist, called unearned income from land a pernicious anomaly; John Stuart Mill saw taxing land as necessary to limit the gains by landlords; Henry George in his widely read book of 1879, *Progress and Poverty*, claimed that the increase in land values from government investment would be sufficient to fund that investment and argued that land-value levies should replace all other taxes.

Many economists support a land value tax on efficiency grounds because, land being immobile and visible, it is hard to evade and does not discourage effort. Even Milton Friedman, neo-liberal mentor of Margaret Thatcher, described the LVT as 'the least bad tax'. Winston Churchill, from an aristocratic landowning family, scornfully dismissed the landlord as someone who 'contributes nothing to the process from which his own enrichment is derived'.

In Britain, the market value of all privately held land quadrupled between 1996 and 2016, and the assets overlying land more than doubled in value, although those possessing the land did little or nothing to justify that increase in their wealth.[20] Much of the increase in value stemmed from public investment in infrastructure and the grant of planning permission for development. That in itself justifies a levy on land-related wealth. In the UK and other rich industrialized countries, the rise in land prices explains about 80 per cent of the rise in house prices since the Second World War.[21] The beneficiaries in effect gained from the waves of enclosure, which made available land scarce and inflated its market value.

The revenue raised from an LVT would depend on the land to be taxed. Taking £5 trillion as the value of all the land in the UK, as estimated by the Office for National Statistics, a 1 per cent LVT would raise £50 billion a year, nearly as much as council tax and business rates combined. There could be an exemption for primary residences (avoiding the 'garden tax' slur), reserving a higher LVT rate for vacant properties and second homes. A 3 per cent LVT, excluding principal owner-occupied residences, but including agricultural land, which is now exempt from business rates, could raise over £33 billion.[22]

Should LVT *replace* current property taxes or be a surcharge on landholdings in addition? An LVT would be a fairer, more progressive system than the current property tax regime. It would be progressive, since large landowners and those owning the most valuable land would pay most. Replacing council tax paid by occupiers with an LVT paid by owners would lessen the burden on tenants and thus benefit the precariat. And an LVT would be fair, since those benefiting financially from public investment or development plans would pay a share of the cost.

The LVT could be set at levels for residential and commercial property that would raise roughly the same revenue as council tax and business rates do now. Extending taxation to agricultural land, unoccupied property and land banks (land with planning permission that is left undeveloped in anticipation of rising land prices) would compensate for scrapping land development charges and Stamp Duty Land Tax on house purchase, which impedes geographical and labour mobility. Revenue from council tax was about £32 billion in

2017–18, from business rates £29.3 billion, and from Stamp Duty Land Tax about £13.2 billion. However, if LVT were to replace council tax and business rates, local government funding would still need to be maintained. At present, revenues from business rates are split between central and local government. Under an LVT system, the revenue claimed by central government should go into the Commons Fund. But LVT rates could be set to raise more than current property taxes, making more revenue available for the Commons Fund.

If an LVT were to be additional to current property taxes, and levied on land now untaxed or undertaxed, all the revenue from the levy could go into the Fund. In that case, it should be accompanied by a reform of council tax to reflect current property values. In England, council tax is based on 1991 property values and occupiers of modest homes can pay the same as those in palatial residences.[23]

There should also be a Planning Permission Levy. When planning permission is granted for property development the value of the land rises sharply, giving landowners a large windfall gain. At least some of that windfall should go to commoners, in whose name the planning permission is granted. The simple act of granting planning permission for one hectare of agricultural land can add as much as £2.5 million to its market value.[24] In 2018 there was enough land with planning permission for 420,000 houses where building had not started, much of it held in land banks by property developers or investment firms.[25] A levy based on the increased land value would not only help build the Commons Fund but put pressure on developers to build and sell houses by making land hoarding more expensive.

Similarly, the privatization of public spaces that often accompanies planning permission grants commercial interests an economic benefit provided by public means. There is an equity case for a POPS levy. And a separate levy, or a higher rate of LVT, should be applied to all housing left unoccupied for more than six months. A Non-Occupancy Levy would encourage landlords and property speculators to make more housing available, at a price or rent that more people could afford.

Commoners should also be compensated for polluted air and for manmade disruption to the earth's climate. A Carbon Levy has moved from the desirable to the essential, a vital component of policies to check global warming.[26] Even a modest tax on carbon emissions would raise twice as much revenue and would be about 50 per cent more effective at cutting emissions than the current cap-and-trade regime adopted in Europe after heavy multinational lobbying.[27] A levy of $70 (about £54) on each tonne of $CO_2$ could raise about 2 per cent of GDP and achieve the commitment made by governments in the Paris Agreement to tackle climate change.

Britain operates a carbon price floor, the Climate Change Levy, which raised about £2 billion in 2016–17. But the implied carbon price is much too low to achieve planned $CO_2$ emission reductions, and it only applies to electricity generation. Introducing a tax on gas and ending the reduced VAT rate (5 per cent instead of 20 per cent) on domestic energy consumption would be more coherent and give households a stronger incentive to reduce fossil fuel use. Additional revenue from a Carbon Levy might come to about £10 billion a year, including an increase in fuel duty.

The revenue from a carbon tax and pollution taxes should go into the Commons Fund, bearing in mind that these depletions of the natural commons hit lower-income groups and areas disproportionately. Other ecological levies are also needed. Vehicle Excise Duty and Fuel Duty are also eco-taxes. In 2016–17 they generated a combined revenue of £34 billion annually, of which fuel duty accounted for £28 billion. However, at present, road taxes do not cover the overall cost to society of accidents, congestion, air pollution, greenhouse gas emissions and health. In 2018, in a dereliction of public responsibility, the government froze Fuel Duty for the ninth year in a row, boasting that it was protecting motorists. Fuel Duty and Vehicle Excise Duty should be raised and the proceeds allocated to the Commons Fund.

Other air-polluting activities should be subject to levies. One is what might be called a Frequent Flyer Levy. Nothing symbolizes the modern plunder of the commons more than pollution of the air and the atmosphere by aircraft. The impact of pollution and aircraft noise on the environment and health is regressive, since lower-income communities tend to be more exposed. In addition, the exemption of the aviation sector from fuel duty and VAT on air tickets amounts to a regressive public subsidy, lowering the cost of travel for flyers who on average are wealthier than non-flyers.[28] A levy on every airline ticket would be a source of income with which to compensate the commoners. It would also be progressive as the wealthy fly more and would therefore contribute more in levies.

A related proposal would repeal the existing Air Passenger Duty and replace it with a Frequent Flyer Levy (FFL) that would vary with the number of flights taken by an individual.[29] The aim would be to limit the rise in passenger demand, obviating the need for more airport runways and reducing greenhouse gas emissions. But it would be simpler to impose the levy on all flights, since checking the number of flights taken by each person would be expensive and bureaucratic.

Demand for flights in the UK is predicted to more than double between 2010 and 2050, causing a huge increase in environmental damage. But while only a minority of the population will be responsible, everybody will suffer from an enhanced risk of ill-health and environmental decay. That justifies imposing a levy and distributing a compensatory dividend to all commoners. And since the environmental damage will be experienced by future generations, the revenue raised from an FFL could fall under the Hartwick Rule, meaning the revenue should not be treated as a windfall, but as money to be put into a permanent capital fund.

Another air-related levy might be dubbed the Cruise Liner Levy. Monstrous ocean cruise liners are causing massive ecological damage. They use dirty diesel fuel that pollutes the atmosphere in the extensive vicinity around where they dock, causing health problems and devastating the natural commons. While cruise liners should be regulated much more stringently, they should also pay a levy based on ship size and fuel use during the time they spend in national waters.

Proceeds from auctioning or licensing the electromagnetic spectrum should be paid into the Commons Fund, since commercial interests – broadcasters and mobile phone operators – are making money from access to a natural commons. This might be called an Airwaves Levy. The UK government raised £22.5 billion in 2000 by auctioning bandwidths for 3G mobile telephony, though in this case companies overpaid. In 2013, it raised £2.3 billion in the auction for 4G and another £1.4 billion for 5G in 2018.

There should also be a Wind Energy Levy on revenue from exploiting wind energy, a rapidly growing economic sphere that has been colonized through privatization. Since we need to shift from fossil fuel to wind and solar energy, a case could be made for a low levy, but the wind across the land and adjoining sea is undeniably part of Britain's commons.

The skyline is part of our commons, but is blighted by unsightly advertising hoardings in urban areas and ugly commercial developments in rural ones. Skyline pollution should attract a Billboard Levy, applied to all outdoor advertising hoardings and rural commercial developments, depending on size and public visibility. How much could be raised by this levy is hard to say, but whatever is raised should be added to the Commons Fund.

Water is the worst case of privatization and colonization of the commons in Britain. A Water Use Levy should be applied to all water used by households and companies. For households the levy could be imposed only on water consumption above a basic threshold, so as to be mildly progressive, but should be designed to discourage wasteful water usage in our era of increasing fragility of water supply. As long as water remains privatized, the water companies should pay an extra commons levy. This should be based on their gross profits because they have artificially manipulated their net profits by loading the companies with long-term debt. A commons levy should also be applied to commercial use of rivers, reservoirs, lakes and the coastline. This might induce a welcome return of some land and amenities to the commons, but it would generate more revenue for the Commons Fund.

Among the biggest potential sources of revenue for a Commons Fund would be a Minerals and Mining Levy, although because the Hartwick Rule dictates that the capital value must be preserved it would not be the biggest source of income for paying current dividends. The latest major commons resources are shale gas and potash; the first for energy, the second for fertilizer.

Shale gas is, regrettably, taking off. Some 2,000 onshore wells have already been drilled for exploration, and production at one well in Lancashire started in 2018, though operations were repeatedly suspended due to earth tremors. In 2017 the government announced its intention to set up a Shale Wealth Fund worth up to £1 billion over twenty-five years, to be used 'for the benefit of people who live in areas which host shale sites'.[30] The Fund is due to receive up to 10 per cent of tax revenues arising from shale gas production, with local communities receiving up to £10 million – which they can decide how to spend, including making direct payments to households. The industry has also agreed to pay £100,000 to local communities for every hydraulically fractured well site at the exploratory stage, and 1 per cent of revenue if it successfully goes into production. In addition, local authorities will be allowed to keep 100 per cent of business rates instead of 50 per cent as now. Landowners will still receive payments for the use of their land. It is perhaps not surprising that the National Union of Farmers, representing landowners, is not opposed to shale gas development.[31]

The proposed Shale Wealth Fund essentially amounts to a bribe to dampen opposition to fracking and is not what is needed. The environmental dangers of fracking are so great that all new drilling should be stopped.[32] However, if fracking is allowed, a levy should be imposed on gross revenues, to be paid into the Commons Fund. The costs of fracking, such as pollution of water supplies and earthquake risk, extend well beyond local communities and landowners. The impact of methane and other greenhouse gas emissions from the fracking process, which some experts argue make fracked gas dirtier than coal, is global.[33]

Jim Ratcliffe, CEO of Ineos, which has spearheaded fracking, has become Britain's richest man with self-reported wealth of £21 billion. In mid-2018, just after being knighted, it emerged that he was moving residence to Monaco to avoid paying British tax.[34] There is no justification for one person to accrue such immense wealth from exploitation of our commons resources. There should be a substantial levy with proceeds placed in the Commons Fund.

The knowledge commons is also a huge potential source of revenue for the Commons Fund. A levy is justified in part by the extraordinary profits gained from colonization of the informational and intellectual commons. Digital data, the 'new oil' of the global economy, have become an important commons resource. Imposing a Digital Data Levy of, say, 10 per cent on all revenue derived from corporate use of personal data would be fair, since we commoners provide those data free of charge to the technology companies. The value of the data to Big Tech is far greater than the cost to the companies of providing the free services that generate the data in the first place.

Virtual reality pioneer Jaron Lanier, in his book *Who Owns the Future?*, proposed that individuals providing data should receive a micro-payment every time their data are used by a company to earn money. Someone who signs up to an online dating site, for example, is matched with a potential partner, but their data will be used by the company to improve its matching algorithms and may be used for other purposes. Lanier argues that the person using the online dating service should be paid the micro-payment.[35] Eduardo Porter has made a similar proposal in *The New York Times*.[36] Eric Posner and Glen Weyl have calculated that paying people for the use of their data would raise US household median incomes by $20,000 a year.[37] But such a system would be administratively complex, costly, somewhat arbitrary and prone to error. It would pay to overuse the technology, increasing its addictive qualities. It would also tend to increase inequality; those on low incomes are likely to use online services less, generating fewer data from which to earn anything.

A more equitable system that would respect the commons character of information would be to impose a levy on the companies harvesting the data, and to channel the income into the Commons Fund from which everybody could receive dividends.[38] It is feasible. In 2018, as an interim fix to tackle tax avoidance, the European Commission set out plans for a 3 per cent digital tax on local revenue earned by digital companies, based on the location of people providing the data. Between 120 and 150 companies would be affected.

The British government later announced a 2 per cent 'digital services tax' on revenues generated in the UK, effective from 2020.

These moves are a response to tax avoidance schemes used by Big Tech and others, enabling them to pay very little tax on their enormous incomes. In Europe overall, digital firms have been paying an estimated effective tax rate of just 9.5 per cent, compared with 23 per cent for 'bricks-and-mortar' companies.[39]

The scale of online data is vast. In 2018, the UK online population was 57.3 million. Facebook had 32.6 million regular users in the country, Instagram had 18.4 million, Snapchat had 16.2 million, and Twitter 12.6 million. Digital advertising revenue in the UK, estimated at £11.4 billion in 2017, is growing rapidly. Google and Facebook between them have over half the market. Google alone accounted for £4.4 billion, 39 per cent of all digital advertising spending, while Facebook's ad revenue was an estimated £1.9 billion.[40]

Amazon's overall UK revenue in 2017 was over £11 billion, yet despite tripling its reported profits over the previous year (understated by giving selected executives shares and deducting them from profits) it managed to halve the amount it paid in corporation tax. Devious tax avoidance arrangements enable Amazon to dodge UK taxes: it paid just £4.5 million in 2017 and even received a tax credit from the government in 2016.

Google in 2016 reported revenues of £1.3 billion, but its US accounts say UK revenue was £5.5 billion, which will have risen in 2017. It, too, is chronically under-taxed in Britain, partly due to the device, also used by Facebook, of booking most of its advertising through Dublin. In 2016, Facebook reported UK revenue of £842 million; others estimated it was really £1.8 billion. Whatever the real figure, Facebook paid just £5 million in corporation tax in 2016–17, less than 1 per cent of revenue.[41] The scope for a Digital Data Levy on enclosure of the knowledge commons by Big Tech is considerable.

Intellectual property rights – patents, copyright, industrial designs and trademarks – are the most artificial and illegitimate source of rentier income. A levy should be imposed on the monopolistic income derived from such 'property' to reflect the fact that the intellectual property rights regime is a capture of the intellectual commons. Even at a modest rate, this would raise a great deal. Though there are no estimates of how much income patents generate in Britain, 'creative industries', almost all of which are protected by copyright, were worth almost £92 billion to the British economy in 2016. And there should be no subsidies for patents. The Patent Box tax break, which lowers corporation tax on revenue deemed to stem from patents, should be abolished. This resulted in £875 million revenue foregone by the Exchequer in 2016–17, mainly benefiting big corporations.

App-driven or online 'tasking' platforms, such as Uber, Deliveroo and Amazon Mechanical Turk, make large monopoly profits for their owners and the private equity funds backing them. Accordingly, an Apps Levy should be imposed on all online labour transactions. At present, 25 per cent or even 50 per cent of what a client pays for the service goes to the owner of the digital platform, not to the person providing the service. These platforms are labour brokers, earning rental income, and should be subject to a rental levy. To give some idea of the potential, Deliveroo booked revenues of £277 million in 2017 and Uber UK had revenues of £60 million, despite suspension of its London licence (provisionally reinstated in 2018). Uber books commissions through the Netherlands as a tax-avoidance device, so a 2 per cent levy on transactions would be a way of capturing at least some of the avoided tax. The array of platforms is expanding rapidly, and an Apps Levy would raise useful resources for the Commons Fund.

Finally, the Fund could be boosted in its initial phase by redirecting some of the billions of pounds paid out in selective subsidies, as well as lost revenue from the edifice of tax reliefs, the benefits of which go overwhelmingly to the wealthy. As of 2017, there were more than 1,000 tax reliefs, resulting in a loss of public revenue of over £400 billion a year. Most of these should be phased out and, say, £100 billion redirected to the Commons Fund. Another source could be an extension of VAT from about half to nearly all spending, which would raise about £80 billion, some of which could be directed into the Fund.[42]

In sum, a set of levies on gains from the commons could be used to build a substantial Commons Fund. The total amount raised could not be predicted with precision, because in some cases the levies would – as intended – lead to a change in behaviour, which might lessen the revenue gained from them.

## Common dividends: a route to basic income

How should the proceeds of the Commons Fund be allocated or distributed? As it would be a 'permanent' capital fund, it should respect the Hartwick Rule of inter-generational equity, so that future generations gain as much as current generations. But the Fund would be made up of levies not only on the use of non-renewable or exhaustible commons but also of renewable and replenishable commons, the revenues from which could be distributed.

One important income source for the Commons Fund would be a carbon emissions levy. But it has two drawbacks – it is a general tax, and is therefore likely to be unpopular, and it is regressive because it would represent a higher proportionate cost for those on low incomes. The challenge is to make it politically popular and progressive. Experience in Canada and Switzerland shows that both these can be achieved if the government makes it clear that the proceeds, or much of them, are paid out as dividends. In Switzerland, for example, two-thirds of the proceeds of the carbon tax is recycled, most of it returned to households as a reduction in their compulsory health insurance premiums. It is very popular. Canada plans to rebate 90 per cent of the revenues from a carbon tax back to individual households, 70 per cent of which will gain more from the rebate than they will pay in higher costs for fuel.

An American study found that, whereas a modest levy on $CO_2$ emissions would be regressive if used to cut personal income tax, it would be hugely progressive, benefiting nearly all the bottom half of the population, if it were combined with recycling the receipts as universal lump-sum payments.[43] Another study also concluded that the levy would be popular if combined with payment of dividends.[44] This idea is attracting support from across the political spectrum, as evidenced in a *Wall Street Journal* op-ed signed by a broad cross-section of Democrats and Republicans and twenty-seven Nobel-Prize winning economists.[45] It would be even better if those receipts were placed in a national Commons Fund and used to help pay for quasi-universal dividends.

In the case of revenue raised from levies on depletable (exhaustible) resources, only the return to the Fund should be paid out, whereas in principle all revenue attributable to levies on non-depletable resources could be distributed annually. What does this mean for permissible spending from the Fund?

A good guide is the Norwegian Pension Fund Global, which pursues an ecological and ethical investment strategy that could be replicated in Britain. Over many years, it has achieved an annual gross return of over 6 per cent, which has yielded a net annual return of 4 per cent after administrative costs have been covered. But as the Fund relies entirely on a depleting resource – oil – only the 4 per cent can be disbursed each year to respect the Hartwick Rule. In the longer term, as oil resources shrink, disbursements are planned to fall to 3 per cent of the Fund value, but by then the Fund will be bigger. By contrast, the proposed Commons Fund would be able to distribute more than 4 per cent each year without jeopardizing its 'permanent' character because income from levies on non-exhaustible commons could be made available for distribution without diminishing the capital.

As it would be a Commons Fund, and as all citizens should be treated as equal, every commoner should receive an equal amount. Pragmatically, the dividends should be paid to every adult resident citizen, with half the amount going to every child under the age of sixteen. Legal migrants would have a waiting period of, say, two years before becoming entitled. Because it would take time before the Fund became substantial, the Common Dividends would initially be small, but even then they would be significant for those on low incomes. They would rise as the Fund grew. To make it progressive and equitable, the dividend could be clawed back from those with higher incomes, perhaps through raising the upper rate of income tax (and corporation tax rate, to deter artificial incorporation). This might enable a higher initial amount to be paid that would benefit those on lower incomes and the precariat.[46] The aim should be to build an income distribution system based on a Commons Fund and Common Dividends that would give people basic security and be ecologically respectful.

Building a Commons Fund and paying out dividends would not be at the expense of spending on social services, the National Health Service or education. On the contrary, these commons must be strengthened – by reversing privatization and commodification and increasing spending paid for by higher taxes and borrowing.

One concern is that, to increase the size of dividends, commoners might support a rapid rate of extraction of commons resources and commons-depleting commercialization. There is no perfect answer, although the same applies to many trade-offs between economic growth and the environment.

It would be more worrying if the Commons Fund and its dividends were to depend solely on income from minerals. But a levy system applied to all forms of commons, including non-exhaustible kinds, would weaken this tendency, as there would be no direct link between any particular levy and the size of dividend. The link between the levies and the dividends would be through the Commons Fund, so commoners could be expected to focus on the performance of the Fund itself, and take pride in its performance, as in Alaska and Norway. Moreover, the investor company or public agency responsible for minerals production would be guided by long-term profit maximization, not by local political preferences, and would be constrained by environmental regulations. The concern also presumes a short-term perspective among commoners – us as citizens – which merely accentuates the need for ecological education.[47]

Common Dividends would in effect be a basic income, a modest regular payment to every legal resident in the community, paid unconditionally as a right, regardless of income, employment or relationship status. Hence the final article in the Charter of the Commons:

> Article 44: Recalling the Charter of the Forest's constitutional commitment to the right to subsistence, the Commons Fund should be a means of introducing a basic income as an economic right, paid as Common Dividends.

Initially, Common Dividends would not be enough to cover a person's basic material needs. But if your net income after paying rent and food is just over £20 a week, as is the case for many people in modern Britain, then even an extra £30 a week would make a significant difference to your standard of living. Pilots and experiments have shown that even a small increase in basic income can have a big positive impact on nutrition, health, schooling, economic activity and social solidarity. Moving towards a proper basic income will be a journey lasting years, just as other major reforms – for example, to pension systems – have required long transition periods.

A basic income would provide an anchor for a fairer distribution system. And it would compensate the precariat in particular, hit by labour flexibility, technological disruption, economic uncertainty and the plunder of the commons that imposes the highest costs on the poor and marginalized.

The case for instituting a basic income as an anchor in a new twenty-first-century income distribution system does not rest on the common assumption that robots and artificial intelligence will cause mass unemployment, or that it would be a more efficient way of relieving poverty than current social assistance, although it would. The main arguments are ethical.[48]

Fundamentally, it is a matter of social justice. Our wealth and income have far more to do with the efforts and achievements of our collective forebears than with anything we do ourselves. If we allow private inheritance, we should accept social inheritance, regarding basic income as a social dividend on our collective wealth.

Moreover, even if pitched at a low level, a basic income would enhance freedom. The political right preaches freedom but fails to acknowledge that financial insecurity constrains the ability to make rational choices. People must be able to say 'no' to oppressive or exploitative relationships, as women know only too well. But the left, too, has ignored freedom in supporting paternalistic policies. Welfare recipients are treated as subjects of charity or pity, subject to arbitrary intrusive controls to prove themselves 'deserving'.

A basic income would enhance 'republican freedom' – freedom from potential as well as actual domination by figures of unaccountable power. A basic income is the only welfare policy for which the 'emancipatory value' is greater than the monetary value.[49] And as a right, it would reduce the precariat's sense of being a supplicant. Basic income would also give people basic (not total) security in an era of chronic insecurity. Basic security is a natural public good. You having it does not deprive me of it; indeed, we gain from others having it. Psychologists have shown that insecurity lowers IQ and 'mental bandwidth', diminishing the ability to make rational decisions, causing stress and mental illness. People with basic security tend to be more altruistic, empathetic, solidaristic and engaged in the community.

Studies have shown that basic income is affordable even with existing tax/benefit systems. The Royal Society of Arts has even suggested that taxing Amazon, Facebook and Apple more would be enough to pay for a basic income.[50] If used solely for individual dividends, a 1 per cent wealth tax alone would be sufficient to pay each adult £2,200 a year, or £42 a week. However, building a Commons Fund would be a more ambitious and better way of raising the money to pay dignifying basic incomes. These would be added to existing incomes so, as the amount paid out rose, more and more people would have an income above the threshold for means-tested benefits, saving public revenue for other purposes.

In the UK a modest 'starting level' basic income paying £40 per week per child and to those over sixty-five, £50 per week for those aged sixteen to twenty-five, and £60 for those aged twenty-six to sixty-four would cost £173 billion a year.[51] If personal tax allowances were abolished and the money reallocated to help pay for a basic income, that would free up over £100 billion a year.

Meanwhile, the Treasury could set a target of rolling back £100 billion of the remaining £300 billion of foregone revenue through tax reliefs. If half of that were added to the funds for what might be called the Base Dividend, the amount available for Dividends would already be £150 billion. At this point, the Commons Fund would come into the picture.

Suppose the levies outlined earlier resulted in the Fund obtaining £100 billion by the end of Year One. Assuming, just for illustration, that the permanent fund rules for exhaustible resources applied to £60 billion, this would leave £40 billion to which the Hartwick Rule would not apply. Half could be recycled as compensation for incursion into the commons, to which could be added the net return to fund investments of, say, £2.4 billion (4 per cent).

This would take the amount available for Common Dividends to over £172 billion after Year One, which is what would be required to pay for the initial target figures. In Year Two, the Commons Fund would be augmented by a further £100 billion. Applying the same rules, the permanent component of the Fund would then be £120 billion, generating a net return of £4.8 billion. The non-permanent component would be nearly £61 billion (£20 billion from Year One plus a 4 per cent return, and £40 billion from levies in Year Two).

Recycling half of the non-permanent component as before would yield about £30 billion to add to the £150 billion base.

At that point the total sum available for paying dividends would be £180 billion. In Year Three and onwards, the Fund's performance could be used to target an average of, say £70 a week. Eventually, if the payable dividends reached half median earnings, any outstanding amount could go to the Treasury for other public spending. Although these numbers are illustrative, it is clear that a Commons Fund could finance a basic income that, while starting at a modest level, would rise steadily over time.

Affordability aside, some argue that a basic income would induce laziness, undermining the 'work ethic'. This is contradicted by all the available evidence, especially if all forms of work and not just paid labour are considered. Besides giving people more energy, confidence and ability to take risks, a basic income would remove poverty and precarity traps embedded in means-tested systems that are major disincentives to taking low-paid jobs.

Basic income would tilt activity towards more reproductive work, away from resource-depleting labour. Official labour statistics should also be overhauled to give value to commoning, including care work. Then we could measure economic growth in ways that better reflect the well-being of society, including more ecologically sustainable activities.

In 2018 the Office for National Statistics estimated that unpaid work by households was worth £1.24 trillion, or £19,000 per person, 80 per cent higher than in 2005 and greater than the total contribution of the non-financial corporate sector. If we gave a value to such work, and legitimized it with a basic income, we might become less obsessed with pushing people into unnecessary and resource-depleting jobs, many of which deserve the title of 'bullshit jobs'.[52]

As for the objection that basic income would be giving 'something for nothing', this is hypocritical. Inherited wealth accounts for about 60 per cent of all wealth in Britain, yet those gaining from private inheritance have done 'nothing' in return. If we allow inherited wealth to persist, we should not oppose distributing dividends from social wealth that would, in any case, not be 'for nothing' but for compensation for loss or depletion of the commons.

How much should a basic income be? The honest answer is that we cannot know in advance. But as it grew from an initially modest level we would be moving towards a reduction of inequalities and insecurity, rather than continuing in the opposite direction as with Universal Credit. The level would be determined by the performance of the Commons Fund. If its income rises and its investments are successful, the initially small dividends will increase. Eventually, that might lead to the question: When is the amount enough or more than enough? Reaching that point would surely be a happy day. Answering the question could be left to the commoners to decide democratically in due course. For the present, that should not be used to defer progress on this transformational journey.

# Epilogue

Imagine a country in which the libertarians and neo-liberals had achieved their aims, in which everything had been privatized and commodified. It would be a dystopia of privation for a majority shovelled into the precariat, unable to pay the entry price to what had been commons, unable to pay for justice, frozen out of cultural channels, deprived of enlightenment education, subject to the whims and manipulations of data-driven algorithms and multinational digital platforms, watching helplessly as plutocrats amassed more and more rental income from privatized 'intellectual property' and other assets, and used their fortunes to fund lobbyists, politicians and parties prepared to serve their material interests. Feted as 'wealth creators', the plutocrats and their political minions could dismiss criticism as mere envy.

That dystopia is not far away. The trends are clear. But they can be stopped and reversed, if we not only recognize the dangers but also reconstruct the commons as a pillar of the state, as a buffer between government and commerce, as the zone where commoners can revive their sense of citizenship and the social and ecological landscape.

The commons are our collective heritage. They cannot be alienated legitimately unless we, as citizens, decide that is what we wish, recognizing that we are custodians for future generations as well as ours. Privatizing and commercializing the commons, and most particularly colonizing them, amounts to theft. It is a form of corruption intended to generate rental income for a few, from newly created 'property rights'. And it is regressive. The loss of the commons most affects those who rely on it the most.

It is they who have the greatest interest in leading a revolt against trespassers on our collective heritage. We should go back to our constitutional roots. The Magna Carta and the Charter of the Forest are charters of reparations, restoring rights to the commons usurped by powerful interests. We need a new reparations charter to restore the commons, which are being snatched so sneakily and illegitimately away from us.

The civil or cultural challenge is to resurrect a widespread awareness of the commons. The president of the International Association for the Study of the Commons, John Powell, who helped draft the Commons Act of 2006 when working in the Department for Environment, Food and Rural Affairs, has lamented the bureaucracy's 'knowledge deficit' on commons issues. Austerity cuts that have thinned civil service ranks and expertise have weakened commons defences still further.

Educating policymakers and the public on the meaning and social significance of the commons is surely vital. All civil servants should be required to take an education course on the commons and the values inherent in them. And all schools, colleges and universities should include teaching the value of the commons in their curricula.

The political challenge is to preserve the commons that have stood the test of time, to mobilize sufficient resources to do so, and to create a regulatory system of stewards and gatekeepers with the capacity and mandate to curtail encroachment and invasion by commerce. For that to happen, the commoners – all of us – must be alert and active. Perhaps it would help if one condition for receipt of those Common Dividends, or basic income, should be a moral (not legally binding) commitment 'to do our bit' to defend and strengthen the commons. And so we should.

There is a paradox with which to conclude this unfolding story. There can be no society without commoning, but we need a commons to common. Expressed less quixotically, commoning is about sharing in activity, but sharing without a structured commons cannot be transformative. Two indigents sitting on the steps outside a church, sharing a loaf, is merely survival. It changes nothing; it is pitiable. By contrast, sharing that takes place in a cooperative or in an occupational guild is about strengthening a sense of belonging, appreciating reciprocity and aspiring to develop one's capacities and the capacities of the group, of the 'club' of commoners. That goes back to ancient Greece and the *agora*, the public place in which citizens had equal status. There they could learn and refine the human values of empathy, dignity and mutual respect, in the context of leisure as *scholé*, imparting civic values and participating in their reinforcement. Without an *agora* these values and the capacity to participate wither from neglect.

A basic income should not be seen in isolation, but as part of a progressive response to the vagaries of globalized capitalism, aiding in the process of building new commons and reviving those that have arisen from time out of mind. It would encourage work rather than labour, leisure (in the *scholé* sense) rather than consumption. It would help build a new 'commonfare' in place of labour-based 'welfare' or its inevitable outcome, 'workfare'. It would help rekindle the values of the right to work, the values of preservation and the right to subsistence that guided that strange and wonderful one-page Charter sealed 800 years ago. Those values applied then, and they apply now, and they will apply in time out of mind to come.

# The Charter of the Commons

## Preamble

The commons are our collective heritage, our common wealth, our collective knowledge and our traditions of sharing in society. They are of most value to those on low incomes, the 'property-less' and the precariat. Shrinking the commons lowers their living standard and worsens inequality. To reduce inequality and strengthen citizenship, it is vital to revive the commons.

The Hartwick Rule of inter-generational equity – the principle that future generations should benefit from the commons as much as current generations – should be respected. Policies must promote and support equitable sharing, while seeking to prevent and reverse 'contrived scarcity' arising from the encroachment, enclosure and privatization of the commons, and the neglect by government.

To revive the ethos of the commons, we should strive to create, and bequeath to coming generations, new commons based on communities of interest and communal forms of management that respect customs of sharing and preserving natural, social, cultural, civil and knowledge resources.

The commons can only be safe if there is strong democratic governance. All spheres of the commons should have identified stewards, responsible for their management and preservation, and adequately funded gatekeepers, without which the stewards may not be held to account.

## Natural Commons

Article 1: Ownership of all land in Britain should be registered with the Land Registry within a year of the order being made, with penalties for non-registration that could include taking land back into common ownership.

Article 2: A new Domesday book should compile a comprehensive record of the public and private ownership of land, including a map showing all commons and Open Access land.

Article 3: Farm subsidies based on the amount of land owned should be abolished.

Article 4: Local authorities should be re-empowered to acquire land for rent to small-scale farmers.

Article 5: In keeping with the spirit of the Charter of the Forest, the Forestry Commission should be obliged to preserve the nation's forests as commons. This means halting and reversing privatization and commercialization, and maximizing public access consistent with conserving the environment.

Article 6: The Charter for Trees, Woods and People, as drawn up by the Woodland Trust in 2017, should be supported by all levels of government.

Article 7: National parks should be preserved as zones of biodiversity, and commercialization should be reversed.

Article 8: The time-honoured right to roam must be preserved. The period for registration of paths and footways should be extended beyond the existing 2026 cut-off. Maps of all open-access green space should be freely available to the public.

Article 9: Public parks must be protected and properly funded.

Article 10: The privatization of roads and squares in cities and towns should be stopped. Privately owned public spaces (POPS) should be rolled back and common rights of use restored. All urban public spaces, including POPS, should be mapped and made publicly available.

Article 11: Urban trees must be preserved and increased in number. Mature trees should not be felled unless they endanger people or property. Privatization of tree maintenance should be reversed.

Article 12: Privatized water companies must be restored to common ownership.

Article 13: The skyline is part of our commons. Those who block or blight the urban skyline with billboards and advertisements should pay a commons levy, as should factories, mass distribution sheds, supermarkets and other non-agricultural constructions that scar our open countryside.

Article 14: Air pollution is a severe subtraction from the commons. It must be regulated and taxed.

Article 15: Wind power is a natural commons that should be converted to common ownership.

Article 16: All resources in or under the ground or sea should belong to the commons and be exploited according to commons principles for the benefit of all commoners.

Article 17: No fracking or other resource extraction should take place in or under any public commons such as national parks.

Article 18: A carbon tax should be imposed to slash greenhouse gas emissions, at a level that will enable the UK to fulfil its pledges to combat climate change. Those on lower incomes should be compensated for the higher energy prices.

Article 19: The Natural Capital Committee must be abolished. Nature is not capital.

## Social Commons

Article 20: The right to a home must be restored. The 'right to buy' and the compulsory sale of social housing must be scrapped, and more social housing built. Local authorities should have the power to requisition unoccupied housing. The 'bedroom tax' should be abolished.

Article 21: Local communities must have more say in the planning and design of local housing, including community ownership.

Article 22: Student accommodation must be affordable for all and comply with normal rules for social housing, including safety, liveable space and access for those with disabilities.

Article 23: We must combat the homelessness epidemic. Conventional hostels and shelters should be replaced by 'housing commons', places where people are assured of shelter and food and can recover a sense of basic security.

Article 24: Cuts in spending on public services and amenities must be reversed. Privatized and outsourced services should be brought back into common ownership or strictly regulated in the interests of users, the commoners.

Article 25: People with physical or mental disabilities should have equal access to public spaces and facilities, including POPS, and equal rights of use. All public spaces and facilities must be made accessible for those with disabilities.

Article 26: The number of allotments should be preserved and expanded. Sites must be protected from privatization or conversion to other uses.

Article 27: Local markets selling fresh and local produce should be encouraged and protected.

Article 28: Policies must ensure food security for all, as part of the right to subsistence. Hunger has no place in an affluent society.

Article 29: The commons traditions of the guilds must be regenerated by reviving occupational communities and encouraging accreditation-based practices in place of licensing.

## Civil Commons

Article 30: Private owners of public spaces should be required to display prominent notices of any restrictions on use of the space and what, if any, 'penalties' exist for contravening them. But private owners of public spaces should not be allowed to impose restrictions and penalties that are not in force in publicly owned public spaces.

Article 31: Legal aid as a right must be granted for both criminal and civil cases. This should include cases brought against the alleged unlawful plunder of the commons by corporations or individuals, who can otherwise exert legal advantage by hiring expensive lawyers and indulging in costly litigation.

Article 32: The probation service must be restored as a common public service. The privatization of prisons and policing must be reversed.

Article 33: If any private social policy provider wrongly denies a claimant some benefit or service to which they are entitled, the provider should be fined, with part going to compensate the wronged claimant. Claimants should not be sanctioned without a fair hearing; there must be no sanctions without due process.

## Cultural Commons

Article 34: The BBC has a unique role as a public service broadcaster. Its governance must be made more democratic and funding through the licence fee must be made independent of the government of the day.

Article 35: The erosion of the cultural commons represents a concealed form of impoverishment and inequality. The public sphere must be revived and funding for the cultural commons restored.

Article 36: To assist in the revival of commoning, in activities involving shared creative activity, fledgling cultural cooperatives should be supported.

## Knowledge Commons

Article 37: Data must be owned by the individuals who
generate them and used only for purposes to which
they agree.

Article 38: Regulation is needed to protect privacy and
require tech companies to meet democratically decided
standards, including removing and barring false or
malicious content.

Article 39: The principles in the European Union's General
Data Protection Regulations should be integrated into
any UK post-Brexit trade deals.

Article 40: Intellectual property rights are too strong
and are depleting the knowledge commons. Patent
applications should be more strictly vetted and their
duration shortened.

Article 41: Copyright protection should end with the death
of the author or artist or, reverting to the old rule,
last for fourteen years after creation of the work if the
author or artist dies within that period.

Article 42: The privatization and commodification of all
levels of schooling and education should be reversed.
All stakeholders, including students, teachers, parents
and the local community, should have a governance
role, along the lines of the multi-stakeholder
cooperative model.

## Commons Fund and Common Dividends

Article 43: A Commons Fund should be set up, primarily
sourced by levies on the commercial use or exploitation

of the commons. The Fund should invest to generate and preserve ecologically sustainable common wealth, and Common Dividends should be paid out equally to all commoners.

Article 44: Recalling the Charter of the Forest's constitutional commitment to the right to subsistence, the Commons Fund should be a means of introducing a basic income as an economic right, paid as Common Dividends.

# Notes

1. G. Standing, *The Corruption of Capitalism: Why Rentiers Thrive and Work Does Not Pay* (London: Biteback Publishing, 2016), pp. 271–4.

---

## CHAPTER 1: THE CHARTER OF THE FOREST

1. All citations from the Charter come from the translation of 1680, with capitals and grammar as in that version. The only two remaining originals from 1217 are in Durham Cathedral and Lincoln Castle. Durham Cathedral also has one of the three remaining copies of the 1225 version, issued when Henry III reached the age when he obtained the royal seal, and one of the five remaining copies of the 1300 issue.
2. N, Robinson, 'The Charter of the Forest: Evolving human rights in nature', in D. B. Magraw, A. Martinez and R. E. Brownell, *Magna Carta and the Rule of Law* (Chicago: American Bar Association, 2014), pp. 311–77. Robinson's paper remains the best descriptive account of the Charter's history, in which he notes that he had been unable to find any book devoted to it.
3. O. Rackham, *Woodlands* (London: Collins, 2006).
4. Implicit in the way the right to work was depicted was an even more radical idea, that the commoners would only do work that was perceived by them as necessary to sustain a way of life.
5. Robinson, 'The Charter of the Forest', p. 311.
6. The permanency is moot. It may have been a temporary promise. But the principle of a right was recognized.

7. The verderers still exist, notably in the Forest of Dean. See C. Hart, 'The history of the verderers', at <http://www.deanverderers.org.uk/verderer-history.html>.

8. The myth of Robin Hood has long been an ideological battleground, with Hollywood films depicting him as a nascent libertarian, against taxes and the state, or as a latent primitive socialist. The latter seems closer to what was happening at the time. Robin Hood may have been mythical, as a symbol of the defence of the commons against encroachment and privatization of land and resources by King John. But his dastardly opponent, the Sheriff of Nottingham, was singled out by name in the Magna Carta (Article 50) as someone who was to be banned from holding any public office.

9. L. Lohmann, 'Forestry, politics and violent conflict', in M. Suliman (ed.), *Ecology and Violent Conflict* (London: Zed Books, 1999).

10. O. Rackham, *The History of the Countryside* (London: J. M. Dent, 1986), p. 66.

11. Rackham, *The History of the Countryside*.

12. Cited in Lohmann, 'Forestry, politics and violent conflict', p. 4.

13. S. Fairlie, 'A short history of enclosure in Britain', *The Land*, Issue 7, Summer 2009.

14. This is documented superbly in P. Linebaugh, *The Magna Carta Manifesto: Liberties and Commons for All* (Berkeley: University of California Press, 2008).

15. Cited in Lohmann, 'Forestry, politics and violent conflict', p. 9.

16. C. D. Liddy, 'Urban enclosure riots: Risings of the commons in English towns, 1480–1525', *Past and Present*, 226 (1), 2015, pp. 41–77.

17. Linebaugh, *The Magna Carta Manifesto*, p. 53.

18. J. Watt, 'Public or Plebs: The changing meaning of "The Commons", 1381–1549', in H. Pryce and J. Watts (eds), *Power and Identity in the Middle Ages: Essays in Memory of Rees Davies* (Oxford: Oxford University Press, 2007), pp. 242–60.

19. Linebaugh, *The Magna Carta Manifesto*, p. 77.

20. Linebaugh, *The Magna Carta Manifesto*, pp. 100–105.

21. Robinson, 'The Charter of the Forest', p. 321.

22. B. Cowell, 'Forests, the Magna Carta, and the "New Commons": Some thoughts for the Forest Panel', Magna Carta Trust, 13 October 2011.

23. The full mouthful of the name of the Act of 1971 testifies to the reinterpretation that had taken place over the centuries. It is *An Act to Abolish Certain Rights of Her Majesty to Wild Creatures and Certain Related*

*Rights and Franchises; to Abrogate the Forest Law (subject to exceptions), and to Repeal Enactments Relating to those Rights and Franchises and to Forests and the Forest Law; and for Connected Purposes.*

24. There is another version. In both, an excellent second stanza goes: 'The law demands that we atone/When we take things that we do not own/But leaves the lords and ladies fine/Who take things that are yours and mine.'

25. Hart, 'The history of the verderers'.

---

## CHAPTER 2: THE COMMONS, COMMONERS AND COMMONING

1. P. Linebaugh, *The Magna Carta Manifesto: Liberties and Commons for All* (Berkeley: University of California Press, 2008), p. 79.

2. For discussion of this dialectic, see S. Gudeman, *The Anthropology of Economy: Commodity, Market and Culture* (Oxford: Blackwell, 2001), p. 27; J. K. Gibson-Graham, J. Cameron and S. Healy, 'Commoning as postcapitalist politics', in A. Amin and P. Howell (eds), *Releasing the Commons: Rethinking the Futures of the Commons* (London: Routledge, 2016).

3. I. Illich, 'Silence is a commons', Asahi Symposium on Science and Man – The computer-managed society, Tokyo, 21 March 1982.

4. For example, P. Kilby, *Forest Camera: A Portrait of Ashdown*, ed. R. Bowlby (Uckfield, Sussex: Sweethaws Press, 1998).

5. C. D. Liddy, *Contesting the City: The Politics of Citizenship in English Towns, 1250–1530* (Oxford: Oxford University Press, 2017).

6. G. Bathe, *Village Greens* (Stroud: Pitkin Publishing/Open Spaces Society, 2016), p. 8.

7. D. Bollier, *Silent Theft: The Private Plunder of Our Common Wealth* (New York and London: Routledge, 2002), p. 3.

8. D. Bollier, 'FabLabs, time banks, and other hidden treasures you didn't know you owned', *Yes! Magazine*, 16 July 2014.

9. 'Economics focus: Commons sense', *The Economist*, 2 August 2008, p. 73.

10. P. Hulm, 'The Swiss commune that changed ecology', *Global Geneva*, 12 December 2016.

11. E. Schlager and E. Ostrom, 'Property-rights regimes and natural resources: A conceptual analysis', *Land Economics*, 68 (3), 1992.

12. E. Ostrom, *Governing the Commons: The Evolution of Institutions for Collective Action* (Cambridge: Cambridge University Press, 1990).

13. For conservation reasons Lincoln Castle, which holds one of the two surviving copies of the 1217 Charter of the Forest and one of the four originals of the 1215 Charter of Liberties, puts them away in darkness every few months.

14. For instance, N. Fernandez, 'How to put an end to the urban commons and "sharing" once and for all', Resilience.org, 19 January 2016, at <https://www.resilience.org/stories/2016-01-19/how-to-put-an-end-to-the-urban-commons-and-sharing-once-and-for-all/>.

15. A. R. Poteete, M. A. Janssen and E. Ostrom, *Working Together: Collective Action, the Commons and Multiple Methods in Practice* (Princeton: Princeton University Press, 2010).

16. 'To the last grain', *The Economist*, 22 December 2018, pp. 69–71.

17. M. Riggulsford, 'Common as marl', *Geoscientist*, July 2017, pp. 16–19.

18. Peter Linebaugh made an attempt to list contemporary American social policies that he thought corresponded to each of the Charter's specified rights. That exercise merely made apparent that in the twentieth century, even before the neo-liberal onslaught, common rights were in retreat. P. Linebaugh, 'The secret history of the Magna Carta', *Boston Review*, Summer 2003.

19. Cited in A. Wood, *The Memory of the People: Custom and Popular Senses of the Past in Early Modern England* (Cambridge: Cambridge University Press, 2013), pp. 117 and 108.

20. Wood, *The Memory of the People*, pp. 201–13.

21. G. Standing, *The Corruption of Capitalism: Why Rentiers Thrive and Work Does Not Pay* (London: Biteback Publishing, 2016).

22. Bollier, *Silent Theft*. See also P. Linebaugh, *Stop, Thief! The Commons, Enclosures and Resistance* (Oakland, CA: PM Press, 2014).

23. N. Robinson, 'The Charter of the Forest: Evolving human rights in nature', in D. B. Magraw, A. Martinez and R. E. Brownell, *Magna Carta and the Rule of Law* (Chicago: American Bar Association, 2014), p. 319.

24. As a Democrat Senator stated in early 2018, 'The President still hasn't nominated a director for the National Park Service and Secretary Zinke has proposed tripling entrance fees at our most popular national parks. His disregard of the advisory board is just another example of why he has earned an "F" in stewardship.' S. Neuman and C. Dwyer, 'Majority of National Park Service Board resigns, citing administration indifference', npr.org, 17 January 2018.

25. This section draws inspiration from Wood, *The Memory of the People*, passim.

26. See, for example, P. Connerton, *How Modernity Forgets* (Cambridge: Cambridge University Press, 2009). Jack Goody suggested that forgetting

can be a creative process, and that creation usually requires some forgetting. J. Goody, *Myth, Ritual and the Oral* (Cambridge: Cambridge University Press, 2010).

27. World Bank, *The Changing Wealth of Nations: Measuring Sustainable Development in the New Millennium* (Washington DC: World Bank, 2011), p. 9.

28. G. Standing, *The Precariat: The New Dangerous Class* (London: Bloomsbury, 2011); G. Standing, *A Precariat Charter: From Denizens to Citizens* (London: Bloomsbury, 2014).

29. See, for instance, D. Mackay, 'New commons for old: Inspiring new cultural traditions', *Landscape Archaeology and Ecology*, 8, 2010, pp. 109–18.

30. C. Borzaga and G. Galera, 'Innovating the provision of welfare services through collective action: the case of Italian social cooperatives', *International Review of Sociology*, 26(1), 2016.

## CHAPTER 3: THE NATURAL COMMONS

1. K. Cahill, *Who Owns the World: The Hidden Facts Behind Land Ownership* (Edinburgh: Mainstream Publishing, 2006).

2. E. Purdy, 'John Locke', in R. P. Carlisle (ed.), *Encyclopedia of Politics*: Vol.2: *The Right* (London: Sage Publications, 2005), p. 286.

3. For a useful account, showing how enclosure was not technologically determined, see S. Fairlie, 'A short history of enclosure in Britain', *The Land*, Issue 7, Summer 2009, at <https://.thelandmagazine.org.uk/articles/short-history-enclosure-britain>.

4. For an affectionate review of the development of commons in land, see G. Bathe, *Common Land* (Stroud: Open Spaces Society/ Pitkin Publishing, 2015).

5. These statistics and others in the section are from the Foundation for Common Land, at <http://www.foundationforcommonland.org.uk/the-commons-lands-of-great-britain>.

6. 'As Brexit negotiations begin, England urged to develop progressive food policy in advance of leaving the EU', Press release, People's Food Policy, 26 June 2017.

7. 'The dukes, their tax breaks, and an £8 million annual subsidy', whoownsengland.org, 8 May 2017, at <https://whoownsengland.org/2017/05/08/the-dukes-their-tax-breaks-an-8million-annual-subsidy/>.

8.  J. K. Boyce, *Inequality and the Environment*, Leontief Prize Lecture, Tufts University, Medford, MA, 28 March 2017.

9.  K. Ashbrook, *Saving Open Spaces: The Campaign for Public Rights to Enjoy Commons, Green Spaces and Paths* (Stroud: Open Spaces Society/ Pitkin Publishing, 2015), p. 3. An early committee member was William Morris.

10. R. Neate, 'UK for sale? Ministers woo world's property developers in Cannes', *The Guardian*, 17 March 2017, p. 33.

11. Foundation for Common Land, 'Rights of common', at <http://www. foundationforcommonland.org.uk/rights-of-common>.

12. 'To the last grain', *The Economist*, 22 December 2018, pp. 69–71.

13. S. Sassen, *Expulsions: Brutality and Complexity in the Global Economy* (Cambridge, MA: Harvard University Press, 2014).

14. M. Grainger and K. Geary, 'The New Forests Company and its Uganda plantations: Oxfam Case Study', Oxfam, London, 21 September 2011.

15. S. Burgos, 'Do land grabs promote food security?', Oxfam America blog, 4 September 2013.

16. Woodland Trust, *The State of the UK's Forests, Woods and Trees: Perspectives from the Sector* (Grantham: Woodland Trust, 2011).

17. O. Bennett and D. Hirst, 'The Forestry Commission and the sale of public forests in England', House of Commons Library note SN/SC/5734, 24 November 2014; EFTEC, *The Economic Contribution of the Public Forest Estate in England* (London: EFTEC, January 2010), Figure 15; Independent Panel on Forestry, *Independent Panel on Forestry – Final Report* (London: Department for Environment, Food and Rural Affairs, July 2012), p. 9.

18. B. Webster, 'Forests are growing . . . into cabin parks', *The Times*, 7 April 2018.

19. C. Davies, 'One of Europe's last primeval forests on the "brink of collapse"', *The Guardian*, 25 May 2017, p. 22.

20. G. Monbiot, 'The Lake District's world heritage site status is a betrayal of the living world', *The Guardian*, 11 July 2017.

21. 'The looting of America's public lands', *The New York Times*, 11 December 2017, p. 13.

22. A. Davies, 'Turning wilderness into theme parks: The great national parks debate', *The Guardian*, 18 December 2018.

23. G. Bathe, *Public Paths* (Stroud: Open Spaces Society/Pitkin Publishing, 2017), pp. 8–9.

24. Open Spaces Society, 'Ten years left to find our way', Henley-on-Thames, April 2016.

25. R. Macfarlane, 'Badger or Bulbasaur – have children lost touch with nature?', *The Guardian*, 10 September 2017.

26. This is the interpretation by Graham Bathe, *Village Greens* (Stroud: Open Spaces Society/Pitkin Publishing, 2016), p. 25.

27. Bathe, *Village Greens*, p. 25.

28. A. Wood, *The Memory of the People: Custom and Popular Senses of the Past in Early Modern England* (Cambridge: Cambridge University Press, 2013).

29. The 27,000 figure was estimated by the Public Parks Assessment conducted in 2001 by the Department for Transport, Local Government and the Regions. The *State of UK Public Parks 2016* report estimated the number as close to 22,000.

30. Cited in R. Shrimsley, 'Putting a price on the perks of parks', *FT Magazine*, 12/13 May 2018, p. 10.

31. E. Hunt, 'London's parks accused of "creeping privatisation" of public spaces', *The Guardian*, 31 August 2018.

32. B. Christophers, *The New Enclosure: The Appropriation of Public Land in Neoliberal Britain* (London: Verso, 2018).

33. J. Vasagar, 'Public spaces in Britain's cities fall into private hands', *The Guardian*, 11 June 2012.

34. 'Erdogan's outsized ambitions', *The Economist*, 28 April 2018, p. 23.

35. See, for example, A. Minton, 'What I want from our cities in 2015: Public spaces that are truly public', *The Guardian*, 30 December 2014.

36. B. Garrett, 'The privatisation of cities' public spaces is escalating. It is time to take a stand', *The Guardian*, 4 August 2015.

37. K. Allen, 'Councils to sell £129m of land and property', *Financial Times*, 1 January 2016.

38. 'How much public land is available for housebuilding', 23 November 2016, at <https://whoownsengland.org/2016/11/23/how-much-public-land-is-available-for-house-building/>.

39. 'Crown jewels', *Private Eye*, Issue 1390, 17 April 2015; <https://whoownsengland.org/> (website run by G. Shrubsole and A. Powell-Smith).

40. 'Awash: Money laundering in London', *The Economist*, 13 October 2018, p. 66.

41. S. Sassen, 'Who owns our cities – and why this urban takeover should concern us all', *The Guardian*, 24 November 2015.

42. Vasagar, 'Public spaces in Britain's cities fall into private hands'.

43. Vasagar, 'Public spaces in Britain's cities fall into private hands'.

44. P. Barkham, 'Introducing "treeconomics": How street trees can save our cities', *The Guardian*, 15 August 2015.

45. S. Daniels, 'The political iconography of woodland in later Georgian England', in D. Cosgrove and S. Daniels (eds), *The Iconography of Landscape* (Cambridge: Cambridge University Press, 1988), pp. 43–82.

46. D. J. Nowak and E. J. Greenfield, 'Declining urban and community tree cover in the United States', *Urban Forestry and Urban Greening*, 32(3), 2018.

47. A. Micu, 'The US lost roughly 1 in every 100 urban trees between 2009 and 2014', ZME Science online, 20 April 2018.

48. F. Perraudin, 'Sheffield puts forward plan to cut down fewer trees', *The Guardian*, 25 October 2018, p. 14.

49. P. Barkham, 'Put a price on urban trees – and halt this chainsaw massacre', *The Guardian*, 11 September 2017.

50. H. Pidd, 'Sheffield trees dispute prompts "scenes you'd expect in Putin's Russia"', *The Guardian*, 28 November 2016.

51. G. Monbiot, 'Look to Sheffield: This is how state and corporate power subverts democracy', *The Guardian*, 24 October 2017.

52. James Maitland, Earl of Lauderdale, *An Enquiry into the Nature and Origin of Public Wealth and into the Means and Causes of its Increase* (Edinburgh: A. Constable and Co., 1819), pp. 41–2.

53. 'Liquid assets: Land owned by the water utilities', 29 August 2016, at <https://whoownsengland.org/2016/08/29/liquid-assets-land-owned-by-the-water-utilities/>.

54. K. Bayliss and D. Hall, 'Bringing water into public ownership: Costs and benefits', University of Greenwich, London, May 2017, mimeo.

55. R. Graham, 'Water in the UK – public versus private', Open Democracy, 19 December 2014.

56. K. Yearwood, 'The privatised water industry in the UK. An ATM for investors', Public Services International Research Unit, University of Greenwich, London, September 2018.

57. J. Ford, 'Water privatisation looks little more than an organised rip-off', *Financial Times*, 10 September 2017.

58. Yearwood, 'The privatised water industry in the UK'.

59. D. Hall and E. Lobina, 'Water companies in Europe', Public Services International Research Unit, University of Greenwich, London, 2010.

60. D. Carrington, 'Thames Water given maximum £8.5 million fine for missing leak target', *The Guardian*, 14 June 2017.

61. Ford, 'Water privatisation looks little more than an organised rip-off'.

62. G. Plimmer, 'London super sewer causes stink over opaque funding structure'. *Financial Times*, 7 August 2017.

63. It is noteworthy that the agreement was made when Ian Pearson, who later became a non-executive director of Thames Water, was a government minister.

64. On options, see *Alternative Models of Ownership*, Report to the Shadow Chancellor of the Exchequer and Shadow Secretary of State for Business, Energy and Industrial Strategy, London, 2017.

65.  D. Bollier, 'FabLabs, time banks and other hidden treasures you didn't know you owned', *Yes! Magazine*, 16 July 2014.

66.  P. Hulm, 'The Swiss commune that inspired a Nobel-prize-winning theory on communal ownership', *Le News*, 13 December 2016.

67.  T. McVeigh, 'As British tourists take to the seas, giant cruise ship flotillas spread pollution misery', *The Observer*, 8 January 2017, p. 10.

68.  A. Chrisafis, '"I don't want ships to kill me": Marseille fights cruise liner pollution', *The Guardian*, 6 July 2018.

69.  In 2018, the International Maritime Organization agreed new rules to reduce sulphur emissions by shipping, but one of several criticisms is that these may result in more sulphur discharges into the oceans. 'Spoil shipping for a ha'p'orth of tar', *The Economist*, 27 October 2018, p. 57.

70.  J. R. Gillis, 'The disappearance of sand', *The International New York Times*, 7 November 2014.

71.  In October 2018, more than a quarter of a million people signed a petition against advertising a horse race on the roof sails of Sydney Opera House, which is a World Heritage Site. It went ahead anyway, despite opposition from the Opera House director. M. McGowan, '"Not for sale": Sydney Opera House racing ad sparks protest', *The Guardian*, 9 October 2018.

72.  M. Taylor, 'All Londoners breathing in toxic air particle at levels above global limit', *The Guardian*, 5 October 2017, p. 4.

73.  D. Carrington, 'Millions of British children breathing toxic air, Unicef warns', *The Guardian*, 21 June 2018.

74.  See, among other studies showing similar findings, M. Pastor, J. Sadd and R. Morello-Frosch, 'Who's minding the kids? Toxic air, public schools and environmental justice in Los Angeles', *Social Science Quarterly*, 83(1), 2002, pp. 263–80.

75.  F. Harvey, 'Air pollution linked to much greater risk of dementia', *The Guardian*, 18 September 2018.

76.  D. Carrington and L. Kuo, 'Air pollution causes "huge" reduction in intelligence, study reveals', *The Guardian*, 27 August 2018.

77.  J. K. Boyce, K. Zwickl and M. Ash, 'Measuring environmental inequality', *Ecological Economics*, 124, 2016, pp. 114–23.

78.  The Offshore Valuation Group, *The Offshore Valuation: A Valuation of the UK's Offshore Renewable Energy Resource* (Machynlleth, Wales: Public Interest Research Centre, May 2010).

79.  *Who Owns the Wind, Owns the Future* (London: Labour Energy Forum, September 2017).

80.  R. Godwin, 'Sonic doom: How noise pollution kills thousands each year', *The Guardian*, 3 July 2018.

81.  J. Vidal, 'The map that shames the world', *The Observer*, 16 August 2015, pp. 18–19.

82.  The most disturbing developments have been in the United States, where there has been a fracking bonanza. In one part of Texas, where there have been no earthquakes for millions of years, there has been considerable seismic activity attributed to wastewater injection linked to fracking. T. Dart, '"Like thunder in the ground": Texans fear link between quakes and fracking waste', *The Guardian*, 5 January 2018.

83.  B. Davey, 'Jim Ratcliffe, Ineos and the empire of trash', Feasta online (Foundation for the Economics of Sustainability), 11 June 2016. For the studies, see J. Hays and S. B. C. Shonkoff, 'Towards an understanding of the environmental and public health impacts of shale gas development: an analysis of the peer reviewed scientific literature, 2009–2015', 2 April 2016, at <https://www.psehealthyenergy.org/>.

84.  L. S. Shaina, S. L. Stacy, L. L. Brink, J. C. Larkin, Y. Sadovsky, B. D. Goldstein, B. R. Pitt, et al., 'Perinatal outcomes and unconventional natural gas operations in Southwest Pennsylvania'. *PLoS ONE*, 10(6), 2015: e0126425; R. Preidt, 'Fracking linked to low birth weight babies', WebMD.com, 3 June 2015, at <https://www.webmd.com/parenting/baby/news/20150603/fracking-linked-to-low-birth-weight-babies>.

85.  A. Vaughan, 'Households near fracking site to receive £2,000 payouts directly from Cuadrilla', *The Guardian*, 7 November 2017, p. 26.

86.  E. Marrington, 'National protections for national parks? What a load of potash . . .', Campaign to Protect Rural England, 24 July 2015.

87.  S. Duke, 'I'm digging the biggest hole in Yorkshire, says Sirius Minerals boss Chris Fraser', *The Sunday Times*, 22 April 2018.

88.  Although there is a legal literature, economists rarely consider the depth and height of land ownership. What depth of land does an owner own? And how high above the land does ownership extend? The Latin aphorism has been cited often enough: *Cuius est solum, eius est usque ad coelum et ad inferos*. It translates roughly as 'Whoever owns the soil, holds title up to the heavens and down to the depths of hell'. But it does not work like that in practice.

89.  G. Monbiot, 'Putting a price on the rivers and rain diminishes us all', *The Guardian*, 7 August 2012; Monbiot, 'Putting a price on nature will only speed its destruction', *The Guardian*, 16 May 2018, p. 4.

90. A. D. Guerry et al., 'Natural capital and ecosystem services informing decisions: From promise to practice', *PNAS – Proceedings of the National Academy of Sciences*, 112(24), 2015, pp. 7748–55.

91. C. Mayer, 'Unnatural capital accounting', *mimeo*, 15 December 2013, p. 3.

92. J. Watts, 'UN poised to move ahead with landmark treaty to protect high seas', *The Guardian*, 22 December 2017.

93. B. Batt, 'Saving the commons in an age of plunder', *American Journal of Economics and Sociology*, 75(2), March 2016, pp. 346–71.

94. L. Lohmann, 'Neoliberalism, law and nature', 5 July 2017, at <http://www.thecornerhouse.org.uk/resource/neoliberalism-law-and-nature>.

95. See, for example, A. Advani and G. Stoye, 'Cheaper, greener and more efficient: Rationalising UK carbon prices', *Fiscal Studies*, 38(2), 2017, pp. 269–99.

96. S. Pace, 'Space development, law, and values', IISL Galloway Space Law Symposium, Cosmos Club, Washington DC, 13 December 2017.

97. Cited in Macfarlane, 'Badger or Bulbasaur – have children lost touch with nature?'

## CHAPTER 4: THE SOCIAL COMMONS

1. G. Standing, *A Precariat Charter: From Denizens to Citizens* (London: Bloomsbury, 2014).

2. P. Butler, 'Report reveals scale of food bank use in the UK', *The Guardian*, 29 May 2017.

3. P. Butler, 'Families with stable jobs at risk of homelessness in England, report finds', *The Guardian*, 15 December 2017.

4. House of Commons Committee of Public Accounts, *Homeless Households*. HC 462, Session 2017–19, House of Commons, 20 December 2017.

5. J. Harris, 'Homelessness has surged for seven years. And it's clear who's to blame', *The Guardian*, 13 October 2017.

6. National Audit Office, *Financial Sustainability of Local Authorities 2018*. HC 864, Session 2017–2019, House of Commons, 8 March 2018.

7. P. Noor, 'What's behind the quiet rise of homelessness in the countryside', *The Guardian*, 10 January 2018.

8. M. Bulman, '4,000 women and children fleeing domestic abuse will be locked out of refuges under government proposals, warns charity', *The Independent*, 29 November 2017.

9. W. Wilson and C. Barton, 'Introducing a voluntary Right to Buy for housing association tenants in England', House of Commons Library research briefing, 25 October 2018.

10. B. Kentish, 'Council house numbers hit lowest point since records began', *The Independent*, 16 November 2017; National Audit Office, *Housing in England: Overview*. HC 917, Session 2016–17, House of Commons, 19 January 2017.

11. Wilson and Barton, 'Introducing a voluntary Right to Buy for housing association tenants in England'.

12. M. Savage, 'Ministers urged to halt right-to-buy scheme', *The Guardian*, 29 January 2019.

13. A. Griffin, 'Grenfell Tower cladding that may have led to fire was chosen to improve appearance of Kensington block of flats', *The Independent*, 14 June 2017.

14. J. Gapper, 'Grenfell: an anatomy of a housing disaster', *Financial Times*, 29 June 2017.

15. D. Batty, N. McIntyre, D. Pegg and A. Asthana, 'Grenfell: names of wealthy empty-home owners in borough revealed', *The Guardian*, 2 August 2017.

16. A. Chakrabortty, 'Jeremy Corbyn has declared war on Labour councils over housing', *The Guardian*, 27 September 2017.

17. R. Booth, 'Londoners miss out as homes built as "safe deposit boxes" for foreign buyers', *The Guardian*, 30 December 2014.

18. O. Wright, 'The government has no idea how many houses have been built on publicly owned land that has been sold to developers', *The Independent*, 24 September 2015, p. 14.

19. P. Collinson, 'UK tenants paid record £50bn in rents in 2017', *The Guardian*, 12 February 2018.

20. 'Britain's buy-to-let boom is coming to an end', *The Economist*, 12 December 2017.

21. P. Greenfield and S. Marsh, 'Hundreds of homeless people fined and imprisoned in England and Wales', *The Guardian*, 20 May 2018.

22. 'Proposed "homeless ban" in Australia cause for concern – UN expert', Press release, Office of the United Nations High Commissioner for Human Rights, 13 March 2017.

23. R. Moore, 'A blueprint for British housing in 2028', *The Guardian*, 21 January 2018.

24. O. Wainwright, 'A new urban eyesore: Britain's shamefully shoddy student housing', *The Guardian*, 11 September 2017.

25. 'Cladding remediation plans still unclear for 129 high-rise buildings', pbctoday, 26 October 2018, at <https://www.pbctoday.co.uk/news/building-control-news/cladding-remediation-high-rise-buildings/48350/>.

26. D. Campbell, 'NHS privatisation would be "political suicide", says thinktank', *The Guardian*, 1 February 2018.

27. 'Policy transplant', *The Economist*, 4 November 2017, p. 34.

28. G. Standing, *The Corruption of Capitalism: Why Rentiers Thrive and Work Does Not Pay* (London: Biteback Publishing, 2016), Chapter 7.

29. Y. El-Gingihy, *How to Dismantle the NHS in 10 Easy Steps* (Alresford, Hants: John Hunt Publishing, 2015).

30. S. Neville and G. Plimmer, 'Non-NHS groups play bigger care role', *Financial Times*, 5 May 2017, p. 2.

31. R. Mendick, L. Donnelly and A. Kirk, 'The PFI hospitals costing NHS £2bn every year', *Daily Telegraph*, 18 July 2015.

32. National Audit Office, *PF1 and PF2*. HC 718, Session 2017–19, House of Commons, 18 January 2018.

33. The Private Finance Initiative Watchdog, 'Meet the investment firms that own your PFI-funded public schools and hospitals', 18 February 2015, at < https://pfeyeblog.wordpress.com/2015/02/18/meet-the-investment-firms-that-own-your-pfi-funded-public-schools-and-hospitals/>.

34. G. Wearden, 'Carillion collapse exposed government outsourcing flaws – report', *The Guardian*, 9 July 2018.

35. National Audit Office, *NHS England's management of the primary care support services contract with Capita*. HC 632, Session 2017–19, House of Commons, 17 May 2018.

36. D. Campbell, 'NHS chiefs tell Theresa May it is time to curb privatisation', *The Guardian*, 7 January 2019.

37. P. Toynbee, 'Now NHS are stripping basic medicines from the poor', *The Guardian*, 17 August 2017.

38. R. Clarke, 'If no one listens to us, the NHS will face its own Grenfell-style disaster', *The Guardian*, 12 July 2017.

39. J. Ford, 'Private equity is the wrong prescription for social care', *Financial Times*, 17 December 2017.

40. S. Duffy, 'The failure of competitive tendering in social care', Centre for Welfare Reform, 12 October 2017.

41. 'The size of the social care problem: Three million hours of care lost in three years', Age UK, 1 June 2018.

42. 'Care system is failing, finds CSA survey', Age UK, 10 May 2018.

43. R. Adams, 'Hundreds of children's playgrounds in England close due to cuts', *The Guardian*, 13 April 2017.

44. R. Ratcliffe, 'Children are being priced out by "pay to play" in public spaces', *The Guardian*, 13 December 2015.

45. C. Lewis, 'Three years on from its sale, the privatisation of Royal Mail is a story of our times', *Huffpost*, 15 October 2016.

46. M. Brignall, 'Royal Mail queues lengthen as depots close across UK', *The Guardian*, 15 December 2018.

47. 'Life in the slow lane', *The Economist*, 5 March 2016, p. 25.

48. G. Plimmer and J. Ford, 'Rail: Frustration grows with Britain's fragmented network', *Financial Times*, 29 January 2018.

49. Plimmer and Ford, 'Rail: Frustration grows with Britain's fragmented network'.

50. N. Flynn, *Public Sector Management*, 6th edn (London: Sage, 2012).

51. R. Davies, 'Network Rail sells railway arches to investors for £1.5bn', *The Guardian*, 10 September 2018.

52. 'Buses in crisis, 2017', Campaign for Better Transport, at <https://bettertransport.org.uk/buses-crisis-2017>; *Buses in Crisis: A Report on Bus Funding Across England and Wales 2010–2016* (London: Campaign for Better Transport, 2015).

53. R. Morrison, 'The arts column: When we cut rural bus routes we cut our vital culture and tourism', *The Times*, 2 December 2016, p. 3.

54. 'Ex-minister slams DWP as £108m spent fighting disability benefit claims', *The Guardian*, 12 February 2018, p. 10.

55. K. Shubber, 'Learndirect faces collapse after failing to suppress Ofsted report', *Financial Times*, 14 August 2017.

56. G. Standing, *Work after Globalization: Building Occupational Citizenship* (Cheltenham: Edward Elgar, 2009).

57. H. Chance, *The Factory in the Garden: A History of Corporate Landscapes from the Industrial to the Digital Age* (Manchester: Manchester University Press, 2018).

58. J. Harris, 'Turf wars escalate in the battle for Britain's allotments', *The Guardian*, 31 May 2013.

59. See 'A people's food policy: Transforming our food system', June 2017, at <https://www.peoplesfoodpolicy.org/>.

60. National Audit Office, *NHS England's management of the primary care support services contract with Capita*.

61. Local Government Association, 'LGA responds to 2015 spending review', Press release, 25 November 2015.

62. G. Kelly, 'We can't all be winners as a new welfare state emerges', *The Guardian*, 28 October 2018, pp. 44–5; P. Butler, 'Deprived northern regions worst hit by UK austerity, study finds', *The Guardian*, 28 January 2019.

63. P. S. Goodman, 'In Britain, austerity is changing everything', *The New York Times*, 28 May 2018.

64. *The Great British Sell Off: How We're Losing Our Vital Publicly Owned Buildings and Spaces Forever* (London: Locality, June 2018).

## CHAPTER 5: THE CIVIL COMMONS

1. A. Wood, *The Memory of the People: Custom and Popular Senses of the Past in Early Modern England* (Cambridge: Cambridge University Press, 2013), p. 125.

2. 'Schumpeter: Jail bait', *The Economist*, 29 October 2016, p. 58.

3. J. Harris, 'Britain's shared spaces are vanishing, leaving us a nation of cliques', *The Guardian*, 4 September 2018.

4. K. Rawlinson, 'Gangs' families should lose council homes – Home Office minister', *The Guardian*, 23 June 2018.

5. Amnesty International, *Trapped in the Matrix. Secrecy, Stigma and Bias in the Met's Gangs Database*, London, May 2018.

6. O. Bowcott, 'Court fees jeopardise Magna Carta principles, says lord chief justice', *The Guardian*, 8 October 2015.

7. 'US: Criminal justice system fuels poverty cycle', Press release, Human Rights Watch, 21 June 2018.

8. L. MacKinnon, 'Top court hears from marginalized offenders crushed by mandatory victim surcharge', iPolitics, 17 April 2018.

9. Equality and Human Rights Commission, *Is Britain Fairer? The State of Equality and Human Rights 2018* (Manchester: EHRC, 2018).

10. S. Krasniqi, 'Are we at risk of losing the right to a fair trial?', *Prospect*, 14 August 2018.

11. R. Davies, '"Recklessness, hubris and greed" – Carillion slammed by MPs', *The Guardian*, 16 May 2018.

12. O. Jones, 'Carillion is no one-off scandal. There are many more to come', *The Guardian*, 17 May 2018, p. 3.

13. N. Cohen, 'In Britain now, the richer you are, the better your chance of justice', *The Guardian*, 21 April 2018.

14. H. M. Devlin and V. Dodd, 'Falling forensic science standards "making miscarriages of justice inevitable"', *The Guardian*, 19 January 2018.

15. D. Neuberger, 'The power of judges in the UK', *Prospect*, 1 November 2018.

16. 'Crime and punishment: England's tragic failure', *Financial Times*, 7 June 2018.

17. J. Grierson, 'Nearly 10,000 police officers have taken second jobs – survey', *The Guardian*, 7 August 2018.

18. M. Rowe, 'Private policing part two: Hampstead', *Professional Security Magazine Online*, 17 November 2015.

19. R. Mason and L. Peacock, 'Billion-pound scandal in welfare-to-work', *Daily Telegraph*, 23 May 2012. The DWP claimed it had investigated the charges. But no public investigation was conducted.

20. K. Brewer, 'Why are privatised probation services using public libraries to see clients', *The Guardian*, 1 November 2017, p. 38.

21. L. Dearden, 'Private probation companies letting convicts commit more crime and allowing them to disappear, report shows', *The Independent*, 9 February 2018.

22. L. Dearden, 'Government's privatisation of probation services "putting public at risk" as offenders monitored by phone', *The Independent*, 14 December 2017.

23. J. Harding, 'Forty years of community service', *The Guardian*, 9 January 2013.

24. HM Inspectorate of Probation, *A Thematic Inspection of the Delivery of Unpaid Work*, Manchester, January 2016.

25. J. Ford and G. Plimmer, 'Drive to expand private prison network loses momentum', *Financial Times*, 12 February 2018, p. 3.

26. J. Elgot, 'MoJ seizes control of Birmingham prison from G4S', *The Guardian*, 20 August 2018.

27. G. Plimmer, 'Mitie criticised for "insanitary" immigration centre', *Financial Times*, 1 March 2016.

28. M. Townsend, 'Detainees at Yarl's Wood Immigration Centre facing sexual abuse', *The Observer*, 14 September 2013.

29. G. Plimmer, 'Serco and Home Office criticised over Yarl's Wood failures', *Financial Times*, 7 July 2016.

30. D. Taylor, 'Former immigration detainees can seek public enquiry over abuse claims', *The Guardian*, 22 May 2018.

31. K. Rawlinson, 'Private firms "are using detained immigrants as cheap labour"', *The Guardian*, 22 August 2014.

32. National Audit Office, *Yarl's Wood Immigration Removal Centre*. HC 508, Session 2016–17, House of Commons, 7 July 2016.

33. T. T. Arvind and L. Stirton, 'Carillion, Capita and the costly contradictions of outsourcing public services', *The Conversation* online, 2 February 2018.

34. A. Travis, 'Seven G4S staff suspended over abuse claims at youth institution', *The Guardian*, 8 January 2016.

35. For an extended discussion of all the rules that have emerged, see G. Standing, *Beyond the New Paternalism: Basic Security as Equality* (London: Verso, 2002).

36. National Audit Office, *Rolling Out Universal Credit*. HC 1123, Session 2017–19, House of Commons, 15 June 2018.

37. J. Pring, 'The PIP files: Nearly one in three Capita assessments were flawed, reports reveal', Disability News Service, 8 February 2018.

38. M. Bulman, 'Nearly half of disabled people reassessed under government's new benefit system had financial support withdrawn or reduced', *The Independent*, 14 December 2017.

39. House of Commons Work and Pensions Committee, *PIP and ESA Assessments: Claimant Experiences*. HC 355, Session 2017–19, House of Commons, 9 February 2018.

40. M. Bulman, 'Mentally unwell woman has disability benefits stopped because assessor failed to turn up to home visit', *The Independent*, 7 April 2018.

41. Press Association, 'Ex-minister slams DWP as £108m spent fighting disability benefit claims', *The Guardian*, 12 February 2018, p. 10.

42. K. S. Jones, 'The revolving door of disability assessments and appeal is still killing people who are chronically ill', 21 May 2018, at <https//kittysjones.wordpress.com/>.

43. 'Why the DWP is happy to lose so many cut-price PIP and ESA appeals', 11 December 2017, at <https://www.benefitsandwork.co.uk/news/3698-why-the-dwp-is-happy-to-lose-so-many-cut-price-pip-and-esa-appeals>.

44. E. Dugan, 'A senior judge has suggested charging the government for every "no-brainer" benefits case it loses in court', BuzzFeed News online, 9 November 2017.

45. See <https://welfareweekly.com/dwp-forced-to-admit-more-than-111000-benefit-deaths/>.

46. UK Independent Mechanism, *Disability Rights in the UK*. Equality and Human Rights Commission, Equality Commission for Northern Ireland, Northern Ireland Human Rights Commission, Scottish Human Rights Commission, February 2017.

47. When asked by MPs how many people had to wait more than ten weeks, Neil Couling, Director General of Universal Credit, first said the DWP did not collect data and then said, 'We do not collect the data, to the extent we

could publish it.' This surely indicated that the department did collect data, and just did not like what they showed.

48. National Audit Office, *Rolling out Universal Credit*.

49. *The Next Stage of Universal Credit: Moving on to the New Benefit System and Foodbank Use* (Salisbury: The Trussell Trust, 2018).

50. G. Bowden, 'Thousands of UC claimants suffer 40 per cent cut to pay back debts', *HuffPost* UK, 9 April 2018.

51. K. Belgrave, 'Universal Credit advance payments fix nothing. They're just loans – and ANOTHER debt for people who have no money', 2 October 2017, at <https://www.katebelgrave.com/>.

52. F. Ryan, 'A landmark legal challenge shows the cruel reality of Universal Credit for disabled people', *Prospect*, 2 May 2018.

53. P. Dwyer et al., *Welfare Conditionality: Sanctions, Support and Behavioural Change* (York: University of York, Economic and Social Research Council, 2018).

54. Cited in P. Butler, 'Benefit sanctions found to be ineffective and damaging', *The Guardian*, 22 May 2018.

55. Butler, 'Benefit sanctions found to be ineffective and damaging'.

56. P. Butler, 'Universal credit "flaws" mean thousands will be worse off', *The Guardian*, 12 April 2018.

57. House of Commons Work and Pensions Committee, *Universal Credit: Supporting Self-Employment*. HC 997, Session 2017–19, 10 May 2018.

58. K. S. Jones, 'The government's eugenic policy is forcing some women to abort wanted pregnancies', 6 May 2018, at <https//kittysjones.wordpress.com/>.

59. C. Jayanetti, 'Revealed: Two-child benefit cap hits 70,000 families', politics.co.uk, 28 June 2018.

60. Among the rules, one bedroom was allowed for anyone over the age of sixteen, one was allowed for two children of the same sex if under the age of sixteen, one for two children under the age of ten regardless of sex, one for non-resident carers if one occupant required overnight care, and one for any disabled child requiring a separate bedroom.

61. R. Curran, 'The bedroom tax is a startling failure – but when will the government admit it was wrong', *The Independent*, 28 January 2016.

62. I. Duncan Smith, 'Britain cannot afford the spare room subsidy', *Daily Telegraph*, 7 March 2013.

63. J. Grierson and S. Marsh, 'Slash "obscene" Home Office fees, say MPs and campaigners', *The Guardian*, 24 June 2018.

64. K. Lyons et al., 'Britain is one of the worst places in western Europe for asylum seekers', *The Guardian*, 1 March 2017.

65. J. Shenker, 'Revealed: The insidious creep of London's pseudo-public land', *The Guardian*, 24 July 2017.

66. This was acknowledged when the new Chancellor of the Exchequer scrapped the scheme. V. Houlder, 'Hammond scraps Osborne's shares-for-rights scheme', *Financial Times*, 23 November 2016.

67. 'Mandatory arbitration in America: Shut out by the small print', *The Economist*, 27 January 2018, p. 10.

68. This is the estimate from a study by researchers at the University of Middlesex, reproduced in N. Clark and E. Herman, *Unpaid Britain: Wage Default in the British Labour Market* (London: Middlesex University and Trust for London, November 2017). See also F. Lawrence, 'Why do ministers do nothing about bosses who steal from the low paid?', *The Guardian*, 30 November 2017.

69. I. Sample, 'Computer says no: why making AIs fair, open and accountable is crucial', *The Guardian*, 6 November 2017, p. 24.

70. V. Eubanks, *Automating Inequality: How High-Tech Tools Profile, Police and Punish the Poor* (New York: St Martin's Press, 2018).

71. C. Doctorow, 'Australia put an algorithm in charge of its benefits fraud detection and plunged the nation into chaos', 1 February 2018, at <https://boingboing.net/>.

## CHAPTER 6: THE CULTURAL COMMONS

1. D. Edgar, '*Cultural Capital: The Rise and Fall of Creative Britain* by Robert Hewison: Review – a Faustian pact', *The Guardian*, 12 December 2014.

2. Cited in Edgar, '*Cultural Capital: The Rise and Fall of Creative Britain* by Robert Hewison: Review.

3. Cited in T. Hunt, 'The threat to local government's heroic, civilising role', *The Guardian*, 25 October 2012.

4. I. Martin, 'The city that privatised itself to death', *The Guardian*, 24 February 2015.

5. New London Architecture, *NLA London Tall Buildings Survey 2018*, London, 2018. See also S. Jenkins, 'Skyscrapers wreck cities – yet still Britain builds them', *The Guardian*, 29 May 2018, p. 3.

6.  This is well presented by Andy Wood, *The Memory of the People: Custom and Popular Senses of the Past in Early Modern England* (Cambridge: Cambridge University Press, 2013).

7.  C. Caldwell, 'Why libraries must perish', *Financial Times*, 16 April 2011.

8.  H. Ellis-Petersen, 'If libraries vanish we will have nowhere else to go', *The Guardian*, 26 October 2016, p. 15.

9.  W. Hutton, 'Birmingham's last hurrah for local pride before civic Britain is culled', *The Observer*, 1 September 2013, p. 38.

10. N. Gaiman, 'Why our future depends on libraries, reading and daydreaming', The Reading Agency Annual Lecture 2013.

11. V. Thorpe, 'A new battle for Hastings and beyond: to save local museums', *The Observer*, 12 November 2017, p. 20.

12. B. Grosvenor, 'Great museums cannot afford to be supplicants of the state', *Financial Times*, 24 January 2015, p. 17.

13. Cited in P. Toynbee, 'Support the National Gallery strikes while they're still legal', *The Guardian*, 11 August 2015.

14. For example, K. Maltby, 'Protests push philanthropy away just when the arts need it', *Financial Times*, 20 May 2017, p. 12.

15. T. Macalister, 'Shell sought to influence direction of Science Museum climate programme', *The Guardian*, 31 May 2015.

16. Cited in R. Spence, 'Who funds the arts and why we should care', *Financial Times*, 19 September 2014.

17. J. Kiss, 'BBC digital expert Tony Ageh poached by New York Public Library', *The Guardian*, 6 April 2016.

18. T. Mills. 'The future of the BBC', IPPR online, 15 September 2017; T. Mills, *The BBC: Myth of a Public Service* (London: Verso, 2016).

19. 'The tech giant everyone is watching', *The Economist*, 30 June 2018, p. 11.

20. A personal favourite, seen in 1986, was daubed across three adverts in a London underground train. 'If Maggie's the answer, it must have been a bloody stupid question.' Rude, offensive, illegal too, but even an admirer of Thatcher might have been tempted to smile.

21. I. Martin, 'The city that privatised itself to death'.

22. Local Government Association, 'Majority of council tax will soon be spent on social care', Press release, 25 March 2015.

23. P. Butler, 'Council tax rises on the way as local authorities try to stay afloat', *The Guardian*, 8 February 2018.

24. A. Harvey, *Funding Arts and Culture in a Time of Austerity* (London: New Local Government Network, April 2016), p. 6.

25. House of Commons Committee of Public Accounts, *Financial Sustainability of Local Authorities 2014*. HC 833, Session 2014–15, House of Commons, 19 January 2015, p. 10.

26. Cited in C. Bennett, 'What future for the arts with these Tory philistines?', *The Observer*, 3 December 2012, p. 41.

27. Cited in 'What Bohemia built', *The Economist*, 13 June 2013, p. 29.

28. N. Vowles, 'Loyd Grossman hails heritage as the antidote to the "placelessness" of globalisation', University of Sussex Alumni News, 4 April 2018.

29. U. Mattei, 'Protecting the commons: Water, culture and nature: The commons movement in the Italian struggle against neoliberal governance', *South Atlantic Quarterly*, 112(1), Spring 2013, pp. 366–76.

## CHAPTER 7: THE KNOWLEDGE COMMONS

1. See, for example, A. Broumas, 'The ontology of the intellectual commons', *International Journal of Communication*, 11, 2017, pp. 1507–27.

2. 'Open government data: Out of the box', *The Economist*, 21 November 2015, p. 55.

3. See also N. C. Kranich, *The Information Commons: A Public Policy Report* (New York: Free Expression Policy Project, 2004).

4. My appreciation of the significance of enclosure of the knowledge commons was enhanced by reading Franklin Foer's book, *World Without Mind: The Existential Threat of Big Tech* (New York: Penguin, 2017).

5. 'The University of Chicago worries about a lack of competition', *The Economist*, 12 April 2017, p. 58.

6. Foer, *World Without Mind: The Existential Threat of Big Tech*, p. 32.

7. F. Pasquale, 'From territorial to functional sovereignty: The case of Amazon', *Law and Political Economy*, 6 December 2017.

8. See M. Sandbu, 'The market failures of Big Tech', *Financial Times*, 19 February 2018.

9. C. Shapiro and H. Varian, *Information Rules: A Strategic Guide to the Network Economy* (Boston: Harvard Business School Press, 1999).

10. E. Morozov, 'To tackle Google's power, regulators have to go after its ownership of data', *The Guardian*, 2 July 2017.

11. One victim is the English language. The Latin word 'data' is a plural of the word 'datum'. Too many writers treat the word 'data' as a singular.

12. D. Fields, 'Rent, datafication and the automated landlord', in J. Shaw and M. Graham (eds), *Our Digital Rights to the City* (Oxford: Meatspace Press, 2017).

13. P. Glikman and N. Glady, 'What's the value of your data?', Techcrunch.com, 13 October 2015.

14. I. Leslie, 'The scientists who make apps addictive', *The Economist 1843 Magazine*, October/November 2016.

15. C. Price, *How to Break Up with Your Phone: The 30-Day Plan to Take Back Your Life* (London: Trapeze/Orion, 2018). See also R. Samadder, 'Breaking up (with my smartphone) is hard to do', *The Guardian*, 11 March 2018.

16. Cited in M. Sarner, 'Meet the tech evangelist who now fears for our mental health', *The Guardian*, 15 March 2018.

17. D. Foster Wallace, 'Deciderization 2007: A special report', *The Best American Essays* (Boston, MA: Houghton Mifflin, 2007).

18. This example is given in J. Shaw and M. Graham, 'An informational right to the city?', in Shaw and Graham (eds), *Our Digital Rights to the City*, p. 4.

19. Foer, *World Without Mind: The Existential Threat of Big Tech*, p. 211.

20. M. Garrahan, 'Facebook and Google tighten digital ads grip', *Financial Times*, 4 December 2017, p. 16.

21. For an account of how they became that way, see A. G. Martinez, *Chaos Monkeys: Inside the Silicon Valley Money Machine* (London: Ebury Press, 2017).

22. R. Benson and V. Pickard, 'The slippery slope of the oligarchy media model', *The Conversation* online, 11 August 2017.

23. N. Scola, 'Facebook's next project: American inequality', *Politico* online, 19 February 2018.

24. A. Hern, 'Royal Free breached UK data law in 1.6m patient deal with Google's DeepMind', *The Guardian*, 3 July 2017.

25. These figures come from K. S. Jones, 'Calibrating academy – Hubert Huzzah', *Politics and Insights* online, 22 March 2018, at <https//kittysjones.wordpress.com/>.

26. 'Les stats, c'est moi', *The Economist*, 22 December 2018, pp. 13–14.

27. D. Reinsel, J. Gantz, and J. Rydning, *Data Age 2025*, Framingham, MA: International Data Corporation IDC (April 2017).

28. J. Naughton, 'The new surveillance capitalism', *Prospect*, 19 January 2018.

29. J. Naughton, 'What price privacy when Apple gets into bed with China?', *The Observer*, 4 March 2018.

30. J. Harris, 'The tyranny of algorithms is part of our lives: soon they could rate everything we do', *The Guardian*, 5 March 2018.

31. Foer, *World Without Mind: The Existential Threat of Big Tech*, p. 103.

32. J. Lanchester, 'You are the product', *London Review of Books*, 39(16), 17 August 2017.

33. Foer, *World Without Mind: The Existential Threat of Big Tech*, pp. 123–4.

34. G. Verhofstadt, 'Tech Vs. Democracy', *Social Europe* online, 27 February 2018.

35. T. Berners-Lee, 'The web can be weaponised – and we can't count on big tech to stop it', *The Guardian*, 12 March 2018.

36. See, for instance, P. Eckersley, 'The malicious use of artificial intelligence: Forecasting, prevention, and mitigation', Electronic Frontier Foundation online, 20 February 2018; A. Selbst and S. Barocas (eds), *AI Now 2017 Report* (New York: New York University, 2017). The latter noted, 'Police body camera footage is being used to train machine vision algorithms for law enforcement, raising privacy and accountability concerns.'

37. Cited in Foer, *World Without Mind: The Existential Threat of Big Tech*, p. 38.

38. See, for instance, N. Srnicek, 'We need to nationalise Google, Facebook and Amazon. Here's why', *The Guardian*, 30 August 2017.

39. N. Shadbolt and R. Hampson, 'Who should hold the keys to our data?', *The Guardian*, 29 April 2018.

40. S. O'Connor, 'Let gig workers control their data too', *Financial Times*, 3 April 2018.

41. For a defence, see J. Hughes, 'The philosophy of intellectual property', *Georgetown Law Journal*, 77, 1988.

42. For a critique of the global intellectual property rights system, see G. Standing, *The Corruption of Capitalism: Why Rentiers Thrive and Work Does Not Pay* (London: Biteback Publishing, 2016), Chapter 2.

43. OROPO, *Who Owns the World's Patents* (Oakland, CA: Open Register of Patent Ownership, June 2015).

44. M. Boldrin and D. Levine, *Against Intellectual Monopoly* (Cambridge: Cambridge University Press, 2008); M. Boldrin and D. Levine, 'The case against patents', Federal Reserve Bank of St Louis, Working Paper 2012-035A, September 2012; E. R. Gold, E. Shadeed and J.-F. Morin, 'Does intellectual property lead to economic growth? Insights from a novel IP dataset', *Regulation and Governance*, August 2017. Also, Standing, *The Corruption of Capitalism*.

45. J. Bessen and M. Meurer, *Patent Failure: How Judges, Bureaucrats and Lawyers Put Innovators at Risk* (Princeton: Princeton University Press, 2009).

46. Gold et al., 'Does intellectual property lead to economic growth? Insights from a novel IP dataset'.

47. UNCTAD, *Trade and Development Report 2017: Beyond Austerity: Towards a New Deal* (New York and Geneva: United Nations Conference on Trade and Development, 2017), p. 133.

48. For a critique, see Standing, *The Corruption of Capitalism*, pp. 74–81.

49. R. Blasiak et al., 'Corporate control and global governance of marine genetic resources', *Science Advances*, 4(6), 6 June 2018.

50. P. Mason, 'Welcome to a new way of living', *The Guardian*, 18 July 2015, p. 3.

51. J. Haskell and S. Westlake, *Capitalism without Capital: The Rise of the Intangible Economy* (Princeton: Princeton University Press, 2017).

52. R. Burn-Callander, 'Companies failing to see value of their intellectual property', *Daily Telegraph*, 13 February 2017, p. 4.

53. M. Blyth, 'America tampers with the Chomsky Trade at its peril', *Financial Times*, 25 August 2017, p. 9.

54. Other reform proposals worth reconsideration are contained in the *Gowers Review of Intellectual Property* (London: HMSO, December 2006).

55. J. S. Mill, *Inaugural address delivered to the University of St. Andrews Feb. 1st 1867* (London: Longmans, Green, Reader and Dyer, 1867).

56. Report of the Special Rapporteur on the Right to Education, Kishore Singh, *Protecting the Right to Education Against Commercialization*, A/HRC/29/30 (Geneva: Human Rights Council, 10 June 2015).

57. H. Williams, 'Elite private schools "get £522m subsidy"', *Metro*, 12 June 2017, p. 26. This was citing a report by business rates firm CVS.

58. W. Mansell, 'The 60% extra enjoyed by England's free school pupils', *The Guardian*, 25 August 2015, p. 33.

59. D. Boffey and W. Mansell, 'Academy chain's fees for "consultants" put schools programme under scrutiny', *The Guardian*, 24 October 2015.

60. R. Adams, 'Academy trust lauded by Cameron falls apart as executive head quits', *The Guardian*, 10 May 2016.

61. W. Mansell, 'Taxpayers to pay investment firm annual £468,000 rent for free school', *The Guardian*, 11 August 2015, p. 35.

62. To call the trusts not-for-profit is surely a convenient misnomer when there is ample evidence that they are paying out large sums of money to themselves and business partners.

63. F. Perraudin, 'Furious parents say collapsing academy trust asset-stripped its schools of millions', *The Observer*, 22 October 2017, p. 10.

64. F. Perraudin, '40,000 children trapped in "zombie" academy schools', *The Guardian*, 3 December 2017.

65. W. Mansell and M. Savage, 'Top academy schools sound alarm as cash crisis looms', *The Guardian*, 27 January 2018.

66. M. Skapinker, 'How to run a school–business partnership', *Financial Times*, 4 December 2007.

67. G. Monbiot, 'In an age of robots, schools are teaching our children to be redundant', *The Guardian*, 17 February 2017.

68. 'Total eclipse of the arts: The quiet decline of music in British schools', *The Economist*, 26 February 2018.

69. For a critique, see G. Standing, *Work after Globalization: Building Occupational Citizenship* (Cheltenham: Edward Elgar, 2009), especially pp. 164–5.

70. M. Bennet, 'Ed tech biz', *London Review of Books*, 22 September 2016, p. 34.

71. L. Crehan, *Cleverlands: The Secrets behind the Success of the World's Education Superpowers* (London: Penguin Random House, 2016). See also M. Benn, *Life Lessons: The Case for a National Education Service* (London: Verso, 2018).

72. J. Andrews and N. Perera, *The Impact of Academies on Educational Outcomes* (London: Education Policy Institute, July 2017).

73. E. Pilkington, 'Koch brothers sought say in academic hiring in return for university donation', *The Guardian*, 12 September 2014.

74. In 2015–16 philanthropic donations to UK universities passed the £1 billion mark. Nearly half of this went to the elite universities of Oxford and Cambridge, further entrenching inequality. S. Weale, 'Annual donations to UK universities pass £1bn mark for first time', *The Guardian*, 3 May 2017.

75. S. Johnson, 'In move towards more online degrees, Coursera introduces its first bachelor's', EdSurge online, 5 March 2018.

76. J. R. Young, 'Here comes professor everybody', *Chronicle of Higher Education*, 2 February 2015.

77. 'The return of the MOOC: Established education providers v new contenders', *The Economist*, Special Report, 12 January 2017.

78. 'The return of the MOOC: Established education providers v new contenders', *The Economist*.

79. P. McDuff, 'The two-year degree shows education has become just another commodity', *The Guardian*, 13 December 2017.

80. D. Morris, 'Be it enacted: The Higher Education and Research Act', Wonkhe online, 27 April 2017.

81. There are higher annual fees for two-year degrees, breaching the government's promised fee cap.

82. R. McFee and H. Siddique, 'Fast-track degrees may hit education standards, government warned', *The Guardian*, 24 February 2017.

83. 'Open science: Time's up', *The Economist*, 25 March 2017, pp. 69–71.

84. A. Spicer, 'The knowledge economy is a myth. We don't need more universities to feed it', *The Guardian*, 18 May 2016.

85. C. Havergal, 'At the heart of the higher education debate: Agents paid an average of £1,767 per non-EU recruit', *Times Higher Education*, 19 February 2015.

86. R. Adams, 'University vice-chancellors' earnings "out of control"', *The Guardian*, 12 November 2015.

87. On this, see G. Standing, *The Precariat: The New Dangerous Class* (London: Bloomsbury, 2011).

88. Cited in Foer, *World Without Mind: The Existential Threat of Big Tech*, p. 78.

89. Standing, *Work after Globalization: Building Occupational Citizenship*.

90. L. Shaw, 'Case study – A quiet revolution: Cooperative schools in the UK', Stories.coop, October 2014.

91. J. Thornhill, 'The march of the technocrats', *Financial Times*, 19 February 2018.

92. G. Keeney, 'Inside views: The bipolar nature of academic publishing', Intellectual Property Watch, 5 May 2016.

---

## CHAPTER 8: A COMMONS FUND FOR COMMON DIVIDENDS

1. The word sabotage is surely correct. If a Chancellor of the Exchequer reduces public revenue by cutting taxes and then declares that the public deficit must be erased by slashing spending on social commons and cultural activity, that is a deliberate act to shrink the commons, especially as there was no evidence that cutting those taxes had any economic benefit.

2. This is a variant of what is proposed elsewhere. See, for example, G. Standing, *Work after Globalization: Building Occupational Citizenship* (Cheltenham: Edward Elgar, 2009).

3. The concept of a commons levy proposed in this section differs from that applied to property owners living within three-quarters of a mile of Wimbledon Common, which has been in operation since 1871.

4. Rahul Basu, Research Director of the Goa Foundation, an Indian environmental NGO, has made a cogent case for treating all minerals and other commons as capital assets. R. Basu, 'Catastrophic failure of public trust in mining: Case study of Goa', *Economic and Political Weekly*, L(38), September 2015, pp. 44–51.

5. 'Free Exchange: We the shareholders', *The Economist*, 22 September 2018, p. 62.

6. 'Norwegian blues', *The Economist*, 10 October 2015, p. 68.

7. C. Wedmore, *Funding the Future: How Sovereign Wealth Funds Benefit Future Generations* (London: Intergenerational Foundation, November 2013).

8. K. Myers and D. Manley, 'Did the UK miss out on £400 billion worth of oil revenue?', resourcegovernance.org, 17 November 2015.

9. P. Barnes, *With Liberty and Dividends for All: How to Save Our Middle Class When Jobs Don't Pay Enough* (San Francisco: Berrett Koehler, 2014).

10. C. Roberts and M. Lawrence, *Our Common Wealth. A Citizen's Wealth Fund for the UK* (London: Institute for Public Policy Research, April 2018).

11. A. Painter, J. Thorold and J. Cooke, *Pathways to Universal Basic Income. The Case for a Universal Basic Opportunity Fund* (London: Royal Society of Arts, February 2018).

12. S. Schifferes, S. Lansley and D. McCann, *Remodelling Capitalism: How Social Wealth Funds Could Transform Britain* (London: Friends Provident Foundation, 2018).

13. S. Lansley and H. Reed, *A Basic Income for All: From Desirability to Feasibility* (London: Compass, January 2019).

14. F. Alvaredo et al., *World Inequality Report, 2018*. World Inequality Lab, 2018, Figure E6.

15. For a detailed description, see <https://en.wikipedia.org/wiki/Panama_Papers>.

16. C. Roberts and M. Lawrence, *Wealth in the 21st Century* (London: IPPR Commission on Economic Justice, 2017).

17. R. Former, 'Monday's macro memo: Tax reform: A proposal for the Chancellor', National Institute of Economic and Social Research (NIESR), 17 November 2017. This counts Stamp Duty on property and shares, Capital Gains and Inheritance Tax, but excludes Council Tax.

18. 'Death of the death tax', *The Economist*, 25 November 2017, pp. 23–5.

19. R. Partington, 'Has the time come for a wealth tax in the UK?', *The Guardian*, 4 March 2018.

20. A. Turner, 'Capitalism in the age of robots', lecture at Johns Hopkins University, Washington DC, 10 April 2018.

21. K. Knoll, S. Moritz and T. Steger, 'No price like home: Global house prices, 1870–2012', *American Economic Review*, 107(2), 2017, pp. 331–53.

22. J. Jones and C. Wilcox, 'A strategy for replacing Council Tax and Business Rates with a Land Value Tax: A first step towards a more equitable tax system', London: Labour Land Campaign, 2015.

23. P. Collinson, 'Council tax should be fair and progressive. Ours is neither', *The Guardian*, 3 March 2018.

24. N. O'Brien, *Green, Pleasant and Affordable: Why We Need a New Approach to Supply and Demand to Solve Britain's Housing Problem* (London: Onward, June 2018).

25. B. Kentish, 'Developers leave 420,000 homes with planning permission unbuilt, new figures show', *The Independent*, 16 February 2018.

26. Intergovernmental Panel on Climate Change, *Global Warming of 1.5 C* (Geneva: IPCC, United Nations, October 2018); J. Hickel, 'The hope at the heart of the apocalyptic climate change report', *Foreign Policy*, October 2018.

27. I. Parry, V. Mylonas and N. Vernon, 'Mitigation policies for the Paris Agreement: An assessment for G20 countries', Washington DC: IMF Working Paper, 2018.

28. P. Lockley and S. Dresner, 'Flying in the face of fairness: Intergenerational inequities in the taxation of air travel', Report for the Intergenerational Foundation, October 2012, at <http://www.if.org.uk/wp-content/uploads/2012/11/Aviation_Report_Intergenerational_Foundation_FINAL.pdf>.

29. S. Devlin and S. Bernick, *Managing Aviation Passenger Demand with a Frequent Flyer Levy* (London: New Economics Foundation, 2015).

30. 'Communities to decide how to spend shale cash windfall', Press release, HM Treasury, 11 November 2017.

31. *Getting Shale Gas Working* (London: Institute of Directors, May 2013).

32. For recent support, see R. Edwards, 'Fracking is damned by international tribunal', *The Herald* (Scotland), 10 June 2018.

33. G. Lean, 'Fracking to prompt sharp rise in greenhouse gas emissions, study says', *The Independent*, 12 March 2016.

34. R. Neate, 'Britain's richest person to leave UK for tax-free Monaco', *The Guardian*, 9 August 2018.

35. L. Dormehl, 'If data is the new oil, are tech companies robbing us blind?', Digital Trends online, 25 September 2017.

36. E. Porter, 'Your data is crucial to a robotic age. Shouldn't you be paid for it?', *The New York Times*, 6 March 2018. See also Shadbolt and Hampson, 'Who should hold the keys to our data?'

37. E. A. Posner and E. G. Weyl, *Radical Markets: Uprooting Capitalism and Democracy for a Just Society* (Princeton, NJ: Princeton University Press, 2018).

38. See, for example, K. McFarland, 'United States: Ex-CIA officer Bryan Wright proposes data mining royalties', Basic Income Earth Network (BIEN) online, 27 May 2016; C. Rhodes, 'Funding basic income through

data mining', BIEN online, 29 January 2017; G. Standing, *Basic Income: And How We Can Make It Happen* (London: Pelican Books, 2017), Chapter 12.

39. 'The old one-two', *The Economist*, 24 March 2018, pp. 60–61.

40. 'Digital duopoly to remain dominant in UK ad race', eMarketer online, 18 September 2017.

41. H. Stewart, 'Treasury targets Facebook and Google with "fair" tax system', *The Guardian*, 22 February 2018.

42. 'Fishing for funds', *The Economist*, 17 February 2018, pp. 30–31.

43. A. Fremstad and M. Paul, 'A short-run distributional analysis of a carbon tax in the United States', Political Economy Research Institute Working Paper No. 434, University of Massachusetts, Amherst, MA, August 2017.

44. D. Klenert, L. Mattauch, E. Combet, O. Edenhofer, C. Hepburn, R. Rafaty and N. Stern, 'Making carbon pricing work for citizens', *Nature Climate Change*, 8, 2018, pp. 669–77.

45. 'Economists' statement on carbon dividends', *Wall Street Journal Opinion*, 30 January 2019.

46. There is an accounting dilemma here. As the savings from clawing back the dividend from higher-rate tax payers would go to the Exchequer, not the Fund, another option might be to consolidate the dividend in the personal tax allowance (and freeze the allowance). This would benefit households whose incomes are too low to pay tax, but would have the disadvantage that the dividend would not be visible to all.

47. The moral hazard might be a bigger challenge in small island developing countries. For a proposed Commons Fund for such economies, see A. Standing, 'Avoiding the curse of blue growth: A blue Commons Fund?', CFFA-CAPE online, 29 August 2018, at <https://cape-cffa.squarespace.com/new-blog/2018/8/27/avoiding-the-curse-of-blue-growth-a-blue-commons-fund>.

48. The points made in this section are developed in more detail in Standing, *Basic Income: And How We Can Make It Happen*.

49. 'Why basic income's emancipatory value exceeds its monetary value', *Basic Income Studies*, 10(2), December 2015, pp. 193–223.

50. Painter et al., *Pathways to Universal Basic Income. The case for a Universal Basic Opportunity Fund*.

51. Schifferes, Lansley and McCann, *Remodelling Capitalism: How Social Wealth Funds Could Transform Britain*, p. 33.

52. D. Graeber, *Bullshit Jobs: A Theory* (New York: Simon and Schuster, 2018).

# Index

**PELICAN BOOKS**

PELICAN BOOKS

PELICAN BOOKS